MATTERING PRESS

Mattering Press is an academic-led Open Access publisher that operates on a not-for-profit basis as a UK registered charity. It is committed to developing new publishing models that can widen the constituency of academic knowledge and provide authors with significant levels of support and feedback. All books are available to download for free or to purchase as hard copies. More at matteringpress.org.

The Press' work has been supported by: Centre for Invention and Social Process (Goldsmiths, University of London), European Association for the Study of Science and Technology, Hybrid Publishing Lab, infostreams, Institute for Social Futures (Lancaster University), OpenAIRE, Open Humanities Press, and Tetragon, as well as many other institutions and individuals that have supported individual book projects, both financially and in kind.

We are indebted to the ScholarLed community of Open Access, scholar-led publishers for their companionship and extend a special thanks to the Directory of Open Access Books and Project MUSE for cataloguing our titles.

MAKING THIS BOOK

Books contain multitudes. Mattering Press is keen to render more visible the unseen processes that go into the production of books. We would like to thank Anna Dowrick, who acted as the Press' coordinating editor for this book, Joe Deville for his work on the book production, Steven Lovatt for the copy editing, Melanie Mallon for the formatting, Alex Billington and Tetragon for the typesetting, Alice Ferns for illustrations, and Will Roscoe, Ed Akerboom, and infostreams for their contributions to the html versions of this book.

COVER

Cover art by Julien McHardy.

THE
ETHNOGRAPHIC
CASE

SECOND EDITION

EMILY YATES-DOERR

AND

CHRISTINE LABUSKI

Mattering Press

Second edition published by Mattering Press, Manchester.

ISBN: 978-1-912729-34-0 (pbk)
ISBN: 978-1-912729-32-6 (pdf)
ISBN: 978-1-912729-07-4 (epub)
ISBN: 978-1-912729-33-3 (html)
DOI: http://doi.org/10.28938/9781912729340

Mattering Press has made every effort to contact copyright holders and will be glad to rectify, in future editions, any errors or omissions brought to our notice.

CONTENTS

LIST OF FIGURES

AUTHOR BIOGRAPHIES

AARON ANSELL is a cultural anthropologist who specializes in Brazilian state formation, patron-client politics, social policy, and rural community life. His ethnographic writings employ methods from linguistic anthropology to analyse emerging expressions of democratic subjectivity and counter-democratic reactivity. He is currently Associate Professor of Religion and Culture at Virginia Tech.

ANDRÉ MENARD holds a PhD in Sociology from the École des Hautes Études en Sciences Sociales (EHESS) and is Professor and researcher at the Department of Anthropology of the Universidad de Chile. His work has centred on Mapuche political history, focusing on the political uses of the notion of race in Chilean and Mapuche context. In this frame he has edited, with Jorge Pavez the photographic album *Mapuche y Anglicanos, vestigios fotográficos de la Misión Araucana de Kepe (1896-1908)* (Santiago de Chile: Ocho Libros, 2008), and more recently the manuscripts of the mystical Mapuche leader Manuel Aburto Panguilef, *Libro Diario del Presidente de la Federación Araucana, Manuel Aburto Panguilef (1940-1951)* (Santiago de Chile: CoLibris, 2013). His current research focuses on the theories of fetish and their applications to the analysis of materiality, magic and politics.

ANNA HARRIS writes about the sensory, bodily, material practices entailed in medical work. She has conducted ethnographic research concerning migrant doctors, genetic testing and sound in hospitals. Her chapter relates to a project she is currently leading on technologies in medical education called Making Clinical Sense (funded by the ERC, grant #678390). She is author of *A Sensory Education* (Routledge, 2020), and co-author of *CyberGenetics* (Routledge, 2016) and *Stethoscope* (Reaktion, 2022). Her current book project is called *Learning Materials*. Anna works as Associate Professor in the STS research group at Maastricht University in the Netherlands.

ANNA WILKING is a writer, anthropologist, documentary filmmaker, and adjunct professor in Brooklyn, NY. She is also a community organizer, working with undocumented Latina sex workers in the South Bronx. She earned her Ph.D. in cultural anthropology from New York University in 2015. Her research focused on street prostitution in Quito, Ecuador and she is currently writing a book about her work. *Sea La Luz* (Let There Be Light) won the AAA's award for best graduate student film of 2014 and has screened in festivals internationally.

ANNEMARIE MOL is Professor of Anthropology of the Body at the University of Amsterdam. In her work she combines the ethnographic study of practices with the task of shifting our theoretical repertoires. She is author of *The Body Multiple: Ontology in Medical Practice* (Duke University Press, 2002), *The Logic of Care: Health and the Problem of Patient Choice* (Routledge University Press 2008), and *Eating in Theory* (Duke University Press 2021).

ATSURO MORITA teaches anthropology at Osaka University. He did ethnographic research on technology development in Thailand focusing on how ideas, artefacts, and people travel in and out of the country. His interest has recently shifted to techno-social movements for transition for sustainability in Japan. His research has been recently published in *Science, Technology and Human Values*; *HAU: Journal of Ethnographic Theory*; and *Ethnos*.

CAROLE MCGRANAHAN is Professor of Anthropology at the University of Colorado. Her research focuses on issues of colonialism and empire, history and memory, power and politics, refugees and citizenship, nationalism, senses of belonging, gender, war, and anthropology as theoretical storytelling. Her book *Arrested Histories: Tibet, the CIA, and Memories of a Forgotten War* (Duke University Press, 2010) tells the history of the grassroots Tibetan Chushi Gangdrug army through the ethnographic study of veterans' lives and the politics of memory in exile.

CHRISTINE LABUSKI is an anthropologist and Associate Professor of Science, Technology and Society and Women's and Gender Studies at Virginia Tech.

She teaches courses about sexual medicine, queer tech, and ecofeminisms, she directs the Gender, Bodies & Technology initiative at VT, and she is a founding member of the Mayapple Energy Transition Collective.

CHRISTY SPACKMAN is Assistant Professor at Arizona State University, jointly appointed between the School for the Future of Innovation in Society and the School of Arts, Media and Engineering. Writing of this article was supported in part by a Hixon-Riggs Early Career Fellow in Science and Technology Studies at Harvey Mudd College. Her book on the taste of water is forthcoming with the University of California Press.

CONSTANZA TIZZONI is a social anthropologist from the Universidad de Chile. She currently works as a Research Assistant at the Pontificia Universidad Católica de Chile. She has conducted different ethnographic studies on parenting and care with women living in low-income neighborhoods in Santiago de Chile. Her research interests are motherhood, care, everyday lives and neoliberalism.

ELIZABETH LEWIS is a medical anthropologist based at the Texas Center for Disability Studies in Austin, Texas. Her research examines the social life of complex disability diagnoses, and she is engaged in multiple applied disability projects on health and family experiences in the United States. Additional information on her work, research, and writing is available at lizlewisphd.com.

EMILY YATES-DOERR is Associate Professor at the University of Amsterdam and Oregon State University. Her work on this book project was supported by an NWO Veni grant (#016.158.020) and a European Research Council grant for research on global maternal nutrition (#759414). She is author of *The Weight of Obesity: Hunger and Global Health in Postwar Guatemala* (University of California Press, 2015) and is writing a second book focused on maternal malnutrition projects and American genocide in Guatemala.

FAYE GINSBURG and RAYNA RAPP (aka Fanya Rappburg when writing together) are both faculty members in the Department of Anthropology at New York

University. Since 2007, they have been carrying out research on cognitive disability and cultural innovation, with an ethnographic focus on New York City. Their book, *Disability Worlds*, will be published by Duke University Press. They founded NYU's Center for Disability Studies in 2017, where Faye is co-director. With support from the National Science Foundation, and along with colleague Mara Mills, Fanya has assembled a team of researchers learning how people with diverse disabilities fared during the pandemic, leading to a forthcoming book, *How to Be Disabled in a Pandemic* (NYU Press).

FILIPPO BERTONI is the founder of FILOtypes, a consultancy for transdisciplinary research and publishing based in Amsterdam. After doing obtaining their PhD with Annemarie Mol's research team to learn about "The Eating Body in Western Theory and Practice", Filo worked on the Aarhus University Research on the Anthropocene programme, an interdisciplinary and experimental project led by Anna Tsing and Nils Bubandt, as well as in the Museum fur Naturkunde Berlin with Tahani Nadim, exploring the entanglements and ecologies of knowledge making at the intersections between social and life sciences and beyond. Putting their experience in transdisciplinary research into practice, Filo now helps other projects in academia and beyond to navigate the shifting landscapes of knowledge production.

ILDIKÓ ZONGA PLÁJÁS studied anthropology and cultural studies in Romania and Hungary and then earned a degree in visual ethnography from Leiden University. She was a PhD candidate at the University of Amsterdam in the RaceFaceID Research Project led by Amade M'charek, where she researched how visual technologies in governance enact certain groups as racial others. Currently, she is a Postdoctoral Researcher in the project "The Security Politics of Computer Vision" at Leiden University and a lecturer of visual anthropology at the University of Amsterdam. *Swamp Dialogues* is her first anthropological film.

JANELLE LAMOREAUX is Associate Professor of Anthropology at the University of Arizona. She is author of *Infertile Environments* (Duke University Press, 2022), which is an ethnographic exploration of epigenetic toxicology and the intersection of environmental and reproductive health in China. She is also co-editor of the *Routledge Handbook of Genomics, Health and Society* (Routledge, 2018), and is currently researching postgenomic understandings of reproductive cells and cryoconservation movements.

JASON DANELY is Reader of Anthropology and Chair of the Healthy Ageing & Care Research and Innovation Network at Oxford Brookes University. He is the author of *Fragile Resonance: Caring for Older Family Members in Japan and England* (Cornell University Press, 2022), and *Aging and Loss: Mourning and Maturity in Contemporary Japan* (Rutgers University Press, 2015). He also co-edited *Vulnerability and the Politics of Care* (Oxford University Press, 2021) and *Transitions and Transformations: Cultural Perspectives on Aging and the Life Course* (Berghahn Books, 2013). He is currently conducting research with formerly incarcerated older adults in Japan and England.

JENNA GRANT is Associate Professor of Anthropology at the University of Washington, where she teaches anthropology of medicine, technology, visuality, and Southeast Asia. Her book, *Fixing the Image: Ultrasound and the Visuality of Care in Phnom Penh* (University of Washington Press, 2022) explores histories and contemporary practices of medical imaging in Cambodia's capital. She is currently studying the interface of experimental global health sciences and border practices in the Mekong subregion and working with the Faculty of Social Sciences and Humanities at the Royal University of Phnom Penh to support their graduate programs.

JENNIFER CARLSON is a cultural anthropologist specialising in the energy humanities. She lectures in anthropology at Southwestern University and is a visiting research fellow at Rice University's Center for Energy and Environmental Research in the Human Sciences. She earned her Ph.D. in Anthropology from the University of Texas at Austin in 2014. Her research focuses on the everyday, affective dimensions of energy transitions and political repercussions in Germany and the United States. Over the course of this work, she has become interested in the relationship between life and infrastructure, asking how life forms are appropriated in—and articulated through—energy development projects.

JOHN BODINGER DE URIARTE is Professor of anthropology and serves as the Chair of the Sociology & Anthropology Department at Susquehanna University. He also directs the Museum Studies and Diversity Studies Programs. His research interests include questions of identity, representation, and Native American sovereignty, and how such issues are engaged in contemporary museum, casino, and photographic practice. He is the author of *Casino and Museum: Mashantucket Pequot Representation* (University of Arizona Press, 2007); most recently he served as lead editor for *Study Abroad and the Quest for an Anti-Tourism Experience* (Rowman & Littlefield, 2020).

KEN MACLEISH is Associate Professor of Medicine, Health, and Society and Anthropology at Vanderbilt. He studies how war, broadly considered, takes shape in the everyday lives of people whose job it is to produce it—U.S. military servicemembers and their families and communities. His book, *Making War: Everyday Life at Ft. Hood* (Princeton University Press, 2013), examines the everyday lives of the soldiers, families, and communities who personally bear the burden of America's most recent wars.

MELISSA BIGGS is a social anthropologist specializing in issues of representation and critical cultural heritage. She serves as Assistant Director of the Humanities Institute at the University of Texas at Austin, and has taught at Colorado College, the Culinary Institute of America in San Antonio, Southwestern University, Texas State University, and the University of Texas at Austin. From 2016-2017, she was a Fulbright García-Robles Scholar in Guadalajara, Jalisco, Mexico.

NICHOLAS COPELAND is a social anthropologist and Associate Professor in the Department of History at Virginia Tech. His book, *The Democracy Development Machine: Neoliberalism, Radical Pessimism, and Authoritarian Populism in Mayan Guatemala* (Cornell University Press, 2019) examines recent transformations in Mayan political experience, illuminating continuities between counterinsurgency, development, and neoliberal democracy. His new research uses politically engaged anthropology and participatory science methodologies to explore the role of water and water science in grassroots defences against extractive development and movements for food sovereignty and buen vivir.

RIMA PRASPALIAUSKIENE is a medical anthropologist and historian. She received her PhD in the UC Davis Anthropology Department. Her book *Enveloped Lives: Caring and Relating in Lithuanian Health Care* (Cornell University Press, 2022) is an ethnography of health care practices in post-socialist Lithuania in the times of neoliberal reforms. Her research investigates the relationship between health, care, and money.

RUTH GOLDSTEIN is Assistant Professor in Gender and Women's Studies at the University of Wisconsin, Madison. She is interested in the gendered aspects of human and nonhuman health, a quickly heating planet and environmental racism. Her current book project *Life in Traffic* examines the socio-environmental consequences of transnational infrastructure projects and climate change along Latin America's longest longitudinal thoroughfare, the Interoceanic Highway. Her subsequent research on mercury as a global pollutant, analyzes the racialized weight of toxic body burdens and impacts on parent/child health.

SAMEENA MULLA is Associate Professor of Women's, Gender and Sexuality Studies at Emory University. Her book, *The Violence of Care: Rape Victims, Forensic Nurses, and Sexual Assault Victims* (New York University Press, 2014), details all of the labor that forensic nurses put into examining sexual assault victims. It was awarded an Honourable Mention in the 2015 Eileen Basker Prize competition, and also earned Mulla the 2017 Margaret Mead Award. Her second book, a collaborative ethnography with Heather Hlavka, *Bodies in Evidence: Race, Gender, Science and Sexual Assault Adjudication* (New York University Press, 2021) follows the evidence collected during forensic examinations to stages of adjudication, this time in a Milwaukee, Wisconsin felony court.

STEPHANIE KREHBIEL is the Executive Director and co-founder of Into Account (www.intoaccount.org), a nonprofit that works directly with survivors confronting churches and other religious institutions. As an advocate, she accompanies survivors through reporting processes, investigations, media coverage, and public storytelling. She has worked with over a hundred individual survivors from a range of denominational backgrounds, from Catholic to Amish to nondenominational evangelicals. Her work has been covered in the *New York Times*, *National Catholic Reporter*, the *Star-Tribune*, and numerous smaller publications. She holds a PhD in American Studies from University of Kansas with a concentration in Women, Gender, and Sexuality studies, and her work as an advocate began during ethnographic research on institutional violence against LGBTQ+ people in the Mennonite Church USA. She is a frequent guest speaker in university and seminary classrooms.

SUSAN REYNOLDS WHYTE, Professor of Anthropology, University of Copenhagen, carries out research in East Africa on social efforts to secure well-being in the face of poverty, disease, conflict, and rapid change. For three decades she has worked with African colleagues on Enhancement of Research Capacity projects. She is the author of *Questioning Misfortune: The Pragmatics of Uncertainty in Eastern Uganda* (Cambridge University Press, 1998) and co-author of *Social Lives of Medicines* (Cambridge University Press, 2003).

TERESA A. VELÁSQUEZ is Professor of Anthropology at the California State University, San Bernardino. Her research on the intersection of anti-mining activism and state resource policy in the Ecuadorian Andes examines the reconfiguration of farmers' relationship to their watershed. She is especially interested in writing about women's political subjectivities and their efforts to defend water as life. She is the author of the book *Pachamama Politics: Campesino Water Defenders and the Anti-Mining Movement in Andean Ecuador* (University of Arizona Press, 2022).

ZOE TODD (MÉTIS) is from Amiskwaciwâskahikan (Edmonton) in Treaty Six Territory in Alberta, Canada. She writes about fish, art, Métis legal traditions, the Anthropocene, extinction, and decolonization in urban and prairie contexts. She also studies human-animal relations, colonialism and environmental change in north/western Canada. She is Associate Professor in the Department of Sociology and Anthropology at Carlton University.

0

FOREWORD

Christine Labuski and Emily Yates-Doerr

WE LAUNCHED THIS BOOK IN 2015 WITH A QUESTION: WHAT IS AN ETH-
nographic case? As ethnography is a process and practice of authorship, this
question produces another: what can it be made to be?

The contributions to this book explore what cases can generate and our
reasons for resisting or embracing them as modes of analysis. There is a rich and
variable history to 'thinking in cases' (Forrester 1996; Creese and Frisby 2012;
Grasswick and Arden McHugh 2021). The expository medical case, attentive to
the unusual and particular, has long been used as a tool for both diagnosis and
instruction. The psychoanalytic case is built from fragments of remembered
details with therapeutic objectives. The legal case establishes a precedent,
while the criminal case comes to the detective as a mystery to be solved. In the
twenty-seven chapters of this book we show the ethnographic case to be all of
these things at once: instructing, dis/proving, establishing, evoking. We also
show that it may achieve different ends altogether.

What follows is a series of 'ethnographic cases' by scholars whose essays
illuminate, even as they unsettle, how we work with this genre.[1] In medical,
law, and business schools, exemplary cases have long been used as pedagogical
tools. Similarly, we hope this collection can serve as a resource for teaching.
You might use these cases to encourage your students to consider how to narrate an occurrence or event from the material of the everyday. Along the way,
you'll find that ethnographic cases produce a very different form of expertise
than those produced in medicine, law, or business. Often told in the form of

a story, the ethnographic case can be an example or an exception. It can also distort distinctions between the micro and macro, demonstrating that what is big can be small, or that significant power resides in that which may be very hard to see. Though explicitly incidental, cases distinguish themselves from other short forms of narrative by way of the expertise they invoke. Solving, learning from, or interpreting the case requires a level of engagement that presumes both knowledge and curiosity, the proficient habitus that makes improvisation possible. Interpretive expertise, in other words, transforms the extemporaneous into the routine, the anecdote into the lesson. Case closed. Or is it?

The book was also a case – an indexical instance – of a collective experiment in digital publishing. The essays themselves began as a web series on *Somatosphere* that ran biweekly over the course of a year. A year or so after its completion, we worked with Mattering Press to put the essays into digital conversation by publishing a 'living book' where readers – including series contributors – could make comments and pose questions as part of a broader conversation. This experiment in public peer review has a unique DOI and lives on as a virtual publication. It was always the plan for the publication with Mattering Press to eventually assume a printed form, a book that could be held, marking both a closure and a new kind of life.

We were scheduled for final editing and publication in 2020. Then the Covid pandemic hit, and we paused all work on the book. Our energy was spread thin as deaths climbed from thousands to hundreds of thousands to millions. It was a time filled with emergency and crisis, and we could not find time for the slow and patient work that books demand.

Yet still, through all the calls of urgency we heard as Covid unfolded, the meticulous, patient methods of ethnography began to seem ever more important. Though the fieldwork in this book all predates the Covid pandemic, the lessons our authors offer about medical knowledge, claims to truth, experiences of illness and engagements with vitality have continued relevance for how we think about – and live through – pandemic times.

The pandemic also ushered in a renewed interest in cases, as r-nought (R0) measurements, daily Covid counts, social distancing, fatality rates, hospital bed counts, community transmission, flattening the curve and contact tracing all became part of everyday vocabulary. 'How many cases are there today?' was a question garnering widespread public attention as the broader question of how cases amplify into a prevalence came to have clear policy stakes in our daily lives. During the earliest months of the pandemic, the distinction between cases and stories felt obvious and important: the former a metric tally of ever-growing risk, the latter a way to imagine and personalise the suffering. Both loomed as potential futures, as we struggled to map our realities onto metrics and stories. For months, there were very few cases where Christine lived. A prominent aerosol expert lived in her university town, and knowledge about the dangers led to early and almost universal protocol following. Christine kept saying that she felt like she was in a play about a pandemic – what was this a case of?

Though most of our writing was concluded before the onset of the pandemic, we are publishing in a new context, where the word 'case' is now part of the daily lexicon. Much of what we learned from our contributors pertained to the role of interpretation in case work. Regardless of why we were drawn to a case, what made our cases 'ethnographic cases' was that we undertook the work of asking questions about meaning and materiality to parse out what the case could say. Though many of our pieces are in dialogue with 'the medical case', none of us could have imagined how familiar we would all become with this vernacular and experience over the coming years.

What role did interpretation now play with respect to cases of Covid? Those of us trained to think with medical anthropology likely maintained that mode of attention; that is, we paid attention to the differences in experience – racialised, gendered, geopolitical – that emerged from and gave shape to the pandemic. As the cases mounted, we were joined by many non-anthropologists in parsing and piecing together what there was to learn about structural inequalities from these case patterns. But this time, our role as interpreters was discouraged, often quite vociferously, by state and professional actors: listen to us, they urged, as we have the answers. This isn't/wasn't the time for interpretation, no matter how much expertise on the topic we brought to bear.

For some of us, Covid was quite personal. People that we knew and loved fell ill, and some died, adding to the numeric spectacle of cases that shaped our days. Our lives were circumscribed in new ways. Covid accentuated social hierarchies and inequalities, but it also generated some broadly shared experiences. In the language of our contributors, it inspired, took the shape of, mapped on to, or helped us to access a sense of a connected reality. This is still what cases do.

Both Copeland and Grant caution that, once attuned, the anthropologist might begin to see cases everywhere – and that observation and description persistently become sites for intervention. How does this provocation shift when cases are, literally, everywhere? What is the ethnographic case of Covid cases? This is not just word play but, rather, a question about how to leverage the power of cases. Back to our original question: what can a case be made to be and what are cases of Covid made of? What is the ethnography of isolation?

For many, Covid slowed us down. There have, of course, been many phases to the pandemic, from dark experiences of intense isolation and quarantine, to the opening up of new possibilities for world-building, to staving off a return of complacency. Through illness and fear, rising Covid cases confronted us with questions about how we want to live. What should our days include? What do we need and who needs us? What matters today, this week, next month and how can I participate in these actions? The press's name of Mattering Press couldn't feel more resonant with the moment: do these stories matter?

We would argue yes. We have followed through with the publication of this book, many years after the project first began, as a statement about the endurance of knowledge gained through ethnography. Ethnographic casework is a slow process, with the knowledge that developed about its case frequently taking years to develop. Covid did not so much change the relevance of ethnography as show ethnography's slow, temporal commitments to be as vital as ever. Although Covid was transformative and life altering, the cases in this book did not need to be radically rewritten as a response. The lessons offered already anticipated and illuminated many of Covid's lessons about how systems reproduce themselves, and also about how people can intervene in and transform these cycles of reproduction. Ultimately, the ethnographic case teaches its readers how to simultaneously cultivate attention to particularities and to the knotted interconnections of world-systems. Our cases illuminate deep connections, but also how particular stories can diverge. They draw reader attention to something different and unexpected, something which does not fit the common stories so far told. They teach us that you do not have to be large, loud or reproducible to matter.

In many ways, 'the case' and ethnography may seem antithetical: the former a short reflection, the latter based on a commitment over time. What we show, however, is that the skill of the ethnographic case lies in its ability to situate the narration of any one event within other narratives, many of which have been listened to and attended to over a long period of time. Ultimately the particularities of ethnographic cases do not aspire to generalised knowledge, but they may nonetheless change the practice of and possibilities for generalities. They teach us how to ask questions that do not need definitive answers but lead on to other questions. They help us to open up and turn the situations we have encountered around, and around again. It is by changing the arc of the questions we ask, and the stories we can tell, that the ethnographic case acts upon the worlds in which we live.

ENDNOTES

1 To pay homage to the traditional ethnographic monograph, the pieces were initially assembled as an expanding bookCASE on Somatosphere (Yates-Doerr and Labuski 2015). The digital Mattering Press book, composed from this series, was later published with Mattering Press (Yates-Doerr and Labuski 2018).

REFERENCES

Creese, G., and W. Frisby, *Feminist Community Research: Case Studies and Methodologies* (Chicago: University of Chicago Press, 2012).

Forrester, J. 'If p, Then What? Thinking in Cases', *History of the Human Sciences*, 9.1 (1996), 1–25.

Grasswick, H., and N. Arden McHugh, *Making the Case: Feminist and Critical Race Philosophers Engage Case Studies* (Albany, NY: SUNY Press, 2021).

Yates-Doerr, E., and C. Labuski, eds., 'The Ethnographic Case', *Somatosphere*, 2015. http://somatosphere.net/ethnographiccase/.

——, eds., *The Ethnographic Case* (Manchester: Mattering Press, 2018). https://processing.matteringpress.org/ethnographiccase/.

I

INTRODUCTION

Emily Yates-Doerr & Christine Labuski

THE BOOKCASE

One day, early on in the series that would eventually become this book, we received two submissions. Their similar anatomy was striking. Each featured a medical waiting room. Someone entered the space with a gift for the clinical personnel, the gift was accepted, and something shifted in the resulting care.

In Aaron Ansell's case, set within the gardens of an informal clinic in Piauí, Brazil, the gift was a small satchel of milk. Rima Praspaliauskiene's was set in a Lithuanian public hospital and the gift was a rich chocolate cake. Aaron, who works and teaches on legal orders, analysed the exchange as a challenge to hospital norms of egalitarianism. He helped us to see how the give-and-take of milk interrupts the requirements of a deracinated liberal democracy, offering instead the warm sociality of personal affinity. Rima, who focuses on medical care and valuing, used the object of the chocolate cake to query the social scientist's impulse to explain why people do what they do. She shows us how this impulse may rest upon the linearity and equivalence of rational calculation, uncomfortably treating sociality as a commodity.

The juxtaposition of these submissions is emblematic – a case, if you will – of something we collectively illustrate: the art of ethnographic writing resides in a relation between what is there and what is done with it. Each of the twenty-seven chapters that follow offers a meditation on how social scientists work with cases.

BEGINNINGS

We might trace the origin of the book to a Science, Technology and Medicine business meeting at the American Anthropological Association annual meeting, when we offered the idea of 'the ethnographic case' as a theme for a series to be published on the web journal *Somatosphere*. We were inspired by Tomas Matza and Harris Solomon's series, 'Commonplaces', which offered a 'cabinet' organised as short reflections on how commonplace technologies shape social life (2013). In proposing the theme, we were imagining a bookCase of short fieldwork stories that would showcase the power of anthropological attention to specific, situated stories while also querying the relationship between these stories and generalisations of knowledge. The idea was quickly picked up and moved around by the group. Almost everyone had something to add. Medical cases, detective cases, legal cases, psychiatric cases: the similarities and differences between how ethnographers think with and in cases, and the use of cases in other fields, were intriguing.

We might also trace the origins to fieldwork. Many of the authors in the series noted that there was *something* – an interaction, encounter, object, or image – from time in the field that had become haunting. Participation in our bookCase series, which would publish a new case every other week on *Somatosphere*, offered a chance to flesh out how messy interactions over many months of fieldwork become condensed into ethnographic moments, where the already understood folds together with that which is yet to be tamed (Strathern 1999).

From the beginning, Christine knew she would write about Judy – a patient she had encountered in her research on vulvar pain. Judy's presence shaped Christine's book, although Christine had not yet had a chance to write specifically about their encounter. Christine titled the case '3 millimetres' – a reference to a closure as much as an opening, for lichen planus, an autoimmune disease, had fused Judy's labia to this small size, causing embarrassment and pain. The details of Judy's story are unique, but taken together they crystallised a problem that Christine had grappled with during her months at the Vulvar Health Clinic: people do not know how to talk about genitals, and an inability to verbalise genitalia contributes to their medical neglect. Silence was not a space of nothingness; it was a space where tissue fused and pus accreted as the vulva, an object erased precisely by its hypersexuality, becomes unthinkable, and thereby untreatable, in preventative practices of care. Writing the vulva, speaking the vulva in her case – as with speaking it in the clinic – would help to develop a new linguistic ecology, making vulvas matter in better ways.

Emily didn't contribute a case herself but used the time of editing the cases as an opportunity to think through challenges of casework that she had encountered while doing research. In her fieldwork on obesity, public health workers had argued that case-based treatment approaches, no matter how personalised, ignored that obesity was an illness of complex systems, built up over generational time. As its causes were not individual, treating patients as if there was anything that they – personally – could do to prevent being sick saddled them with an impossible responsibility that often made things worse. These public health workers instead advocated treating obesity as a problem based on political and economic structures.

While this made sense, Emily feared that a focus on structures quickly slipped into a domain of knowledge that prioritised metrics, not ethnography. To offer a quick observation: people routinely expressed concern that obesity was a structural problem with numbers, implying that a measurable demographic was suffering or sick. The problem she saw was that metric-based descriptions risked mobilising plans for treating quite dissimilar people and experiences and afflictions, as if this heterogeneity did not matter. Concern for *ontological violence* – alongside violence that is structural – made Emily cautious about constraining anthropologists to the role of illustrating, with our stories, what the economists or epidemiologists already know.

It was as much out of curiosity for ethnographic structures as for ethnographic cases that Emily began to wonder what would happen to obesity if she uncased it, followed it outside the clinical setting. Listening to this curiosity, she started tracking obesity across kitchens, schools, farms and laboratory science—although tracking is not quite the right word, for it turned out there was no stable object leaving footprints in the sand. Obesity in kitchens, where women struggled to square their expertise in cooking with dietary counselling that treated them as ignorant, was not the same as obesity in grade schools, where children learned not to eat fattening 'junk food' but had only candy and soda available at recess. In farms, where people used toxic pesticides to grow healthy vegetables for far-away consumers worried about their weight, obesity was a matter of chemicals and trade. And in scientific centres, where researchers travelled into rural communities and then returned to their urban laboratories with swabs of saliva or vials of blood, it became a problem of ancestral deprivation – yet different again.

The intricacies of the structures Emily was encountering began to turn her understanding of the relation between the particular and the general on its head. She was beginning to see the case not as a part of something larger (a unit to be added together with others). Instead, the very practice of adding things together changed the substance under evaluation, such that there was simply no way to add it up.

Both Christine and Emily were drawn to the intrigue of 'the ethnographic case', in part, from conviction gained by living in the mess of anthropological fieldwork that things need not be patterned nor predictable to have efficacy – that particularity is its own form of power. We were also drawn to it because it posed a critical question for a field organised by participant observation: how does one make an analytic intervention that is situated and still expansive enough to address global injustices and violence? (This is an especially troubling question considering that expansion – a colonial practice if there ever was one – so often furthers injustice and violence).

And so we began to assemble a group of ethnographers to think about how the practice of telling stories shapes the worlds we study. An important postcolonial critique of anthropology notes that we too often get our case materials in the peripheries while doing our so-called theory in colonial centres (Oyèrónké Oyěwùmí 1997; Law and Lin 2016). There is a highly gendered dynamic to this division between the particular and the general as well (Behar and Gordon 1996). We began to wonder if a possible way forward might be found in the assertion that *the case is the theory*. But before making this argument, we thought we'd find out what anthropologists were doing with their cases. 'What is the ethnographic case?', we asked in our opening call for contributions. And then, to be more precise about the question, 'what can it be made to be?'

DESIGN

Every other week, for over a year, our bookCase grew larger by one installation. In fashioning the bookCase, we worked with graphic designers to emphasise texture over pattern. If anthropologists have long sought to make generalities by looking for replications, reproductions and repetitions of culture, this was a chance to try out something else. The design we settled on was one where the cases were each connected but also stood apart. While they shared a basic design, they also varied in their thinness and thickness. The texture chosen to illustrate the cover of each case was selected by the author to offer a hint at something that would lie within the case, encouraging, from the outset, what Anna Tsing has called an 'art of noticing' (2015). In emphasising specificity over pattern, we wanted to stress a practice of noticing how we notice: what do we keep in the frame of the stories we tell; what do we set aside; what travels between cases and what stays put? The push, from the outset, was to think of ethnography as the study of the techniques by which cultures are made to materialise, rather than the study of culture as if such a thing could ever stand by itself (see Landecker 2007, 2016).

CASEWORK

The twenty-seven contributors to this volume related stories about cases that immediately drew them in and haunted them long after the fact; about people or events that both indexed and interrupted broader patterns, and about places and contexts where being *a case of* something was either routine or exceptional. Several authors use their stories to *make a case for* something: a compelling idea or a perspectival shift, for example. Others understand their cases to be points of departure, an episode or figure that appeared to be one thing but turned out to be another, and that left them thinking as much or more about the source and routes of their ethnographic curiosity as about what questions their cases did or did not answer. If our initial interest lay in the question of what the case can be made to be, we quickly learned that the answer was wide and unsteady: with every entry, 'the case' shifted from what it was the week before.

The series began with Annemarie Mol's case, which recounts the story of a country doctor who injected turpentine into the leg of a dying farmer to activate his immune system, thereby saving his life. She uses the story to suggest that cases, be they medical or ethnographic, serve to evoke and inspire, generating resources in one place that might be used elsewhere – though there are never guarantees about how these resources will travel.

Anna Harris' case addresses the condition of autophony, in which patients cannot screen out sounds that most people do not notice, hearing, for example, their eyeballs moving left to right. She counterposes medical cases, which aim to normalise that which is bizarre, with ethnographic cases, which turn something as mundane as a tapping finger into a point of fascination. She asks about the strangely familiar place of the ethnographer's body in the generation of our stories: 'How do we listen in? And when we do, what does it do to our stories of the world when we use our own sensing, moving, living bodies as a case for others?'

Nick Copeland also focuses on an atypical condition: that of facial paralysis accompanying an epidemic of Bell's Palsy in Guatemala's Western highlands. At least medical doctors might call it Bell's Palsy, and calling it this might stabilise it enough to offer some prescriptive treatments. But whereas clinical understandings and prescriptions of bodily disorder allowed the diagnosis to travel far, he found they also failed to characterise the suffering of people who experienced momentary intensities *and* systematic violence. He reads the case of paralysis through a patterned failure of human and planetary systems. But if the case hints at something larger, there is also something tellingly nervous about the very possibility of 'the system'.

Systems thinking forms the basis of Atsuro Morita's case which takes up the relation between holist and partial systems through a story of sailing along the Noi River in Thailand with a firm of Japanese engineers who are studying Dutch irrigation canals. If this sounds complex, the point is rather that the trip has been carefully arranged. Intricate, yes, but not here wild, although this binary becomes a point of departure for the essay since the nature they are studying has been designed to be transformed. Through a series of deft ethnographic manoeuvres that bring together the field and its representation, Morita illustrates (or to turn from visual-based language toward action-based language – he *does*) the field site as an always-experimental space.

REPRESENT-ABILITIES

Questions of representation loomed large throughout the series. While representation may, in some academic corners, still be taken as a reflection of a stable truth, we drew upon numerous cases of political, legal or activist representation in which representation took a different form. Here representation rather connotes *advocating for* – an idea, a political position, a group of women and so on – entailing a stance, an engagement and an assailable commitment.

What's in a name?, Ruth Goldstein asks, facing us with the long-neglected representational problem of choosing pseudonyms. One solution might be to work with people to select the names they want to use. But in Goldstein's research on mining and sex work in the Peruvian Amazon, she found that in some cases it was not safe to use the names people wanted, and in others, the names they wanted were not theirs to give. Eschewing an ethics based in prefigured rules Goldstein takes naming to be an active, negotiated process of labour, fraught with asymmetry. We may work to perfect it – to express ourselves better – but if we are to fashion a goal for ourselves, it might lie in attending to the labour of naming and not in the ideal of coming up with a perfect name.

Teresa Velásquez further explores relations of collaboration with and between anthropological interlocutors to address a situation in which Ecuadorian anti-mining activists refused to be represented in her writing. They were worried, Velásquez explains, about extractivism in ethnographic practice and wanted to maintain their own words, even as they were learning how to speak from others. Everyone in this case is in drag, referent indistinguishable from sign – and yet claims to the power of 'the real' continue to have efficacy. One ends this essay with a clearer sense than ever of how the powers of the spoken word are in awkward (read: productive) relation with the material powers of earth, violence and gold.

That representation reinforces certain kinds of power is a worry that animates Anna Wilking's case. She entered fieldwork wanting to make a film that would celebrate the motherhood of Ecuadorian sex workers, whom she knew to be using sex work to be 'good' mothers in many of motherhood's most romantic terms. But the medium of film, though highly editable, could not be predetermined, and the story that found Wilking was a story of a 'good father' who filled an absent mother's place. The case was unusual – it was, as Wilking writes – a *mis*representation of most sex workers who choose sex work to stay active in their children's lives. And yet, letting go of the sociological mandate that a case must stand in for a majority allowed Wilking to focus on the vulnerable, nurturing masculinities that are surely there but so often left out of stories of sex workers' lives. She represented the story of fatherhood not because it was broadly *representative* but because it was a future that deserved to be made visible.

Jenna Grant's case similarly positions representation as a technique for *fixing* things, in a double-meaning of the term that implies giving ontological stability to fluid objects – not because there is one real underlying truth to the form of these objects, but because this can sometimes help to improve (fix) the matters of concern. Lest you worry that this is difficult to grasp, the argument – as with the arguments in each of the twenty-seven cases – is made accessible through field-work. The aunt of Puthea, a woman in Phnom Penh, sees a small cat in an ultra-sound image of Puthea's fetus. The image hints at a porousness between humans, images, animals and machines while also giving biological shape to the being-in-formation. The ethnographer, she makes clear, is part of the mess and the mix:

> Exceptional stories fix ethnographers, too. I did not hear about another cat-like scan, yet after talking to Puthea and Ming, I listened more closely for image stories. I asked different questions. I worked to make this story into an exemplary ethnographic case. Can it bear this weight? Perhaps. If representations fix—whether with words, images, or as cases—that fixing is a process, impermanent yet consequential. Fixing the image fixes the fate. Fixing the case shifts what is possible.

Her case ends by shifting what is possible and, indeed, with many of the cases, 'the future' is at stake. Yet also apparent in our series is that by writing cases we do not only author other, future, conditions of possibility; in the practice of authoring we make evident 'other' conditions that are already t/here.

This point is made clearly in Sameena Mulla's consideration of different ways prosecutors and defendants depict the skin around the vagina in rape trial testimony. Court outcomes may be swayed by the use of hair scrunchies or timing belts or by the presence of blood or its absence. But regardless of what jurors see and how they see it, there can be violence even when there are no visible wounds. Things can be real ('really real') without being apparent – and still the practice of making-evidence through expert intervention must be drawn upon to make them so.

Also taking up the question of laws and borders, Zoe Todd's case bends established Euro-Western legal statutes to not just recognise but reciprocate the implicit Indigenous legal orders 'all around'. She draws attention to the micro-sites where human-fish transspecies collaborations are actively resisting and reshaping colonial logics and Inuvialuit territories. Her goal is not simply to raise awareness – produce knowledge – of these sites for an academic community. This is a case that seeks to *change* the ongoing violence of academic 'iterations and interpretations of Indigenous philosophy'.

The essay by André Menard and Constanza Tizzoni further troubles the role of anthropological knowledge through a comparison between legal and ethnographic case work. Their essay unfolds through the following puzzling situation: A Mapuche defendant is accused of killing his wife. The language of culture is drawn upon, for exoneration requires linguistic and cultural sleights of hand that perform the man as insane, and, with this, perform the techniques of anthropology as insane as well. This is a case that questions the very project of ever having a case stand in for – speak for – a totality.

Carole McGranahan's case also marks the shifting horizons between factual and legal representation. This is the scene she sets: Tashi, a Tibetan man, must prove that he is the father of his children upon moving to Canada as a refugee. A DNA test suggests to Canadian officials that he is not the father, so the anthropologist is called upon to show that kinship – and not genetics – make fatherhood in Tibet. It is clear that this defies Canada's existing legal parameters of family, which ask that fatherhood fit into a genetic 'yes' or 'no'. What is less clear is how much ethnography can make courts bend; how much can our differences make a difference?

The cases thus far in the collection had taught us not to expect that this question could be answered in general terms. In some of the cases, anthropological interventions sought to illustrate the value of materially recognising human difference. Faye Ginsburg and Rayna Rapp's 'No judgments' narrates events that took place during a day of fieldwork with the autism theatre initiative, a group that works to make Broadway theatre accessible to people with disabilities, along with their families and allies. For these performances, the theatre space is modified to account for particular sensory issues involving light and sound, fidget toys, safe spaces and a high tolerance for diverse behaviour. Ginsburg and Rapp's contribution makes a case for upholding the aspirations, rights and accommodations of people with disabilities, articulating 'life with a difference' as an aspect of human variation too long neglected in anthropology.

Susan Reynolds Whyte's polygraphic casebook describes a process of collective and transnational authorship to tell stories of unexpectedly living through Uganda's AIDS epidemic. The many authors involved seek to document the individual and diverse experiences of people whose lives were extended by ARVs. In writing ethnography through cases they seek to 'capture' readers and not only the lives of the people whose stories they tell. These are representations that aim to grab attention and make an impact.

Meanwhile, Ken MacLeish's case emphasises a call to pause over (or perhaps *as*) a call to action. He focuses on the production of violence through a 'non-event' – here, a soldier who might have fired on a harmless vehicle but did not. The tension made material in the account he re-scribes is that the distribution of agency into an 'actor network' may impede the very sorts of response-abilities that ANT's critique of the liberal subject sought to encourage. What emerges is a challenge to both the sovereignty of the individual and the displacement of this sovereignty into the mess of bureaucratic orders. This is a case, as with many of our cases, that raises far more questions than it answers; in doing so, the tactic of relentless questioning emerges as a possible way forward.

SOCIAL LIVES OF CASES AND CONCEPTS

That cases have social lives is a truth that emerges from our bookCase. And another truth: it is not simply 'the case' for which this is the case, but *all* concepts that we deploy and study –sociality here being a case in point. A few decades ago Bruno Latour critiqued 'the social' for its celebration of the human (Latour 1992). That argument had its place then and there, but if the sociality that our cases highlight today is human, it is 'not only' (de la Cadena et al. 2015) this. Anthropologists have long argued that *nature is social*. Complementing this, many of our cases demonstrate that *the social, too, is natural*—an argument sustained by ethnographic consideration of nature as a swamping, smelly, ugly, active and unpredictable thing.

Ildikó Zonga Plájás, for example, writes of how life within the Danube Delta Biosphere is infused with fog and rays of light. This swamp-nature, with its incongruous refuge and wonder, *produces* ways of knowing and living. The weight of the camera she holds accompanies the gravity of the documentary task, giving shape to stories that in turn shape this landscape. This is representation that is *after* something in the world.

In Janelle Lamoreaux's case of the DeTox Lab in Nanjing, China, the synthetic pesticides and pollutants that settle into earth and bodies have been rendered, by both scientists and activists, as 'the environment'. Narrative and statistical accounts alike strategically naturalise the effects of industrialisation to make the case that ugly sperm make ugly futures. Accounting for nature in this way, Lamoreaux shows, may not be a general but an inspirational project.

Christy Spackman's case unpacks the chemistry of sociality through discussion of a sweet, liquorice-like smell that permeates the lives of residents of Charleston, West Virginia. A spill of 4-methylchycloheanemethanol damaged the region's water supply. Instruments designed to measure the ghostly toxin could not detect it; and still the contaminant persisted, if unevenly, in people's sensorial experiences. Spackman describes how nature becomes domesticated in a laboratory while the impurities of domestic activities – cooking, seeing, smelling tasting – are held at bay. In this case, scientific purification comes with a price, as contingency's mess would yield better knowledge about the presence of chemicals than lab technologies. Or perhaps we should consider this as *producing* a price, since the inequalities in who bears the burden of toxicity sustain inequalities of industrial production.

In Jennifer Carlson's discussion of energy transition in Germany, 'nature' also pertains as much to financial as to biological futures. Her case, set amid a rapidly transitioning solar panel installation project in the hamlet of Dobbe, examines the psychosomatic afterlives of green energy to illustrate the entanglement of ecology with capitalist speculation. Life that was supposed to be made good is instead filled with fibreglass, rust and plastic ruins; anxiety and stress emerge from the wreckage of now abandoned glasshouses. As does so much else: compassion, friendship, family meals. Consumers (or are they citizens? or mothers? or lovers? or friends?) struggle to make sense of their condition through the categories of social analysis, but even as they do so, life, like weeds, takes shape outside these bounds.

PLASTIC BOUNDARIES

How do you know a case when you see one? Elizabeth Lewis writes of a single encounter, well before she began extensive fieldwork that would become a 'flashpoint' for later analysis of disability care in Texas. At first the encounter seemed to be an outlier. The blind and non-verbal woman, locked in a cage in a Central American institution, was anything but typical. Over time, however, the woman edged ever-closer to the centre of Lewis' analysis. The woman may remain enclosed in a wooden box in a far-away place – but this was not all that happened. Absent was made present; what was locked away was also leaking out. This is not an arena where cases lie waiting to be known and seen; it is one where they are done through narrative relations.

'Cases set boundaries; cases draw you in', note Biggs and Bodinger de Uriarte. They use the constantly mirrored reflections of a Native American casino to make their point. The Casino is a mimetic world, interiors containing a complicated mix of referents, exteriors gesturing outward while embracing their own design as part of the sign. So too might we understand the halls of anthropology to be mimetic. We 'reveal' – but less because there is one possible truth to be known and more because this act of demonstration is part of the performance. A practice of mirrors, whose reflection also changes how we see.

Every other week, we collectively participated in remaking 'the case'. We could not make cases out of nothing – we could not make things that didn't matter. Nevertheless, the condition of being material in no way suggested that cases could freeze their form. Case by case, to borrow from Jason Danely's entry, the case was adjusted and transformed. Stomach tubes are Danely's entry into this argument. Decisions about whether to use tubes in elderly care homes, fraught with uncertainty by all involved, must be negotiated case-by-case. Cases are specific, unique, grounded in the variable textures of the everyday – what he refers to as a 'constellation of contingencies'. Here, however, Danely intervenes to shift the implications of contingency. For if cases are exceptional, *that* they are exceptional is commonplace. It is this connection that serves as a point through which to begin a conversation. Here, becoming a case facilitated processes of sharing without aspirations of becoming identical. Mutuality without replication.

'Are the truths of the case's contingency and plasticity ontological truths?' you might wonder. 'Let's try out different answers and follow what happens', we might respond.

ALTERNATIVES AND AUTHOR-ITIES

Sharing across different sorts of differences turns us toward matters of politics, which is to say, matters of relating. Through his study of earthworms, Filippo Bertoni asks us to consider what happens to relating if we think not through the mode of argumentation but through metabolic pathways of incorporation, digestion and excretion. What arises from this exploration is that 'the purpose of *making a case* may not be to be right, but to offer resources that we can use to metabolize and live with the world in alternative ways'.

It is worth pausing to consider Bertoni's emphasis on living in 'alternative ways' given the focus on the plasticity of nature made above. Many readers will have heard of claims to 'alternative facts' made by conservative pundits who reproduce a longstanding tactic of fascist politics by claiming that assumed truths are not what they seem. Some may wonder if this isn't somehow uncomfortably resonant with what we are doing here, with our unstable ontologies and our futures and actualities that are worlded through representational practices. Let us point to a difference.

Alternative facts – war is peace; freedom is slavery – are still rooted in ontological claims upon a one-world world in which there is one, and only one, correct reflection of that world. These so-called facts are not giving up their singular authority – the authority that comes from locking things up. The science of this series meanwhile asks how things come to be bounded and then sets out to understand the effects of binding things one way or another or another yet again. We ask this not because there is just one answer to be known, but because some questions, and some answers, are better than others – better not in general terms but in specific cases.

Bertoni notes that through ethnographising earthworms he learned about how they are already engaged in politics otherwise, which gave him ideas for how he might do this as well.

> The living together of worms can serve as a reminder to Euro-American social scientists that there are no guidelines out there on how to live together well. Instead, politics, when understood as living together, calls for makeshift arrangements that are both radical and specific, as well as for experimenting with alternatives. If composting might work through certain standard passages, composting guides never give any final word, but rather suggest some possible alternatives to tinker with. This is a togetherness that is not constrained by the limits of closed systems and of the categories that Euro-Americans commonly use to think about the world. It is instead a togetherness enlarged by the imaginative openings that worms, like anthropology, can offer us.

If Bertoni's case has a lesson for Euro-American sciences, we hope that our series might have a lesson for Euro-American politics. We could respond to the fascist claim of alternative facts by saying that, no, 'facts are facts', thereby initiating a fight over whose facts are right. Yet to replace the myriad truths of ethnography with the single truth of 'truth' would be a short-sighted tactic that undermines both scientific and political possibilities. In Bertoni's case the facts of science are facts that are open to, even welcoming of, alternatives (note the multiplicity). Not just anything can become a fact. After all, methods matter. Here, a precondition to becoming a fact was that you were not closed to other possibilities. To be science is to be challengeable, not certain. We might wish something similar for politics, creating systems designed to be both contested and recursively transformed.

Rather than concede that our *alternatives* were misdirected to those who abuse this term, this book suggests that it is especially crucial to stay close to the study of how truth-making proceeds and truth-telling gains power. *That* something *is*, is merely a starting point for asking *how* something *is* – a starting point, in other words, for thinking about how we are acting and how we might act otherwise. In the face of toxic lies that intend to close down the project of enquiry, the project of engaging alternatives becomes more necessary than ever.

Stephanie Krehbiel's case is a good one on which to wrap up. In her entry, case-making facilitated the production of violence. She writes of being transformed into a case, her analytic capacities and professional qualifications stripped from her. This is not an accidental metaphor; producing persons as cases – and cases as woman, as body – can privilege ways of knowing that facilitate abuse – and do so very often in the name of furthering good. The cultivation of intimacy, long taken as a hallmark of anthropological legitimacy, in her site becomes a means for the twisted, suppressed eroticism of power to take hold, subverting what is known in the name of more stable knowledge.

Krehbiel makes a point about authority and power that has been with us throughout the series. The man she writes about deploys his authority to subvert the power that she holds and does so through terms and ideas that resonate with her own. He speaks to her of examining how knowledge is gained and legitimised; he emphasises the importance of *discerning* what is good. But he does this, she shows, to bolster his authority over her. He is not interested in a flourishing of possibilities but in using his truth (in the singular) against her. She realises that she cannot talk back to him because he will take up and twist her words. Eventually, she begins to ignore him, putting her energies elsewhere. He engages power in the name of finding truth; she finds power, making space for her authorities, by cutting the relation.

This book attempts to respond to critiques of ethnography, whether these come from positivist scientists who find the methods too disorganised and lacking in both rigor and replicability, or decolonial scientists who question anthropology's extractivist legacies (and with whom we see ourselves aligned). Instead of arguing against these critiques, we adopt the tactic of celebrating ethnography by doing it well. In twenty-seven installations, we show ethnography to be vibrant, curious and committed. But this does not mean that ethnography is *always* vibrant, curious and committed. For we've also given it space to be none of these: to be focused on mundane details that call into question a need to be vibrant; to ask how curiosity may activate and further the exploitation of capitalism; to consider when we might lessen and not strengthen our commitments.

What we learn from the ethnographic case is a way to practise authoring, and authority, with care for the situation and the story. We attempt to neither ask nor answer the question of what 'the case' is in general terms. Instead, we take up the challenging truth that it is not only the objects we study that have social lives: so do our theories about them. This, then, sets us on a path of caring not only for what is inside our cases. It compels us to also care for what their walls are made of and to ask how these structures can be done differently and moved.

REFERENCES

Behar, R., and D. A. Gordon, *Women Writing Culture* (Berkeley, CA: University of California Press, 1996).

de la Cadena, M., et al., 'Anthropology and STS: Generative Interfaces, Multiple Locations', *HAU: Journal of Ethnographic Theory*, 5.1 (2015), 437–75.

Landecker, H., *Culturing Life: How Cells Became Technologies* (Cambridge, MA: Harvard University Press, 2006).

——, 'It Is What It Eats: Chemically Defined Media and the History of Surrounds', *Studies in History and Philosophy of Science. Part C. Studies in History and Philosophy of Biological and Biomedical Sciences*, 6.57 (2007), 148–69.

Latour, B., *One More Turn after the Social Turn* (Notre Dame, IN.: University of Notre Dame Press, 1992).

Law, J., and W. Lin, *The Stickiness of Knowing: Translation, Postcoloniality and STS*, 2016. http://heterogeneities.net/publications/LawLin2016TheStickinessOf Knowing.pdf.

Matza, T., and H. Solomon, 'Commonplaces: Itemizing the Technological Present', *Somatosphere*, 2013. http://somatosphere.net/commonplaces/.

Oyèrónké, O., *The Invention of Women: Making an African Sense of Western Gender Discourses* (Minneapolis, MN: University of Minnesota Press, 1997).

Strathern, M., Property, *Substance, and Effect: Anthropological Essays on Persons and Things* (London: Athlone Press, 1999).

Tsing, A. L., *The Mushroom at the End of the World: On the Possibility of Life in Capitalist Ruins* (Princeton, NJ: Princeton University Press, 2015).

2

EXEMPLARY: THE CASE OF THE FARMER AND THE TURPENTINE

Annemarie Mol

IN 1976, WHEN I WAS EIGHTEEN AND HE WAS EIGHTY-FOUR, MY GRAND-father told me the case of the young farmer and the turpentine. By then this case was more than fifty years old. It stemmed from the time that my grandfather, Chris Mol, worked as a general practitioner in what was then a poor, sandy region of the Netherlands. When he settled there, the people and the land still looked pretty much as they had when, forty years earlier, Vincent van Gogh had been drawing and painting the local farmers. At the time, being a family practitioner meant receiving people who came to see 'the doctor' in his house throughout the day. His was a big house, painted a warm yellow, in the style of Vienna (where after graduating in Amsterdam my grandfather had extended his studies). Farmers regularly came for a consultation after Sunday mass, when they had already made the walk to the village centre. And when a young boy running or a neighbour with a bicycle were sent to fetch him, my grandfather would go and pay house visits to the widely dispersed farms, traveling by the motorbike that he had bought as soon as he could afford it.[1]

The case of the young farmer began with such a house visit. The doctor found the young man in bed with a fever and a nasty, infected wound in his left leg. He made a cut in the skin of the abscess, to allow for the escape of the *pus bonum et laudabile*: the good and praiseworthy pus. A body liberated of pus would heal faster. But the young farmer didn't heal. When the next day the doctor was called in once again, he feared an imminent sepsis, from which the patient was likely to die. What to do? There were as of yet no antibiotics. There were no other treatments either. Or were there? My grandfather remembered a case history that he had heard from an older colleague. In that case, too, the problem had been an infection in a leg that had become compartmentalised, festering and putrefying, while the rest of the body had not got itself involved in the defence.[2]

This is where the turpentine comes in. Chris Mol asked the young farmer's permission to engage in an experiment. The patient readily agreed. 'Yes doctor', he said, 'if you do nothing I will die, I feel I will'. So my grandfather steered his motorbike to the workshop of the local painter and asked for dirty turpentine. Back in the farm he injected a small amount of this into the dying man's right leg, the other leg. The experiment worked out well. The injected turps aroused a fierce, overall reaction of the immune system. This vehement immune response also reached the wound in the left leg and the bacteria infecting it. For a while the patient was critically ill, but he healed. That is the case of the young farmer and the turpentine. My grandfather told it to me as a lesson about both the human body and medical practice, a layered pedagogy that is typical of medical case histories. This is the lesson about the human body: it is complex and not quite predictable. And this is the lesson about medical practice: don't just depend on your textbooks, they may fail you. If they do, be inventive, daring. Case histories may help here as they relate what, often surprisingly, worked out well in other sites and situations.

As I reiterate this story here I seek to add another lesson, a lesson about sharing knowledge. To my mind 'the case of the young farmer and the turpentine' is an exemplary case of a *case*. A case carries knowledge, not in the form of firm rules or statistically salient regularities, but in the form of a story about an occurrence that, even though it may have happened just once, is still telling, indicative, suggestive. It condenses expertise that is not general, but inspirational. As cases are idiosyncratic, those who seek inspiration from them still have to think for themselves. They have to adapt the lessons learned to the situation in which they find themselves.

Cases, then, do not transport knowledge smoothly. It requires work to draw on them. The implications *here* of a case that occurred *elsewhere* have to be carefully thought through and tinkered with. Such tinkering may serve highly varied goals. Medical cases may inspire doctors who, under slightly different circumstances, with other specificities kicking in, have to solve a similarly intractable problem. Judges may seek guidance from cases as they consider how to judge the next particular intractability. For ethicists, discussing past cases or imaginary vignettes is a way of sharpening their skills of appraisal. For historians a case begs questions about its conditions of possibility: what all had to be in place for this particular event to occur?[3]

Cases are also good for those of us who craft theory as we work with empirical materials. For even if cases index situated events, it is still possible to make them pertinent elsewhere. Not everywhere, mind you. It remains to be seen where a lesson travels and where it doesn't hold. The genre of theory that cases inspire does not aim to be empirically encompassing or universally valid. Instead, it carries a set of sensitivities that emerge from the case at hand. And then begs the question what might be different elsewhere. For example, the case of anaemia may exemplify relations between clinical and laboratory ways of separating out the normal from the pathological (Mol and Berg 1994) (But in cancer the clinic relates differently to the lab [Jain 2013]). The case of diabetes may be used to argue that 'choice' is not a particularly helpful term in the context of living with a chronic disease, where other terms, like 'care', make better sense (Mol 2008). (But within caring practices there are moments when choices impose themselves [Callon and Rabeharisoa 2004]). The case of meat may illustrate the multiplicity of natures within the so-called West – for however much this 'West' is mono-naturalist in theory, in many of its practices, meat-practices included, reality multiplies (Yates-Doerr and Mol 2012). (This is a complicated message, for there are also instances where mono-naturalist visions impose themselves upon practices (Bonelli 2012).

And the case of the young farmer and the turpentine? Since 1976 I have tenaciously kept it in the back of my head as I worked on other cases. And as, finally, I now write it down, I am curious if beyond my specific situation, that of a granddaughter to whom it was passed on as a heritage, it may hold up as both a compelling story *and* a convincing case of a case.

ENDNOTES

1 For the separation between work and private space and time of general practitioners in the course of the twentieth century (in Britain, but the Dutch case is strikingly similar), see D. Armstrong, 'Space and Time in British General Practice', in M. Lock and D. Gordon, eds., *Biomedicine Examined* (New York: Springer), pp. 207–25.

2 For the immunology that was rising at the time, see Cohen, E., *A Body Worth Defending: Immunity, Biopolitics, and the Apotheosis of the Modern Body* (Durham, NC: Duke University Press (2009).

3 A great example of an historical quest for conditions of possibility is M. Foucault, *The Birth of the Clinic*, trans. A. Sheridan (London: Tavistock Publications, 1973/1963).

REFERENCES

Bonelli, C., 'Ontological Disorders: Nightmares, Psychotropic Drugs and Evil Spirits in Southern Chile', *Anthropological Theory*, 12.4 (2012), 407–26.

Callon, M., and V. Rabeharisoa, 'Gino's Lesson on Humanity: Genetics, Mutual Entanglements and the Sociologist's Role', *Economy & Society*, 33.1 (2008), 1–27.

Jain, S. L., *Malignant: How Cancer Becomes Us* (Berkley, CA: University of California Press, 2013).

Mol, A., 'Lived Reality and the Multiplicity of Norms: A Critical Tribute to George Canguilhem', *Economy and Society*, 27.2 (1998), 274–84.

——, *The Logic of Care: Health and the Problem of Patient Choice* (London: Routledge, 2008).

Mol, A., and M. Berg, 'Principles and Practices of Medicine', *Culture, Medicine and Psychiatry*, 18.2 (1994), 247–65.

Yates-Doerr, E., and A. Mol, 'Cuts of Meat: Disentangling Western Natures-Cultures', *Cambridge Anthropology*, 30.2 (2012), 48–64.

3

AUTOPHONY: LISTENING TO YOUR EYES MOVE

Anna Harris

ONE DOCTOR, SEVEN MEDICAL STUDENTS AND AN ANTHROPOLOGIST CROWD into the patient's very small hospital room. The doctor places his briefcase next to the bed, introduces himself to the patient and turns to his students. Whose turn to do a respiratory examination? Mumbling, shuffling, staring at shoes but soon a volunteer. First inspection, palpation and then the tricky techniques of percussion and auscultation; that is, tapping out body sounds with one finger over another and listening to the patient's breathing through a stethoscope. The student isn't sure if he is finding a dull note when he percusses one part of the patient's back, as she hunches awkwardly forward in her cotton gown. The other students are watching and sneaking a few taps on their own chests, practising their swing. How to tell if the note is dull? The doctor teaches the students a trick, while the patient looks on, listening in to the lesson too. The students should tap their own thighs, for that is a dull sound and a dull feel. You always have yourself as a gold standard, he tells them; use this! Excuse yourself to the toilet if you have to, tap away and remember that sensation.

I have observed many instances of self-percussion during my long-term fieldwork researching how doctors learn the sensory skills of diagnosis. In self-percussion, medical students sounded out their own bodies, practising the technique by feeling for 'dullness' or 'resonance'. This knowledge was then to be applied during their examination of patients, where dullness or resonance in the 'wrong' place or in uneven distribution, may indicate disease. Tom Rice (2013) also observed similar acts of self-listening in a London hospital, in the form of auto-auscultation. Rice found that the first sounds a medical student listens to, when they buy their first stethoscope, are often their own. *What does it mean to use your body as a case for others?* Medical students (and indeed many other practitioners of the body) do this all the time. It is a common way of learning new bodily skills and bodily knowledge.

When students take their own body as a case, they are learning not from a pickled body part or cadaver, nor from written descriptions of symptoms and signs, but from their living, breathing body that creaks and pulses and moves. There is a sense of delight and discovery as students learn to listen to their heartbeats through stethoscopes, when they discover hollow and dull spaces in their abdomen and chests. There is fear and trepidation too, as students learn that there may be abnormalities among themselves, heart murmurs often being discovered at this moment, disrupting neat distinctions between pathology and normality, between the healers and the sick (see Nott and Harris (2023) for more on this). Through self-listening and other forms of self-sensing, students experiment with their bodies, learning through the sensations they experience and bring about with their own bodily practices.

Doctors and medical students are not the only ones listening to their own bodily sounds in medical settings. Patients do too, although this is regarded as a pathological rather than pedagogical event. In the medical literature, self-listening is referred to as autophony, a word that could also be used to describe what the medical students are doing. In the medical case, however, autophony is definitely an 'abnormality', described as a form of 'hyper-perception'. For most people, sounds from inside the body are 'screened out', so as to make the outside world audible. For patients with medical conditions inducing the effect of autophony, such as having a small crack in the bone protecting the delicate semi-circular canals in the ear for example, the torrent of internal sounds, necessarily inaudible to most of us, can be heard and is dramatically amplified. That is, normal anatomical features which protect us from constantly hearing our internal workings, are fractured.

Patients may be able to hear their eyeballs moving from side to side, the pulsing of blood or the gurgles of digestion. I first heard of a patient suffering from autophony during my fieldwork from one of the nurses with whom I spent time. Curiosity led me to the medical literature, where I found the condition documented largely through case studies.

Take, for example, two case reports in the *Journal of Neurology, Neurosurgery and Psychiatry* which describe the 'unusual but fascinating' symptoms of autophony (Albuquerque and Bronstein, 2004). The first case is a fifty-three-year-old woman who presents with a tendency to stumble to the left side of her body. Questions about tinnitus reveal that the patient hears sounds of increasing pitch when she rolls her eyes upwards and decreasing pitch when she rolls then down. Case 1 is noted as saying she could play a tune with her eyes. Case 2 is a thirty-two-year-old man, also falling to the left, this time when he hears loud sounds such as a telephone ringing. He can hear his own heartbeats, bone taps and footsteps. Case 2 is reported to complain of 'a soft low pitched sound in his left ear "rather like moving a hard-pressed finger across a clean, wet china dinner plate" when he move[s] his eyes' (Albuquerque and Bronstein, 2004).

For these cases/patients, inner movements of tendons stretching and blood pumping are constantly heard. Their descriptions of these sounds are unusual, which make them such fascinating case studies for medical practitioners. In medical cases the intriguing is plucked from the mundane. Something is learned from the unusual. In ethnographic cases, it is often the other way around, and mundane acts such as tapping on your chest are made more intriguing and fascinating through description and situation within other stories.

Whether rare or mundane, the same question arises for both medical and ethnographic cases as it does for students tapping out their own bodies: how to move from one case to others?

Moving from one case study to others requires interpretation. For a case to become meaningful in other sites, similarities as well as differences are found and compared. A medical student compares sounds from their thigh with those tapped on a patient's back. A clinician reading the medical journals compares case studies with patients in her clinic. An anthropologist compares their ethnographic findings with other accounts in the literature: Melbourne hospitals compared to London hospitals. These cases, like their brief and suit versions, travel. As Annemarie Mol has pointed out in the preceding chapter in this edited volume, though, cases do not always transport knowledge easily; interpretation takes work.

What might be taken from these cases of autophony in medicine, of students and patients listening to their bodily sounds, presented here side-by-side? They might teach us that through acts of self-listening bodily borders are crossed, blurring inside/outside, and in the process not only does one's own vitality, amazingly, horrifyingly, emerge, but the possibility of others' too. Patients suffering from autophony, like tinnitus, might try to pay less attention to these sounds. Both of these are in the end more pedagogical rather than pathological concerns, matters of learning how to listen and what this reveals.

The medical student is taught to be aware, to listen to their own body, a fleshy textbook they carry with them at all times, so as to listen better to the bodies of their patients. As Tom Rice has shown in his ethnography of listening practices in medicine, this can reify and isolate aspects of the body, turning patients' bodies into objectified clinical cases – the beautiful murmur on the wards for example. Self-listening disrupts this too, by showing that medical students can also be one of those cases, when they find a murmur in their own heart or something else that stands out as 'abnormal'.

The case of autophony, this being a more recognised clinical case, helps us to understand how self-sensing can be overwhelming, too. It cannot always be the basis for knowing others, as the roar of inner sounds may distract from noticing the world. For the patients, this inner sensing, more hearing than listening, is unwanted, always in the background. It differs from the medical students' experience of seeking out these experiences and trying to learn to attend to them.

And the anthropologist? How do we listen in? And when we do, what does it do to our stories of the world when we use our own sensing, moving, living bodies as a case for others? As many anthropologists have invited us to do over the last decades, awakening the scholar's own sensuous body has effects, and it may be that we listen or we hear, that we desire to learn through attentive and careful attention, or that we want to ignore the inner roar, so as to better help us notice other details in the worlds we inhabit. Scholars in other fields such as history have shown that attending to these different sensuous practices of knowing bodies is revealing if we look across time and medical frameworks. As anthropologists, we can attend, as this book encourages, to the different kinds of cases in our field sites, and to learn through comparison of their framings, to listen in, in whatever sensory and bodily ways makes sense to us, to how these cases may or may not resonate with each other.

ACKNOWLEDGEMENTS

This chapter has benefited from research conducted as part of a Dutch (NWO, Vici) funded research project entitled 'Sonic Skills: Sound and Listening in the Development of Science, Technology, Medicine (1920–now)', led by Karin Bijsterveld (grant agreement No. 277-45-003), and a project which received funding from the ERC under the European Union's Horizon 2020 research and innovation programme (Starting Grant agreement No. 678390), called Making Clinical Sense. Anna would like to especially thank all interlocutors in the various medical schools for their generosity, Emily and Christine for their incredible editorial support, and Charlotte Bates, Susan Whyte and Christy Spackman for their excellent comments via open peer review.

REFERENCES

Albuquerque, W., and A. Bronstein, '"Doctor, I Can Hear My Eyes": Report of Two Cases with Different Mechanisms', *Journal of Neurology, Neurosurgery and Psychiatry*, 75 (2004), 1363–364.

Nott, J., and A. Harris, 'Teaching the Normal and the Pathological: Educational Technologies and the Material Reproduction of Medicine', *Science As Culture*, 32(2) (2023), 214–239.

Rice, T., *Hearing and the Hospital: Sound, Listening, Knowledge and Experience* (Canon Pyon: Sean Kingston Publishing, 2013).

4

ENCASED: PLOTTING ATTENTIONS THROUGH DISTRACTION

Melissa S. Biggs and John Bodinger de Uriarte

CASES SET BOUNDARIES; CASES DRAW YOU IN. OFTEN IMAGINED AS THEY appear in traditional museums – archipelagos of order in ordered spaces with carefully placed markers for larger narratives – cases partition, sequence and present artefacts and information for visitor attention. As anthropologists interested in museums and other exhibitionary spaces, we consider the parameters around what is encased and what is not encased. Where does the visitor experience of the museum actually begin, and how do they know?

Much of our work in recent years has focused on the establishment and expansion of public exhibition venues for Native American self-representations of histories and sovereignties following the advent of Indian gaming.[1] Our research often oscillates between the realms of public stories presented in museums and at historical landmarks, and the kinds of public stories and thematics employed in casinos and spaces such as gardens, village greens and hotel lobbies. For this project we visited casino and non-casino Native sites in Connecticut, Minnesota and Southern California, and studied casino design in Macau and Las Vegas.

We seek to provoke certain kinds of reading spaces or experiences for the reader. One of the ways we see our writing working in this case is by evoking the kind of dense, overlaying, immersive experience that casinos offer. The images we provide are designed to be evocative; the way the text and the photos work together is part of our analysis.

Our case in point here is the Mohegan Sun, in Uncasville, Connecticut. We choose this site because it wilfully blurs distinctions between casinos and more traditional exhibit spaces. Like all casinos, the design of the Mohegan Sun encloses its patrons within the casino space. The absence of windows, clocks, and a clear exit erases the outside and encourages people to stay in the building, to amble within a set of predetermined choices for attention or directed distraction.

The automated jingles of the slot machines, punctuated by the simulated sounds of coins spilling into their waiting troughs, promise potential gains. The noise distracts patrons and keeps them focused on the opportunities available within the casino confines, absorbed by the casino's narrative. Visitors animate the interior, moving through the space, pushing buttons and turning cards – eating, walking, observing.

Like most casinos, the Mohegan Sun serves up a thematic interpretation of a particular kind of nowhere, a site for generalised and accessible longing. Unlike most casinos, the Mohegan Sun draws on and accentuates a sense of place specifically connected to local imagined identities, what one might call a sense of 'Moheganness'. The Mohegan Sun turns some of the thinking about casino interior design on its head by making design elements focal points for distracted attention, rather than rendering them unobtrusive, as in traditional casino design (see Schull).[2]

Tribal historians worked with a design firm to embed a large number of Mohegan signs and symbols in the casino's interior to create a space for what Tantaquidgeon Museum Director Melissa Tantaquidgeon Zobel called 'ambient learning'.[3] This selective strategy renders other elements of Mohegan identities – like colonial and post-colonial histories of displacement and marginalisation – invisible.[4]

The Mohegan Sun presents an immersive experience that absorbs visitors into saturated interiors crammed with a dense set of Mohegan signs. These signs often intersect with those indicating an imagined 'natural': howling wolves, local plants and crops, stone formations and starry skies. Some of this participates in recent casino design trends that extend fantastic narratives outside the confirming cases of their interior spaces. In Las Vegas, for example, the skyline and roller coaster of New York New York, and the hourly pirate battles at Treasure Island

expand beyond the conventional limits of casino space. However, the imagined referents of many Las Vegas attractions lie far, far away from their footprints in that city. The Mohegan Sun's outward-extending narratives are imagined both large and general, and profoundly local and intimate. The interior design at once effaces and hyper-refers to the outside. The inside folds into outside to indicate its own surroundings, replete with local histories and desires.

Patrons circulate through three interlocking gaming spaces, the Casinos of the Earth, Sky and Wind. Each of the casinos functions as a contained narrative space. Within the Casino of the Earth, visitors move through the four seasons, signalled by the designs of the carpet – blooming flowers or autumnal leaves, for example – and skins printed with traditional seasonal activities, such as planting and hunting. The Mohegan creation story provides the central motif of the Casino of the Sky; the Casino of the Wind offers representations of the winds from the four directions. Some of these design elements immediately stand out. The printed skins suspended from the ceiling and the representations of the thirteen Mohegan moons embedded in the flooring need little explanation.

Other designs require more specialised knowledge: traditional basketry designs replicated by the light fixtures, the repetitions of certain colour combinations and motifs that reproduce particular Mohegan symbols. To enable its visitors to engage with these less visible markers of Mohegan history and identity, the Mohegan Sun provides *The Secret Guide* 'intended to facilitate and enrich' visitor experience 'by explaining the hidden meaning of all that surrounds you at Mohegan Sun'. The guide links design choices to specific aspects of Mohegan cosmology, history and traditional artistry. Once available for the asking at any of the information desks scattered throughout the casino and hotel complex, the guide must now be purchased in the casino gift shop.

Each of the sign sets – the different motifs, the different objects, the different embedded narratives in the casino – whisper (or not) secret (or not) stories about imagined Mohegan spaces and places, groundings and elements. In a space made thick by noise and scent, sight, and the dense tactility of everywhere, jostling for over-layering attention, secret or silent stories weave through everything on display.

The Hall of the Lost Tribes, located in the Casino of the Earth, exemplifies the constant play between visible and invisible, real and imagined, Mohegan and not. The Hall pays homage to thirteen tribes that once occupied territories adjacent to the Mohegans, with many of the tribal identifying symbols either taken from historical documents or created by the casino design firm. The Hall is fully enclosed, included in, but still separated from the Mohegan narrative.

The immersive and multiply distracting interiors recall Walter Benjamin's distraction theory, in particular its relationship to architecture. In contrast to the 'contemplative immersion' demanded by traditional aesthetics, Benjamin posits that architecture offers 'the prototype of an artwork that is received in a state of distraction and through the collective' (1968: 239). While the concentration of the connoisseur allows for the artwork to absorb her, the distraction of 'the masses' allows for their absorption of the artwork into themselves, a productive surrender to vernacular immersion.

The Mohegan Sun presents a grand distractive theatre for such absorption. If the site blurs the distinctions between museum and casino it succeeds, in part, by oscillating between offering sites for contemplation and sites for traversing distraction – the kind of distraction achieved by walking through a space crammed full of Mohegan signs intermixed with the deep distractive strategies of a contemporary casino. The buzzing, ringing, flashing overloads the senses, creating a fully tactile atmosphere through which the patron swims, both enchanted and in a perpetual state of being decentred.

Building from Benjamin, Michael Taussig recognises the 'dialectical image' inherent in the mimetic faculty, 'historicizing nature and naturalizing history'. Mimesis is 'the nature that culture uses to create second nature [...] drawing on the character and power of the original' (1993: 251). While the interior case contains a complicated mix of explained and unexplained Mohegan referents and designs, the case's exterior gestures outward, including and embracing the site as part of its sign. The mirrored, reflective glass exterior of much of the complex serves as a skin that replicates its surroundings, referring to a close elsewhere, covering itself with a mimetic landscape.

We present the Mohegan Sun as a case that troubles distinctions between representational and immersive environments. Writing a case study such as

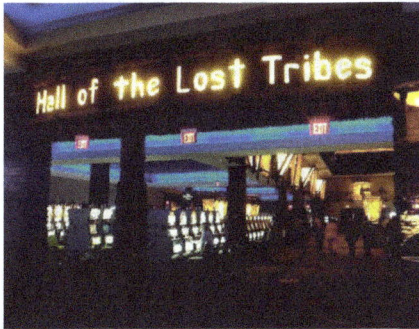

this encourages us to rethink the boundaries between public casino spaces and more traditional exhibition spaces, to recognise them as a continuum. This kind of writing permits a kind of 'sense engagement' with the text, at once immersive and representational, drawing you into a story intended to feel expansive, but which remains carefully bounded. The surrounds of Uncasville and local histories bump against each other, the expectations of non-Native visitors looking for Native markers against a backdrop of the imagined Native mundane, and local uses of Mohegan stories and place- and way-finding practices. While the building holds the mimetic experiences of its interior – the dry-stone walls and trees and bark panels, for example, or its never-changing seasons – it acts as reflective container and embodied story at once.

LIST OF FIGURES, IN ORDER OF APPEARANCE

ENDNOTES

1 Bodinger de Uriarte, J. and M. Biggs, 'Wag(er)ing Histories, Staking Territories: Exhibiting Sovereignty in Native America', *Museum and Society*, 11.2 (2013), 122–57. http://www2.le.ac.uk/departments/museumstudies/museumsociety/documents/ volumes/uriarte.

2 Natasha Schüll's ethnographic study, *Addiction by Design*, considers more traditional forms of casino design and their links to addictive behaviour, specifically machine-based gambling.

3 We interviewed Zobel on 17 October 2009. She was one of the sources consulted by the primary design firm for The Mohegan Sun, The Rockwell Group, based in New York City. From the beginning, the Group worked with tribal historians to identify Mohegan objects and themes to incorporate into the interior design. The firm is particularly known for its dense, thematic interior designs. Please see http:// www.rockwellgroup.com/ for examples. The Group's client base includes a number of casinos and other venues in Las Vegas.

4 Nearby tribally reclaimed sites, such as Shantok, recognised by the Mohegan as their first settlement, and the Royal Mohegan Burial Ground in the neighbouring town of Norwich, acknowledge these more complicated histories.

REFERENCES

Benjamin, W., 'The Work of Art in the Age of Mechanical Reproduction', in H. Arendt, ed., *Illuminations* (New York: Schocken Books, 1968), pp. 217– 51.

Taussig, M., *Mimesis and Alterity: A Particular History of the Senses* (London: Routledge, 1993).

5

NO JUDGMENTS: FIELDWORK ON THE SPECTRUM

Faye Ginsburg and Rayna Rapp

SPECTRUM: A BROAD RANGE OF VARIED BUT RELATED IDEAS OR OBJECTS, the individual features of which tend to overlap so as to form a continuous series or sequence.

The presence of disability in American public culture is at once increasingly visible and yet still segregated and rendered invisible. In our multi-sited ethnographic research for our 2024 book *Disability Worlds* (Duke), we are especially reliant on case studies across the spectrum of disability worlds to help us comprehend how the presence of this category is expanding our understanding of humanity. To understand this uneven process, we have been tracking the presence and absence of disability across sites like schools, labs, families, arts activists and self-advocacy organisations, both mainstream and obscure, all in New York City. Here, we invoke 'the spectrum' in two ways. First, it conveys a sense of our experience of disability in our study as 'the broad range of varied but related ideas... which tend to overlap'. Second, it evokes the diagnostic language used to describe the increasing occurrence of a range of complex symptoms controversially classified together as Autism Spectrum Disorder (ASD) (DSM 5). Since our research often involves projects linked to ASD, our title brings together these two sets of associations.

As our knowledge of disability worlds deepens, we have come to expect that each case study is revelatory of the emergence of (or resistance to) 'the new normal', standing both for itself and the larger project of redrawing the social map of disability inclusion. Indeed, we encountered the new normal emerging in that most public of spaces: Broadway. Denizens and visitors to New York are probably familiar with the TKTS booth in Times Square that offers steeply discounted theatre tickets for day-of performances. It is the public face of The Theater Development Fund (TDF), a well-known non-profit founded in 1968 dedicated to assisting the theatre industry in NYC.

Probably less well-known is TDF's recent vanguard work in making theatrical performances accessible to people with disabilities. TAP (Theater Accessibility Program) offers well-designed accommodations for people with certified vision, hearing or mobility impairments, including audio description headphones, open captioning and sign interpreters at selected performances. In 2011, TDF took a step beyond these physical accommodation programmes, founding the Autism Theatre Initiative (ATI). Beginning with performances of Disney's *The Lion King* and *Mary Poppins*, and moving on to *Elf* matinees, ATI recently offered an autism-friendly performance for older teens and young adults and their supporters for a special matinee of *The Curious Incident of the Dog in the Night-Time* on 30 November 2014. In February 2015, we joined a group of TDF volunteers in training to help out at the first autism-friendly Broadway performance of the play adaptation of Roald Dahl's classic children's book, *Matilda*, a hit about a preternaturally smart and second-sighted girl who saves herself and her beloved schoolteacher by unmasking and banishing the bully who runs their school, while also saving herself from a family that has no appreciation of her talents. The play, which has its harrowing moments, is nonetheless filled with talented child performers, creative stage sets and the triumph of good over evil. In short, this is family fun that pretty much anyone can enjoy, and that underscores the value of being a person who is a bit different, and who has a finely honed sense of right and wrong. This seemed a well-chosen production for the anticipated crowd.

But autistic children and adults have often felt excluded from Broadway theatres, and TDF's ATI set out to remedy structural barriers to their access. Working with actors, directors and a large support staff of ushers, salespersons and attendants, ATI negotiated changes in lighting, sound levels and audience expectations:

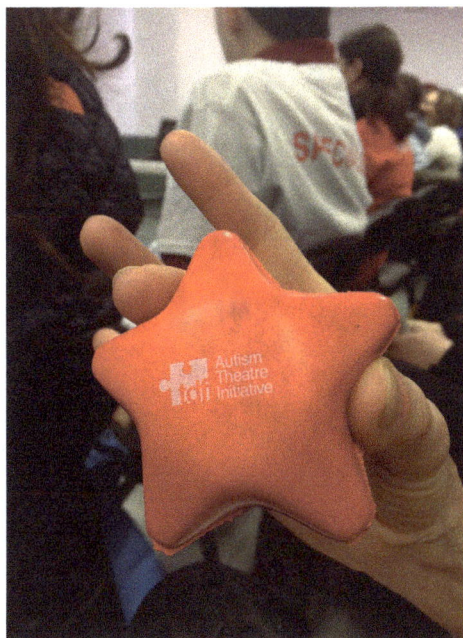

FIG. 5.1 Autism Theatre Initiative 'fidget toy'

the professional staff were taught to expect a different level of noise and movement in *Matilda* audiences when autistic people were welcomed into the Schubert Theater. Likewise, after unfortunate experiences with local restaurants that had evicted autistic patrons who had gone out to eat after prior performances, ATI worked with nearby eateries to be sure they were autism-friendly and received staff training on what to expect. They were listed and promoted on a laminated card – along with other items – and given out to families as they entered The Schubert.

The day of the performance was cold and crisp; we volunteers dressed in bright red TDF knit hats, with identifying t-shirts under our down coats, and carried bright red swag bags with the TDF logo, filled with the aforementioned restaurant directories, clear guides to who's who in the cast and an array of attractive tension-relieving 'fidget toys' and earplugs to be given to those waiting to go in. The Schubert Theater is large; it seats almost 1500 people, and virtually all seats were taken for this performance, which was for autistic audiences and their families, friends and allies only. As Philip Dallman, ATI coordinator, explained to the forty assembled volunteers during our training, the NYC area has enough people meeting that description to fill a Broadway theatre, one of the locational advantages of creating innovative outreach to audiences with disabilities in the city.

Ticketholders had to stand outside as lines were moved in: not an easy wait for anyone. Our job was to make audience members feel welcome as they lined up to enter the theatre. These are people who are routinely made to feel out

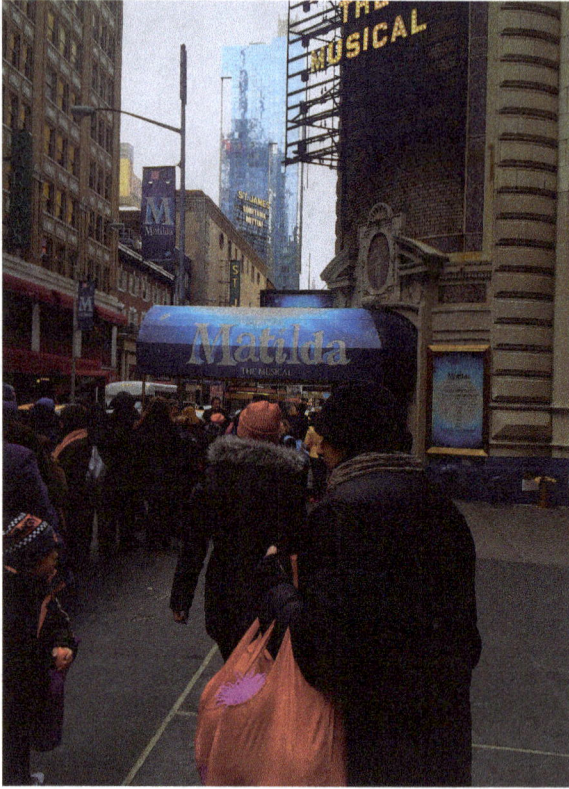

FIG. 5.2 Ticketholders queuing for a performance of *Matilda*

of place and marginal; our directions were to make clear that this experience was going to be different from the minute they spotted the theatre. Indeed, there were so many volunteers eagerly greeting arrivals – like so many good spirited, red-hatted elves – that we may have been a bit overwhelming. We were given clear instructions, spelled out on the introductory PowerPoint, that people we approached may not want to make eye contact, and that though we may find ourselves moved to tears, under no circumstances were we to cry in front of the theatregoers. Five people in white t-shirts, with the word 'specialist' in red letters across the back, had considerable experience working with autistic people; they were available at all times to help in situations that any volunteer could not handle, and we had their cell phone numbers on speed dial.

Inside, we helped families to find their seats, and also pointed out the quiet rooms – waiting areas outside bathrooms repurposed for this occasion — on each floor of the theatre. Padded floor mats, 'fidget toys', bean bag chairs and a quiet atmosphere made these popular locations for this audience having to deal with the sensory overload created by a large crowded theatre. In the quiet rooms, anyone overwhelmed by the adjusted sensory assault of the performance was free to take a break at any point; autistic people were encouraged to return to their seats whenever they were ready.

We spoke with dozens of volunteers, programme coordinators and – of course—families in the audience. Every volunteer had a story that brought them to the performance, ranging from autistic people themselves, to neuroscientists who had autistic kin, to dancers with special education interests, to siblings whose autistic brothers and sisters were in the audience, and parents and kids of all ages. Audience members were spellbound by and enthusiastically voluble and unruly about the magic that is Broadway. The performance was brilliantly orchestrated; the actors appeared unruffled by the noise and occasional shouts, and nobody flinched when a squeeze toy was hurled upon the stage in Act 1, or a low din rumbled through much of Act 2. Specialists were clearly positioned on every level in case of difficulties. Afterwards, we were part of the brigade that helped to clear the theatre efficiently and sympathetically.

One Sunday matinee, one instance of an autism-adjusted performance on Broadway. *Cui bono?* This event engaged many constituencies, we would argue, showing how one case can ramify out into a broad spectrum of public culture. Local restaurateurs learned how to adapt to new clients, theatre staff – especially ushers – learned the meaning of 'no judgment' (the informal ATI motto) and many people got to enjoy a hugely positive experience often denied to them because of the lack of tolerance for autistic people, who are judged as inappropriate and disruptive in many public venues. Beyond this eye-opening, moving and joyful day, TDF proclaims itself the greatest beneficiary: 'We don't just want everyone who participates to have a great day, we want to build new audiences for the future', as Dallman enthusiastically put it during our training. Moreover, the ATI is part of a broader movement for changing the face

FIG. 5.3 Audience members settling into their seats before the performance

of American public culture, part of the remarkable, longstanding Museums Access Consortium (MAC) of NYC, a volunteer-based association that brings together cultural practitioners, people with disabilities and disability advocates to share experiences, learn from one another, and refine best practices with the aim of advancing accessibility and inclusion in cultural facilities of all types in the New York metro area.

Our 'fieldwork on the spectrum' attends to the growing transformation of American public culture. Everyone involved, from toilet attendants to Broadway stars, from restaurant waiting staff to families enjoying a relatively unstressed outing, experienced what inclusion of life with a difference might be like if the aspirations, rights and accommodations needed to include a wide range of people with disabilities are really in place. After all, 2015 marks a quarter of a century since the passage of the Americans with Disabilities Act. Think about how rarely you see the audiences we are describing next time you go to the theatre, the museum or the cinema. Groups like ATI and MAC are in the business of changing that. We were privileged to witness one extraordinary afternoon, one case among many in slow but steady transformation. It's about time.

6

FACIAL PARALYSIS: SOMATICISING FRUSTRATION IN GUATEMALA

Nicholas Copeland

WHILE CONDUCTING ETHNOGRAPHIC FIELDWORK ON INDIGENOUS POLITICAL organising in northwest Guatemala in the mid-2000s, I encountered, quite by accident, an apparent epidemic of Bell's Palsy – an illness involving paralysis of one half of the face, known locally as *derrame facial* (facial stroke) or *parálisis facial*. After conversing with sufferers, I began to wonder what their condition and the prevalence of cases might reveal about how marginalised Guatemalans experienced social life after decades of injustice and reactionary violence in the midst of a failing democratic transition.

US clinicians define Bell's Palsy as a temporary paralysis of one side of the face caused by trauma to the seventh cranial nerve.[1] Researchers in Minnesota found that the condition affected 20–30 in 100,000 people (Hausser 1971). Although there are few identified risk factors, pregnancy and advancing age are understood to play predisposing roles. Central to the dominant US medical model of facial paralysis is a bodily trauma that causes the cranial nerve to swell against the narrow and bony fallopian canal, affecting all functions associated with the seventh nerve: muscular movement of the neck, forehead and face (including its expressions); secretions of the lower jaw; tear duct and salivary gland expression; taste; and outer ear sensation. Although the exact cause is often undiagnosed, the types of injury commonly understood to produce Bell's

Palsy include wounds, blunt force, broken bones in the face, injuries to the brain stem, tumours – specifically acoustic neuroma – and cysts, as well as infections and autoimmune disorders. The lower halves of the faces of those afflicted with Bell's Palsy are usually swollen and one side of their mouth droops down, as if they were smoking an invisible pipe. They have difficulty eating, closing their eyes and mouths, and controlling their facial expressions.

This purportedly universal biomedical description – 'biomedical' in that it focuses exclusively on the bodily causes of disease, pathophysiology – belies its origins in specific studies with distinct populations and erases a potentially heterogeneous set of 'biomedical' practices and definitions (Hahn, Robert, and Kleinman 1983). This fairly standard description has a wide circulation and helps many clinicians – in and beyond North America – to identify cases and treatments. I interviewed a doctor in Huehuetenango who repeated this medical definition nearly verbatim. However, this authoritative description elides the experiences and meanings associated with *derrame* in the rural department of Huehuetenango where I worked. Most cases that I encountered corresponded with intense frustration and emotional trauma, although there were several cases that corresponded with unexpected and uncontained *alegria* (usually translated as joy or happiness).

I met one young Indigenous man who had saved for two years in the hope of migrating to the US with his new bride. When her parents forbade her, their dreams vanished, and his face twisted out of control. His disfigurement covered with a yellow bandana, he explained how he had spent the money instead on a costly regimen of vitamin-B injections. An NGO worker told me that her aunt's face became paralysed when she was robbed, having just withdrawn 20,000 *quetzales* (US$3000) from the bank. The value of a life's work congealed in paper, gone in an instant. An activist friend recounted seeing similar cases among clandestine 'communities of populations in resistance' (internally displaced) during the war, Indigenous villagers who had fled violence and were living in extreme deprivation and fear, constantly moving through mountains and jungle to evade the army. Sometimes the torsion of expression lingered, and at times became permanent, which many attributed to a lack of treatment.

Facial paralysis befell my long-time friend who was defrauded by a bank. After working for three years in the US, he returned to Guatemala and placed his life savings into BANCAFE. In the early 2000s, the bank's owners illegally deposited millions into offshore accounts, declared insolvency and fled the country. Thousands of account holders organised rallies, demanding that the government take action, only to be told that their protests were in vain as it was too late to hold the bank accountable. To punctuate this point, the national police turned water cannons on protestors in Guatemala City. My friend was furious with the crooked bankers and their government accomplices but couldn't do anything. When his anger exploded into a brick wall of intransigence, *derrame* struck.

I began seeing cases everywhere, far more than the North American bio-medical accounts might have predicted. When I dug deeper, I was referred to a pharmacy in a small town near the department capital that offered low-cost home remedies for this peculiar condition: mild electric shocks to the face from a metal wand wired to a hand crank magnetic generator housed in a metal box. The device was invented by a long-deceased doctor, a town founder and Rosicrucian mystic. This I was told by his aging granddaughters, who have been treating a steady stream of cases for over a decade, seven to ten each day. They charged fifteen *quetzales* for a session that lasts about fifteen minutes, far more affordable than the vitamin or steroid injections prescribed by local physicians. I watched them treat patients, who said that the shocks loosened their muscles and provided temporary relief. Some were cured after several visits. During the extreme counterinsurgency violence of the 1980s, the pharmacists remembered that cases of *derrame* more than tripled.

Sometimes emotional and bodily stress combined to cause *derrame*. One poor, middle-aged, dishevelled single mother wrapped her head in a black shawl and avoided bright light. She explained that her *derrame* began when she was lying awake at night worrying about how to pay for her child's education after his school announced they were raising tuition fees. Abandoned by her partner and caring for several children, she made a meagre living selling *tamales* on buses, waking up before 5am to cook them and carrying a heavy basket on her head all day in the hot sun, which gave her a terrible headache. Contrary to the North

American understanding, where *derrame* strikes once and does not recur, this was her third *derrame*. She recounted a previous case caused by *alegria*, nineteen years ago, when she gave birth to her first daughter after having four sons. Another woman linked her *derrame* to *susto* (fright) and *enojos* (angers) – to use oversimplified translation – resulting from routine physical abuse by her husband upon whom she and her children were dependent. The pharmacists reported seeing more women than men patients due to domestic abuse and also, they believed, because of reactions to hormonal birth control injections. However, the medical cases were not always correlated to acute misfortune or unexpected happiness; several sufferers I interviewed claimed that there was no precipitating event, although they might not have wanted to reveal such personal or potentially embarrassing information to a *gringo* holding a camera.

Rather than see all cases as instances of a universal category: 'Bell's Palsy', I follow medical anthropologists who examine how meanings, categories and emotions configure distinct illness experiences, which are further shaped by social, historical and political contexts. I am also interested in bodily intensities and nervous systems, in the plural, as historical and social artefacts. What might these cases of *derrame* reveal about how Guatemalan social and political realities congeal in living bodies and affective imaginaries? How does bodily affect blur the line between individual experience and social worlds? I found one clue in that almost everyone I spoke with narrated their *derrame* as a result of their being forced to *tragar* (swallow) intense and generally negative emotions that could not find an outlet or satisfaction. This metaphor of ingestion and forcible envelopment dramatises the interminable labour of absorbing pain and frustration into the body and speaks to the existence of some kind of habitual disposition of defensive girding associated with this process. *Derrame* only means stroke in the limited context of a brain haemorrhage. It also means to spill out and over: experiences of structural violence that cannot be absorbed or somaticised spill over onto the face, or perhaps in the cases precipitated by *alegria*, spill over to breach the habits and orientations through which subjects shield themselves from the expected harshness of everyday life.

It seemed to me that these sufferers share ingrained dispositions and sedimented responses to frustration with endemic poverty, violence, crime and other forms of victimisation and injustice that are systematically and dispro-portionately inflicted on poor, Indigenous and female bodies in Guatemala in the course of social relations. The high incidence of *derrame* was the tip of an iceberg of social suffering; it rendered legible the extent to which violence assaults lives and social worlds in the low hum of the ordinary.

I see in the lived situations surrounding most cases of *derrame* a distinctive pattern where people struggle against hardship and injustice that they ultimately have to endure and swallow. For those whose *derrame* was related to euphoria, *derrame* might be incited by an intense rush of feeling unleashed by the tempo-rary lowering of a rigid barrier routinely held up as protection against expected misfortune and abjection – the 'swallowing mechanism'. It is hard to say more without careful and extended observation. But it is hard not to draw parallels to Guatemalan history. In 1954, a CIA-sponsored coup upended a decade-long experiment with democracy driven by peasant hunger for land. Military dicta-torship set the stage for the revolution, a spillover of political desire. A vicious counterinsurgency inflicted unspeakable cruelty to vanquish the guerrillas and hope itself. But desire for change persisted and inspired the 1996 peace accords that promised more than they delivered. Neoliberal democracy partially accom-modates political challenges, even embracing human and Indigenous rights, but leaves structural victimisation intact and inflicts new injuries.

The experiences of individual sufferers are always in some respect irreducible, but sufferers can also be read as cases to reveal distinctive patterns of embodiment fashioned by the heterogeneous, unbounded and imbalanced social 'nervous systems' of which they form part (Taussig 1992). The ethnographic challenge is to ponder the distinctive experiences and meanings of *alegria, susto* and *nervios,* which do not translate neatly into the Western conceptions 'happiness', 'fright' and 'nerves', and to understand them as cultural and historical products, distinc-tive ways of being in the world. I read the similarities between these cases of *derrame* to index the limits of some Guatemalans' ability to effectively swallow injustice, exposure and victimisation. I view the epidemic of *derrame* as a trace of structural violence on the most visible, personal and emotionally inscribed bodily surface, the face – a jarring sign of the acute frustration that is an ordinary affect in contemporary Guatemala and much of the postcolonial world.

ENDNOTES

1 Clinicians typically distinguish between facial paralysis caused by damage, respectively, to the central and peripheral nervous systems, the latter being Bell's Palsy.

REFERENCES

Hahn, R., and A. Kleinman, 'Biomedical Practice and Anthropological Theory: Frameworks and Directions', *Annual Review of Anthropology*, 12.1 (1983), 305–33.

Hauser, W. A., W. E. Karnes, J. Annis and L.T. Kurland, 'Incidence and Prognosis of Bell's Palsy in the Population of Rochester, Minnesota', *Mayo Clinic Proceedings*, 46 (1971), 258–64.

Taussig, M., *The Nervous System* (New York: Routledge, 1992).

7

'HE DIDN'T BLOW US UP' – ROUTINE VIOLENCE AND NON-EVENT AS CASE

Ken MacLeish

THIS CASE IS A STORY THAT A SOLDIER TOLD ME. I CALL HER KELLY, AND she said it was 'the craziest story I was gonna get' from her. So for her it was an extreme, a worst case, but also a kind of telos of conditions she lived with and feelings she felt every day in occupied Iraq. It was a case of something not happening. As is fitting for those tensions of normality and emergency and rule and suspension that characterise state violence, it was both exceptional and part of a pattern: the pattern of soldiers' embodied terror and vulnerability (even as they surely inspired terror in vulnerable others) and the pattern of the mechanisms that shaped their thought and action. It was a case of something that might have happened to Kelly but didn't, that she might have done but didn't do, and of things that were treated as if they were real even when they turned out not to be. It was a case of a potentiality or hypothetical attaining a curious afterlife of actuality.

Kelly was a junior enlisted engineer in her early twenties who spent a tour in far western Iraq building bridges to replace ones that had been destroyed by the US counterinsurgency campaign. Kelly was in her unit's headquarters section and so spent a lot of time convoying around with the company commander, making thrice-weekly visits to the bridge construction site. She was the driver for their high-riding utility truck, called an LMTV, in the middle of a small convoy of similar vehicles and Humvees. Her NCO sat beside her in the passenger seat and a gunner stood behind them manning a mounted .50 calibre machine gun. The .50 cal (or M2 Heavy Machine Gun), along with its smaller cousin the M249 Light Machine Gun, is a ubiquitous tool in contemporary US wars. Large and heavy enough that it must be mounted on a vehicle or tripod, it can nevertheless be operated by a single individual, firing rounds the approximate size of an adult's thumb either singly or in a continuous stream, and quite efficiently tearing apart metal, wood, concrete and flesh.[1]

The main threats confronting Kelly and her unit were roadside bombs and what in Army argot are called VBIEDs, for 'vehicle-borne IED', pronounced 'vee-bed' – car bombs delivered into the middle of convoys or checkpoints. Everyone was afraid of these bombs. People Kelly knew in other units had been hurt and killed by them. Once a Humvee right in front of her was hit, another time a trailing vehicle. A Marine tank that had left the FOB (forward operating base) right before her convoy got blown in half. 'In my eyes, in everybody's eyes, we got lucky a lot' when it came to bombs, she said. 'Somebody was totally looking out for us'. These cases didn't belong to Kelly, but she was still being shaped by them. Indeed, they brought into existence her own parallel set of cases: 'getting lucky a lot' in the face of the risk and vulnerability that were affirmed by these other incidents.

One day, on a run to inspect the bridge, their convoy of trucks and Humvees rolled past a long line of oncoming civilian vehicles that pulled over and stopped at their approach. Except one car continued right on toward the lead Humvee in the convoy. From her elevated vantage, Kelly watched anxiously as it came on, and listened over the radio as the soldiers in the lead Humvee found their .50 cal jammed as they prepared to fire at the car. The car pulled over at the last instant and let the Humvee pass. But then it continued to advance directly toward Kelly's oncoming truck. She was terrified; one of the Marines stationed with her unit had been killed in a VBIED attack that occurred in exactly this way. The middle of the convoy, where she was, is a better target, and also a more probable location for a command vehicle. 'I about shit myself', she said. 'I was praying, "Dear Lord, forgive me for my sins!"' Suddenly the death that had been stalking friends and fellow troops seemed to be staring her right in the face. 'It was the perfect scenario of everything that was going wrong with the other convoys, and it was scary as shit.' Kelly yelled to her gunner to shoot, but for reasons she didn't know or explain to me, he didn't shoot. The car came closer, and kept coming, and then drove on past without incident. The command group completed their inspection and their trip back to the FOB. But when she got there, Kelly said, she and a friend who had been riding in another vehicle went to her room and prayed together, 'cause it was that traumatic'. They felt like they had narrowly escaped dying. The violence that they had seen claim other soldiers – people who they resembled in all the ways that mattered in this scene – was all of a sudden that much nearer, even though it remained unrealised. 'It's not your friends anymore, it's starting to hit you'. Virtual or not, false alarm or not, she felt touched by the threat.

So she now had her own case, 'scary as shit', but I wondered what it meant. I asked Kelly how she felt about the fact that the driver had not actually been a bomber. She explained that the escalation of force protocols she had been trained in defined the driver's behaviour as threatening. 'If somebody came at you, if they even get in the vicinity of your convoy, you blow them up. Cause it's considered a threat. Cause they know the rules, they know they're supposed to pull over. And that was scary because there was clearly people pulled over' – other civilians – 'knowing that that was what they were supposed to do'. The driver 'knew what he was doing was wrong'. And Kelly, it seemed, knew that she had to fear him as a result.

She allowed that the driver may just have been impatient, as she said she probably would be herself if convoys of armed foreigners were constantly jamming up traffic as they pushed their way through her hometown, or that he may have been in the grips of some emergency, as she had seen earlier in her deployment when a family with a sick child were shot by soldiers as they rushed through a checkpoint on their way to a hospital. The specifics of the driver's case were unknown to her, but they were not impossible to imagine. If her gunner had listened to her, 'this dude would've been dead'.

The story tacked between two poles: the intensity of this 'traumatic' brush with death and a vague sense of reflection and relief that the gunner hadn't fired. 'The fact that he didn't blow us up was just astonishing to me, because in our minds, it was like, that was what was gonna happen'. The 'we' of this shared mind remains unclear in her telling, since her NCO and gunner didn't appear to share her assessment of the situation, even if some of the soldiers in the lead vehicle, the one with the jammed .50 cal, did share it. But the fact remained that for Kelly, the threat was not just potential, but actual, an ontological reality that extended to her fellow soldiers, endangered along with her even if, in her telling, many of them did not share her perception of the situation. 'His actions *were* threatening', she asserted of the driver, and she wondered, 'Why didn't he blow?' 'I would've felt terrible', she said at one point right before the subject changed and our conversation moved on. At another she used language that was curiously contingent, acknowledging, 'I almost feel bad [...] I had the intention of killing him and it wasn't a threat. It's weird. I'm sure it happens a lot' – this disastrous bad luck paralleling, but somehow not equal to, how she and her soldiers 'got lucky a lot'. 'That's probably the best story you're gonna get out of me!' she said. And then she laughed.

The thing that made this story eventful for Kelly was not the narrowly averted killing of an innocent civilian, described in vague and contingent 'almosts' and 'would haves', but the sense, articulated far more concretely, of narrowly avoided death: his actions *were* threatening, she said, she *did* pray in the terror of the moment and afterwards, and she believed she was almost killed. Despite the sympathy with which she was able to regard the driver's perspective – in his situation, she said, 'I'd be like "fuck that!"' – and the divergent perceptions of her fellow soldiers – some contravening her call to shoot and others sharing her sense of narrowly-avoided death – her telling of the story remains framed by the fact that she was following the well-established escalation-of-force rules while the driver 'knew what he was doing was wrong'.

In this story, as in many others I heard from soldiers, the proverbial 'fog of war' is something both less and more than the morass of potential moral and existential hazards depicted in popular representations. The battlefield is frequently a chaotic and ambiguous environment, but one in which discipline, training, mission objectives and rules of engagement provide both a technical, procedural rubric, and a sort of embodied, affective pedagogy that makes otherwise benign behaviour and objects into deeply felt mortal threats (MacLeish

2012). Such knowledge and action are technical, automatic, systematised and distributed – an effect of the way that, as Michel Callon and John Law put it, 'the knowing individual' disappears into the capacities and obligations of the network (Callon and Law 1997). This particular network happens to have the necropolitical mission of identifying killable, 'rule-breaking' bodies and deputising killer actors. At the same time, individual knowledge and capacity to act do not emerge seamlessly and uniformly from that network; they are irregular, perspectival and vexingly partial ways of knowing and doing. Kelly's training told her that the driver was a threat, just as it told the crew and gunner in the Humvee in front of her, who tried and failed to fire on the car before she even started yelling to her gunner. The decision whether to fire wasn't hers alone. It only arose because of the accident of the jammed weapon in the lead vehicle, without which the Iraqi driver would probably have been killed before he got anywhere near Kelly's truck, and then it fizzled with the intercession and inaction of Kelly's gunner and NCO. Such circumstances demand careful consideration of what it means to make a decision in the first place: who the deciding agent is, how an action takes shape, and how an aftermath is sorted out. What Kelly describes is less an instance of morally anguished trade-off or a brush with transgression than it is a moment of powerful but strangely non-eventful certainty in the face of seemingly glaring contradiction.

I want to conclude by suggesting a couple of ways to think about this case anthropologically. The first is via its exemplarity, not just as a piece of data but as part of a project of understanding human experiences of routinised violence. Do we imagine Kelly's case to be a distortion, attenuation or exception to this human experience? Or can we take it as an expression of that humanity, however discomfiting that might be? What does it mean to take Kelly's terror seriously while taking equally seriously the Iraqi driver's terror as he made his way through overlapping fields of high-calibre fire? And might a careful understanding of the former help trouble the notion that the latter is simply an inevitable side effect of well-intentioned liberal war-making? This seriousness of consideration does not have to be a matter of somehow letting Kelly off the hook – as if most of us are not in one way or another hung on that same hook – or of confining our analysis to the narrow moral economy of this particular scene of sovereign violence. It can instead be cause for interrogating a far less questioned mode of liberal subjectivity that is both given responsibility for acts of violence and cast as the thing being defended by such acts. In the name of defending a highly unimaginative vision of freedom, this subjectivity stubbornly and violently privileges autonomous action and individual responsibility. So this is a case in another way too, one that precludes possibilities for sensing and responding to the agency of others, for recognising that doing and knowing are always ours and not-ours, and for unsettling just what defines the 'us' to which these things belong.

ENDNOTES

I There is a widespread apocryphal claim that it is illegal under the Geneva Conventions to use .50 calibre rounds against human targets, but no such prohibition exists. It is common, however, for unit-level rules of engagement to limit the use of the M2 and other large-calibre weapons to non-human targets, though in urban combat that involves shooting at buildings or vehicles, such distinctions may in practice be meaningless.

REFERENCES

Callon, M., and J. Law, 'After the Individual in Society: Lessons on Collectivity from Science, Technology and Society', *The Canadian Journal of Sociology / Cahiers Canadiens de Sociologie*, 22.2 (1997), 165–82.

MacLeish, K., 'Armor and Anesthesia: Exposure, Feeling, and the Soldier's Body', *Medical Anthropology Quarterly*, 26.1 (2012), 49–68.

8

WHAT'S IN A NAME? A CASE OF TRAFFICKING IN OTHER PEOPLE'S STORIES

Ruth Goldstein

> 'Is writing seemly? Does the writer cut a respectable figure? Is it proper to write? Is it done?'
>
> — Jacques Derrida, 'Plato's Pharmacy', in *Disseminations*

'I CHOOSE... *ESTRELLA*. YES, YOU CAN CALL ME *ESTRELLA* WHEN YOU WRITE'.

'Are you sure?' I asked.

Estrella nodded her head, a wisp of dyed honey-blonde hair coming loose from behind her ear. Her long earrings, the gold paint flaking around a plastic ruby, swayed back and forth as she nodded in affirmation. Yes, she was sure.

'You can write, if you want', Estrella gestures to my notebook that sits on the table. I write instead on a napkin. It feels less official and thus less obtrusive. 'Unless you prefer napkins... This is what you call anthropology?' She laughs and pats my hand, the pen hovering over the flimsy paper.

I look at my scrawl on the napkin. I have written the date, 'Estrella' – her chosen pseudonym, and the name of the café where we sit. 'Yes', I tell her. This is what I call my anthropological practice of ethnography. I bring out my field notebook, already swollen with the additions of drawings and pressed plants that women have given me. The drawings are the result of trying to keep sex workers' children occupied while I talk with their mothers, which at times becomes a baby-sitting arrangement if a client interrupts our conversation. Estrella has several children of her own, but they live with her mother in another part of Peru. That childhood home is far from her adopted one, which is a place of work in the brothels of the Peruvian Amazon's region of *Madre de Dios*.

'Do you always ask people what name they want to use?' Estrella asks.

'Yes'.

At the time of my initial conversation with Estrella in 2011, this was true. But as my research unfolded, I realised just how much my ideas and ethnographic practices would need to evolve to keep up with the dynamism of people's stories and everyday lives. I offer this interactive process of 'choosing names' and adaptive research strategies as my ethnographic case. Choosing names can mean several things: usually, it meant inviting participants in my research to choose their own pseudonym. Of course, it could also mean that I honoured someone's refusal to be named at all – the more typical kind of ethnographic practices of anonymity. Or, as I highlight in this case, my refusal to employ the name that Estrella's former colleague chose, because it put Estrella at risk. The more interactive naming practices, as well as certain kinds of refusal, constitute one way that ethnographers might consider furthering relations of trust with people whose lives and stories we analyse. I hesitate to write 'reciprocity', a charged term so dear to anthropology (Mauss 2000 [1950]; Graeber 2014; Strathern 1990), because of what are often socioeconomic differences between researcher and study participant – and it's the researcher who should be bound with social debt if not also moral obligation, rather than the participant.

My longest round of fieldwork, which had begun in 2010, examined three modes of 'traffic': in women destined for the sex-trade, plants employed by sex-workers for reproductive health that were also targeted by biopirates for commercial production,[1] and gold, made solid via liquid mercury along Latin America's Interoceanic Road.[2] Completed in 2011, this transnational infrastructure project has enabled more than just the transport of soybeans from Brazil to Asian markets, its proposed purpose (Daniels 2011; Fleck et al. 2010; Gadea 2012; IIRSA 2011). It has allowed heavy machinery and people to enter the rainforest mining areas, and for gold and wildlife to be smuggled out. As an increasingly rich 'roadology' set of scholarship has shown, building new roads often has unforeseen consequences (Dalakoglou and Harvey 2014; Harvey 2018; Uribe 2018; Zhou 2014). Not everyone experiences socioeconomic mobility and motor-ability. From 2010–2012 and then again between 2016 and 2018, I travelled the 3500-mile road from the Brazilian Atlantic to the Peruvian Pacific coast, traversing the Brazilian, Peruvian and Bolivian Amazon. From rainforest to laboratory, from brothel to bank, 'traffic' functioned as my analytic to examine physical encounters and collisions as well as entwined questions of the dynamic value of people and things travelling across borders and through global commodity-chains (Goldstein 2015). As a methodological approach, I realised that I was also 'trafficking' in other people's stories, capitalising on the tales they told me about themselves (Goldstein forthcoming). This underscored my desire to create a more interactive ethnographic approach. Asking people if they wanted to choose their own pseudonyms seemed easy enough. But 'what's in a name' can signify ethnographic enrichment as well as present challenges, as my case suggests.

FIG. 8.1 'Welcome' sign over the start of the South leg of the Interoceanic Road, from Cusco all the way to São Paulo in Brazil

FIG. 8.2 Traffic(king) of people and things along the Interoceanic Road

FIG. 8.3 Map of road integration, Peru–Brazil

The gold mining, which fuelled interdependent economies, had its greatest concentration in Madre de Dios where I first met Estrella. Situated near the border of Brazil and Bolivia, Madre de Dios had earned the nickname 'El Wild West' for its implosion of lawlessness and prostitution reminiscent of the North American gold rush. The fall of the US dollar and the rise of the price of gold had coincided with the construction of the Interoceanic Road, which was the first paved thoroughfare in the region (marked in black on the above map). Where artisanal mining had previously meant backbreaking work for little return, the price was now right for a liveable wage. Male miners from Brazil, Bolivia and Peru streamed into the rainforest mines. Female sex-workers hailed from these countries, in addition to Colombia and Ecuador. During my two years conducting research along the Interoceanic Road (2010–2012), I would ask miners and sex-workers, along with environmental engineers, biologists, Indigenous leaders and government officials what name they would like me to use when I wrote.

Government officials almost entirely chose their own names for accounts written about them. Sex-workers already operated under a host of fake names to protect themselves and their families from embarrassment and, in some cases, violence from clients and police (who were often one-and-the-same). Miners similarly conducted their operations illicitly. They did not employ their legal names (if they had a national identity card from Peru or a neighbouring country) – not among one another in the mines, not with the environmental engineers who tried in vain to regulate the proliferating artisanal application of liquid mercury in the mines, and certainly not with me. I asked people how they would like to be 'named' because people's words have a different quality when their narratives become legible as a creative process and practice of interactive research when co-authorship is not an option.

Despite my desire to make my ethnographic fieldwork as interactive as possible, I soon realised that I could not always uphold a practice of inviting people to choose without any intervention on my part. As I became more ensconced in fieldwork, I realised the high stakes in employing people's legal names, even when they encouraged me to do so. When it came to writing about Indigenous activists, I did not always feel comfortable honouring a person's request to employ their full or legal names. Gaining one's identity card and displaying

FIG. 8.4 Gold 'changing' – burning the mercury to leave pure gold; a highly toxic procedure

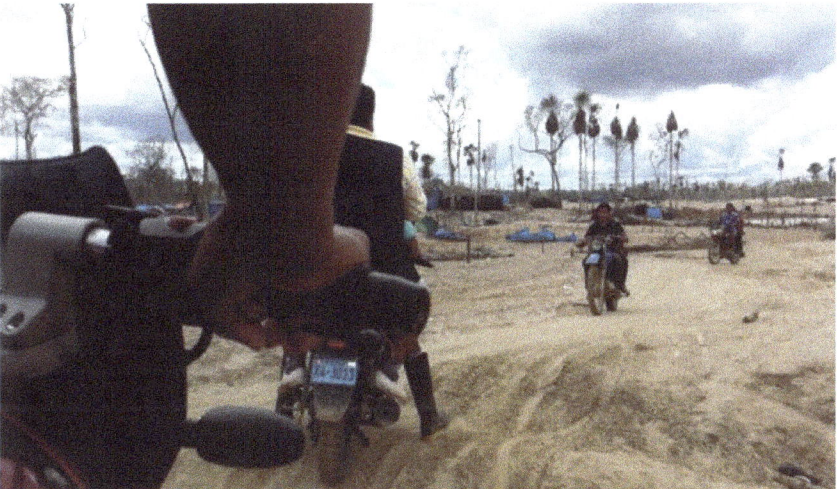

FIG. 8.5 Transport in the gold mines; mercury turns the rainforest landscape into desert

FIG. 8.6 Regional Peruvian health team performing rapid HIV/AIDS tests anonymously for sex-workers and gold miners in rainforest mining camps, pictured here outside a brothel

nametags has become a proud gesture for people – Indigenous or not (and that category of the person also goes up for debate) – so often ignored by the State. This process echoes Marcel Mauss's notion that having a name forms a critical step in taking on an identity as a person (Mauss 1985). Yet while Indigenous activists may have felt confident in their personhood and in asking me to use their full names, environmental activists, particularly Indigenous ones, represent easy assassination targets for disgruntled loggers, oil speculators, miners and drug traffickers. Naming people in full might not only undermine their efforts but might also put their lives in danger.

Sex-workers, unlike Indigenous activists, did not tell me their real names and I did not ask for them, knowing that they protected their own identities from their customers as well. I may never have learned Estrella's full legal name had not a competing exotic dancer taken it as her 'stage-name' and asked me to employ it when I wrote. 'Véronica' became the first person who selected a pseudonym that I refused to employ on ethical grounds. Instead, I chose 'Véronica' for her, after making sure there would be no confusion with – or danger for – another sex-worker. My desire to increase interactive and participatory ethnographic methods had met its limits. By using Estrella's real name, Véronica exposed Estrella to social harassment at best and to police violence at worst. Most worrying for Estrella, however, was that in the event of a police raid, the news media – armed with video cameras – would take footage and reveal her identity. Family members did not know about her line of work, and Estrella feared that they would find out. She hid under the beams of police searchlights and news cameras as best she could. It was she who pointed out to me some of the similarities and differences between sex-workers and Indigenous activists. 'We are both trying to stay alive… they need and hate us'. Estrella's comment that politicians both needed and hated sex-workers and Indigenous activists came from her observation that both were necessary for a strong tourist industry. But both were too often found dead.

While Indigenous environmental activists tend to participate in local and international politics with their full names – traveling to conferences with identity cards and passports tends to necessitate this – the stakes for being outspoken and visible are high. In November 2014, just as Peru prepared to hold climate talks in Lima, four Indigenous activists were murdered by illegal loggers. Death threats have become common for activists and leaders at the Indigenous federation of Madre de Dios (*Federación Nativa del Rio Madre de Dios y sus Afluentes* – FENAMAD). Hunt Oil, the powerful petroleum conglomerate, began its drilling in 2006. It's unclear whether the Peruvian army, police officers, company cronies or all of them together physically attacked protesting Indigenous groups. The Peruvian government has since renewed the nine-year contract with Hunt Oil for another three years, without consultation with the Indigenous communities living on the land under extraction (FENAMAD).

In 2020, with oil and gold ever more extractable, and with growing infrastructure, people and information travelled faster than they had along rivers when I first arrived in 2010. I began to question how quickly – or slowly – my own words and naming practices might also travel. Such questions might not have been an immediate concern if the violence of extractive economies had not intensified, nor if my first round of fieldwork had not come to an abrupt and undesired end in March of 2012, when a gold mining strike in Madre de Dios turned bloody. It was not the first, nor has it been the last clash between the Peruvian government and illegal and informal gold miners in Madre de Dios.[3] In 2012, The Peruvian government sent its army to pacify protesting miners, joined by the Indigenous federation of Madre de Dios. An estimated 15,000 gold miners went on strike to continue working, demanding an alleviation of environmental regulations. Several thousand sex-workers joined them. The Indigenous federation, misjudging the political climate, walked with the gold miners in the hope of entering negotiations with the state over land claims. The plan backfired. The Peruvian media painted the Indigenous federation as betraying the earth by making an alliance with the gold miners. Already targets if

FIG. 8.7 Peruvian Army extracting illegal gold miners from a rainforest conservation area

they did not cooperate with marauding loggers and miners, Amazonian activists once again became the focus of the Peruvian government's 'extraction' efforts (large-scale protests in 2009 along the Inter-Amazonian Highway had also turned violent). The choice of the word 'extraction', as Peruvian secret service-men explained to me while asking me to provide names and information to help them, was a euphemism for 'extermination'.

Forced to leave and worried that I would endanger people who had trusted me with their words, I set about destroying identifying data. Without a strong internet connection to digitally save interviews, everything went onto a small external hard-drive. This ended up pressed between my skin and the elastic of my clothing. I jammed the RAM on my computer so that it would not turn on anymore. I explained to the government agents going through my bags that the rainforest humidity, former ethnographic foe-turned-friend, had destroyed my digitised data.

Making ethical decisions about how to protect the people that anthropologists work with during ethnographic fieldwork is, as cultural anthropologist Paul Stoller notes, 'a very messy business'. Stoller's comments were made in response to the debates about ethnographic integrity and ethics surrounding Alice Goffman's book, *On the Run* (2014). The book sparked interest and ire for multiple reasons: Goffman is a white woman conducting research in black Philadelphia neighbourhoods, she documents what appears to be her participation in a crime as the driver of a car, and she refuses to give people's real names and often, their ages, blurring their identities. This means that when journalists attempted to fact-check her bombshell book, they couldn't do it. The sensational reaction to Goffman's book – both positive and negative – was further heightened by Goffman's status as the daughter of Erving Goffman, famed US sociologist.

The academic and journalistic response gave me pause because I too am a white woman ethnographer, conducting research where I keenly see a power imbalance – one so closely tied to anthropological origins and practice. I meditated on the similarities as well as the stark differences between long-form journalism and ethnography. Whereas journalists must check their facts, the very concept of a fact and what constitutes truth has become part of a critical enquiry for social scientists. Ethnography is not about 'fact-checking', Stoller notes, but rather a weaving of personal and professional interactions into fruitful, if not fruitfully frustrating, entanglements. The 'truth' is not an objective one, existing outside social interaction, but rather something made collaboratively. And laws are often unjust. Acknowledging the precariousness of other people's lives, a precariousness that the writer often does not share, may necessitate blending the 'facts' to protect people's identities. At least, this becomes a necessity if one cares about people beyond the publication of their story.

Goffman's deployment of pseudonyms and anonymity for the people portrayed in her book reignited debates that dance around the issue of race (Lewis-Kraus 2016) in social science research. While I find the critiques from journalists on this question of fact-checking easily addressable (or dismissible) on ethical grounds to protect people's identities, the dynamics of race, and of what it means for a white social scientist to do an ethnography in and of an African-American community, merit deeper questioning. The concerns about the colonial roots of social science bear further thought. The power dynamics that play a role in qualitative research are reflective of greater social hierarchies. The structural inequalities in academia are not singular to institutions of higher learning, but they can be exposed by researchers as well as institutional policies and practices. Whether one agrees or not with Goffman's fieldwork location and subsequent analysis, I can appreciate the care that she took to blur details, places and events. She gave pseudonyms – which I understand was also done out of respect – to protect people who shared their lives or interacted with her.

The conflict around Goffman's book, scholarship on 'ethnographic refusal' (Simpson 2007; Tuck and Yang 2014; Zahara 2016; Velásquez, this volume), as well as conversations with colleague-friends about potentialising collaborative and multimodal futures of anthropology (Goldstein, Edu, and Alvarez 2017) gave me cause to reflect on Derrida's questions that I posed at the beginning of this piece. 'Is writing seemly? Does the writer cut a respectable figure? Is it proper to write?' And not just: 'Is it done?' but also 'How is it done?' I continue to bring these questions with me into (and out of) the field because they not only urge me to consider my whiteness and privilege when I write, but also *how* and *how much* I write. Which is to say, if I am to be trafficking in other people's stories in the academic context – that is, to be capitalising on telling the tales of other people's lives – is there a 'proper' and more 'respectable' way to do so?

These are questions that I continue to ask myself as a practice of integrity. They are part of a reflexive toolkit, one which I find myself adding to on a regular basis. Kahnawake Mohawk scholar Audra Simpson's questions for herself also resonate with me: 'Can I do this and still come home; What am I revealing here and why? Where will this get us? Who benefits from this and why?' (2007: 78). While 'home' can be an elusive concept, let alone an actual place, positioning myself to be invited back into people's homes strikes me as a very good way to cut a respectable writerly figure.

Simpson's critical reflections on ethnographic refusal (2007) have been foundational for me to think with, as have subsequent interventions by Unangax̂ scholar Eve Tuck and her collaborator, K. Wayne Yang (2014). Simpson advocates for limits to what the ethnographer writes, something that is especially acute for her when returning to her Mohawk community. She highlights the kinds of conflict that arise when creating and controlling silences in the text: 'To speak of limits in such a way makes some liberal thinkers uncomfortable, and may, to them, seem dangerous. When access to information, to knowledge, to the intellectual commons is controlled by people who generate that information [participants in a research study], it can be seen as a violation of shared standards of justice and truth.' (Simpson 2007: 74). While Simpson takes up histories of colonialism in the Americas that are specific to Indigenous peoples, I do think the limits that Alice Goffman set vis-à-vis pseudonyms and the journalistic outrage speak to a European Enlightenment standard of singular truth and justice.

The kinds of ethnographic refusal and 'stances of refusal in research', are, as Tuck and Yang write, 'attempts to place limits on conquest and the colonization of knowledge by marking what is off limits, what is not up for grabs or discussion, what is sacred and what can't be known' (Tuck and Yang 2014: 225). In many cases, it is also a question of why something must be known by a wider, reading public. Colonial European legacies of voyeurism are in play. Such grand expository writing usually indicates that the writer is not intent on staying – or returning – to the communities and people written about. Certainly, I wanted to be able to return, to continue research relationships and friendships. I also consider there to be a moment of reflective ethnographic empathy. 'Would I want to be named in such a way?'

Attempting to collaborate in the choosing of pseudonyms is one way I try to answer the questions of what it means for the writer to cut a respectable figure when analysing the lives of others. Paulo Freire, Brazil's revolutionary thinker and writer, espoused a pedagogy that was a 'naming' of the world, engaging in a dialogue with others. 'If it is in speaking their word that people, by naming the world, transform it, dialogue imposes itself as the way by which they achieve significance as human beings' (Freire 1970: 88). This resonates with Mauss's assertion that to become a person, one must first have a name. Freire's formulation, however, goes one step further in highlighting (as he does throughout *Pedagogy of the Oppressed*) human relationality, how we bring one another into existence through naming practices. For Franz Fanon, being called a name other than one's own – that is, hailed as 'Negro' in a racialised pejorative way – creates a severe sense of trauma and alienation from one's self (Fanon 1967). One's 'own name' may not be the one given by parents or typed into a legal document; it is the name that feels comfortable to inhabit.

This is why inviting people to participate in their pseudo-naming, as well as telling them why I may not be able to honour their requests, meant something more important – perhaps even more truthful – than 'fact-checking'. It meant explaining to Véronica, who had stolen Estrella's true name for her nightly activities, why I would not do as she wished. This did not provoke a positive response from Véronica, but it did mean that trust with Estrella and her network of sex-workers deepened. Fortunately, it also enabled a different conversation with Véronica to occur. This in turn enriched my connections with all of them. Certainly, that is a 'best ethnographic case scenario'. However, it can only enrich ethnographic renderings by requiring us to reflect on our own motivations. Mauss's concluding words, after considering whether the stable category of the person and naming might someday fade away, brings my own ethnographic case to a close: 'Let us labor to demonstrate how we must become aware of ourselves, in order to perfect our thought and to express it better' (Mauss 1985: 23). That strikes me as a seemly and respectable answer to my own questions of how writing might be done.

ENDNOTES

1 Biopiracy is the stealing of entire plants and animals, or simply seeds, eggs or genetic material *as well as* the associated ethnobiological knowledge. It is part of a larger multi-billion-dollar wildlife trafficking industry (UNODC 2020). In my research, I focus on three plants in particular: Maca (*Lepidium meyenii*), which is Peru's most biopirated plant (INDECOPI 2014; Smith 2014; Tavui 2016), Coca (*Erythroxylum coca*), sacred in the Andes as a leaf, but refined into cocaine, and Ayahuasca (*Banisteria caapi*), an Amazonian vine revered for its potent medicinal-psychedelic effects, which has led to an increase in its pharmaceutical testing, principally for depression and Parkinson's disease (Domínguez-Clavé et al. 2016; Djamshidian et al. 2015; Dos Santos et al. 2015).

2 While it is more commonly referred to as the Interoceanic Highway in English news media, the Spanish and Portuguese don't necessarily differentiate so clearly between 'road' and 'highway'. In Spanish, the paved infrastructure project is known as *La Carretera Interoceánica* and in Portuguese, as both *A Estrada do Pacífico* and *A Rodovia Interoceânica. Carretera* in Spanish is more commonly applied to 'roads' and *autopista* for 'highways'. Similarly, in Portuguese, *rodovia* translates as 'highway' but *'estrada'* as road. Both are used interchangeably. Brazilians, Peruvians and Bolivians who came to see the 2011 inauguration of the transnational infrastructure project in Madre de Dios noted that the route's two-lane bridges were very narrow. For this reason, they referred to it as a road, not a highway.

3 The Peruvian government differentiates between illegal and informal mining. The latter means that there is a process to become 'formalised', that is, legalised. It is a moment of limbo, however, for miners, as they work through the government registration process.

ACKNOWLEDGEMENTS

This piece is dedicated to Estrella as well as Juana and Jorge Payaba Cachique, two Indigenous Shipobo activists in Madre de Dios, Peru. Jorge passed away in November 2014. His sister, Juana, fights illegal loggers and gold miners on Shipibo community land while facing death threats. She continues to support the work her brother did, advocating for 'Indigenous communities living in voluntary isolation' who live along the Peruvian and Brazilian border, as well as trying to keep extractive industries at bay.

Juana Payaba's name is not a pseudonym. From 2011 onward, she has been a public figure as president of her community, creating videos to publicise the illegality and danger of mining in her community. I have chosen to honour her requests for visibility by employing her real name.

REFERENCES

Dalakoglou, D., and P. Harvey, 'Roads and Anthropology: Ethnographic Perspectives on Space, Time and (Im)Mobility', *Mobilities*, 7.4 (2012), 459–65. DOI: 10.1080/17450101.2012.718426

Daniels, A., 'La Transoceánica: un sueño peligroso', *BBC Mundo*, 7 September 2010. https://www.bbc.com/mundo/america_latina/2010/09/100809_carretera_transoceanica_interoceanica_peru.

Derrida, J., *Disseminations*, trans. B. Johnson (New York: Athlone Press, 1981), 74.

Fanon, F., *Black Skin, White Masks* (New York: Grove Press, 1967 [1952]).

FENEMAD, *Gobierno amplía por tres años contrato de licencia a Hunt Oil para explorar Lote 76, Noticias Fenamad*, 5 August 2015. http://www.fenamad.org.pe/noticias/gobierno-amplia-por-tres-anos-contrato-de-licencia-a-hunt-oil-para-explorar-lote-76/.

Fleck, L. C., and others, *Estrategias de conservación a lo largo de la Carretera Interoceánica en Madre de Dios, Perú: Un análisis económico-especial*. Lima, Peru: Conservation Strategy Fund, 2010.

Freire, P., *Pedagogy of the Oppressed*, trans. M. Bergman Ramos (New York and London: Bloomsbury Academic, 2000 [1970]).

Gadea, R. S., ed., *Integración Física Sudamericana 10 años después: Impacto e Implementación en el Peréu*. Lima: Banco Interamericano de Desarrollo, Centro Peruano de Estudios Internacionales Universidad del Pacífica. 2012.

Goffman, A., *On the Run: Fugitive Life in an American City* (Chicago: Chicago University Press, 2017).

Goldstein, R., *Life in Traffic: Women, Plants, and Gold Along the Interoceanic Highway* (Berkeley, CA: University of California Press, forthcoming).

Goldstein, R., 'The Triangular Traffic in Women, Plants, and Gold: Along the Interoceanic Road in Brazil, Peru, and Bolivia' (Dissertation, University of California, Berkeley, 2015).

Goldstein, R., U. F. Edu and P. A. Alvarez, 'Collaborations: Envisioning an Engaged Multimodal Future for Anthropology', *History of Anthropology Newsletter* 41 (2017): https://histanthro.org/notes/an-engaged-multimodal-future/.

Graeber D., 'On the Moral Grounds of Economic Relations: A Maussian Approach', *Journal of Classical Sociology*, 14.1 (2014), 65–77.

IIRSA: EJE INTEROCEÁNICO PERÚ-BRASIL-BOLIVIA, 2011. http://www. iirsa.org/admin_iirsa_web/Uploads/Documents/mer_bogota11_extension_ eid_pbb_esp.pdf.

Lewis-Kraus, G., 'The Trials of Alice Goffman', *The New York Times*, 12 January 2016. https://www.nytimes.com/2016/01/17/magazine/the-trials-of-alice-goffman. html.

Mauss, M., 'A Category of the Human Mind: The Notion of Person; the Notion of Self', trans. W. D. Halls, in M. Carrithers, S. Collins, and S. Lukes, eds., *The Category of the Person: Anthropology, Philosophy, History* (Cambridge; New York: Cambridge University Press, 1985), pp.1–23.

——, *The Gift: The Form and Reason for Exchange in Archaic Societies*, trans. W. D. Halls (New York: W. W. Norton & Company, 2000 [1950]).

Simpson, A., 'On Ethnographic Refusal: Indigeneity, "Voice", and Colonial Citizenship', *Junctures* 9 (2007), 67–80.

Soros, A., 'Local Activists Are Paying with Their Life to Protect Their Forests in Peru', *The Guardian*, 17 November 2014. http://www.theguardian.com/ environment/2014/nov/17/environ.

Stoller, P., 'Alice Goffman and the Future of Ethnography', *Huffington Post*, 15 June 2015. http://www.huffingtonpost.com/paul-stoller/alice-goffman-and-the-future-of-ethnography-_b_7585614.html.

——, 'In Defense of Ethnography', *Huffington Post*, 24 August 2015. http://www. huffingtonpost.com/paul-stoller/in-defense-of-ethnography_b_8028542.html.

Strathern, M., *The Gender of the Gift: Problems with Women and Problems with Society in Melanesia* (Berkeley: University of California, Press, 1990).

Tuck, E., and K. W. Yang, 'R-Words. Refusing Research', in D. Paris and M. T. Winn, eds., *Humanizing Research: Decolonizing Qualitative Inquiry with Youth and Communities* (Thousand Oakes, CA: Sage Publications, 2014), pp. 223–47.

Uribe, S., 'Illegible Infrastructures: Road Building and the Making of State-Spaces in the Colombian Amazon', *Environment and Planning D: Society and Space*, 37.5 (2019), 886–904. doi:10.1177/0263775818788358

Watts, J., 'Spotlight on Murders of Activists as Peru Prepares for Lima Climate Talks', *The Guardian*, 17 November2014. http://www.theguardian.com/ environment/2014/nov/17/activists-murders-peru-lima-climate-talks.

Zahara, A., 'Ethnographic Refusal, A How to Guide', *Discard Studies*, 8 August 2016. https://discardstudies.com/2016/08/08/ethnographic-refusal-a-how-to-guide/.

Zhou, Y., 'Branding Tengchong: Globalization, Road Building, and Spatial Reconfigurations in Yunnan, Southwest China', in T. Blumenfield and H. Silverman, eds., *Cultural Heritage Politics in China* (New York: Springer, 2013), pp. 247–60. https://doi.org/10.1007/978-1-4614-6874-5_13.

9

NORMALISING SEXUALLY VIOLATED BODIES: SEXUAL ASSAULT ADJUDICATION, MEDICAL EVIDENCE AND THE LEGAL CASE

Sameena Mulla

WHAT CONSTITUTES EVIDENCE OF SEXUAL ASSAULT? I AM SEATED IN A courtroom as a sexual assault forensic nurse is asked to explain, by a prosecutor, the basic tenets of genital anatomy. During the sexual assault trials I observe in Milwaukee, WI, testimony is highly orchestrated. Sequestration orders bar the presence of witnesses from the courtroom unless they are testifying. The first witness, almost always the complainant, is not present when the forensic nurse testifies. Early in the forensic nurse's testimony, the prosecution provides a body map, and the map is introduced as an evidentiary exhibit so that the jury can consider this anatomy lesson in its search for truth. The map depicts two views of a vulva, referred to as a 'vagina' in the shorthand of the court, more or less from the perspective of someone standing or sitting between a patient's legs as they are held in stirrups. One of the views on the map includes a detailed view of the cervix, which can be visualised with the assistance of a speculum. The images are neat and simple, with black line drawings that bely the fleshiness of human bodies. The absence of the victim-witness during the forensic nurse's testimony further alienates the corporeality of the body from its sanitised renderings.

The sequestration order reproduces the work of the drape in gynaecological examinations, separating persons and pelvises (Kapsalis 1997; Mulla 2014). As adjuncts to the testimony of the victim-witness, these maps serve as the basis for the jury to move forward in their deliberations over whether or not there is evidence beyond a reasonable doubt that a crime, in this case sexual assault, has been committed.

During the trial, the nurse responds to the prosecutor's questions, explaining how and what we are seeing, and how these body parts function. When they describe the tissue of the 'vagina', the forensic nurses testify that vaginas are 'made to have sexual intercourse often'; 'lubricated'; 'very stretchy'; 'similar to the membrane of the mouth – a mucus membrane'; 'like a scrunchy' in reference to a tool for holding back the hair; 'able to accommodate something the size of

ANATOMICAL DIAGRAMS-SKIN SURFACE ASSESSMENT

Utilize diagrams to document all injuries and findings including cuts, lacerations, bruises, abrasions, redness, swelling, bites, burns, scars and stains of foreign material on patient's body. Distinguish pre-existing injuries from those resulting from the incident. Record size, color and appearance of all injuries. If an Alternate Light Source is used to assist in visualizing secretions, denote areas of (+)findings with "+ALS".

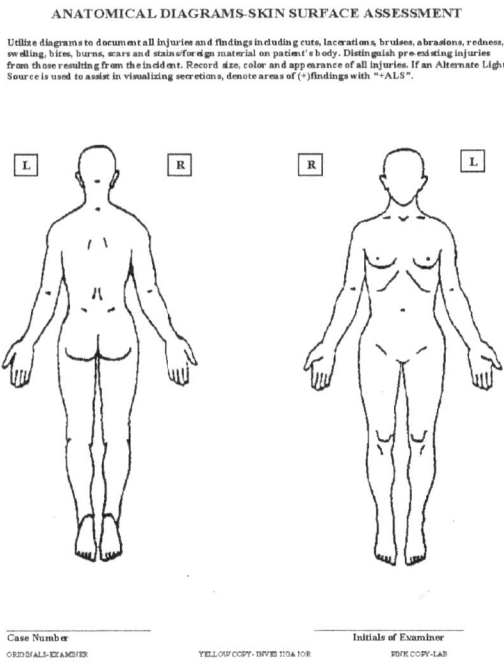

| Case Number | | Initials of Examiner |
| ORIGINALS-EXAMINER | YELLOW COPY-INVESTIGATOR | PINK COPY-LAB |

FIG. 9.1 Gender neutral body map (produced and made freely available by FORGE – forge-forward.org)

a watermelon'; and 'a self-cleaning vessel'. These descriptions of a lubricated, stretchy, self-cleaning membrane that is likened to the mouth ('Think how quickly your mouth heals when you bite it or have a sore?', a nurse might ask) assist the jury's understanding of the minimal or absent injury in the sexual assault case being adjudicated. One nurse told us that once when she had testified, she removed her scrunchy from her ponytail, demonstrated its elasticity, and replaced it as a demonstration from the stand. Even as the testimony supports the jury's ability to render a verdict, it also normalises the vagina as distinctly gendered by invoking the qualities of a 'vagina' through the feminised person of a nurse who uses gendered language to speak to the jury (Martin 1991). The nurse herself belongs to a profession which is over 90% female in the US, with deep roots in female religious orders, while the form of labour associated with nursing practice is itself intensely feminised. This normalisation of gendered bodies participates in the normalisation of sexual violence as heterosexual and heteronormative (Gavey 2005).

Returning to the testimony of the forensic nurses, one can ask about the purpose of the nurses' demonstratives. Why use a scrunchy to illustrate the tensile nature of vascular tissues? Why not a timing belt, or a rubber band, or some object with a less (or differently) gendered provenance? The nurses' testimony largely explains why there is 'nothing to see'. The injured vagina, in these cases, is cast as inscrutable (and objectified, universal, capacious, yielding, heteronormative, resilient, reproductive, and a slew of other, mostly troubling, things). Pratiksha Baxi has productively described the relationship of medical expertise to the law in her in-depth ethnography of the sexual assault trial in India, *Public Secrets of Law*. Critiquing the longstanding reliance on the medical category of the sexual *habitue* in India's law courts, she argues that there is no medical knowledge outside the law. It is the law that determines the status of disciplinary expertise, exemplified, for Baxi, in the enduring use of the two-finger test in the Indian court of law.

This also holds true in the context of law courts in the US, where, accounting for the lack of injuries on a sexual assault victim, the nurse's descriptions give context to a body that does not give up its secrets through the revelation of physical evidence. The experts – forensic nurses in these cases – can sometimes locate the microinjuries that laypeople will not see. These will be described by the forensic nurse as she testifies to what she saw when she conducted her examination. During the proceedings, the prosecutor often asks the forensic nurse to render the injuries onto a body map. This body map is then proffered as yet another evidentiary exhibit (Figure 9.1). This visual representation of the wound is still devoid of its fleshiness. Photographs of the genital examination, which are often a part of the medical trial, do not make their way into the law courts, as prosecutors find that body maps, helpfully narrated by forensic nurses, are more effective conveyances of information. The body maps, unlike photographs, do not invite the same visceral response of disgust from the jury, a phenomenon that many prosecutors seek to avoid (Mulla 2014).

While microinjuries are sometimes present, more often, formulating the pathology of sexual assault as Canguilhem might in *The Normal and the Pathological*, the symptoms of sexual assault cannot be localised. It may be a productive slippage to substitute 'injury' for 'pathology' and wonder how to teach

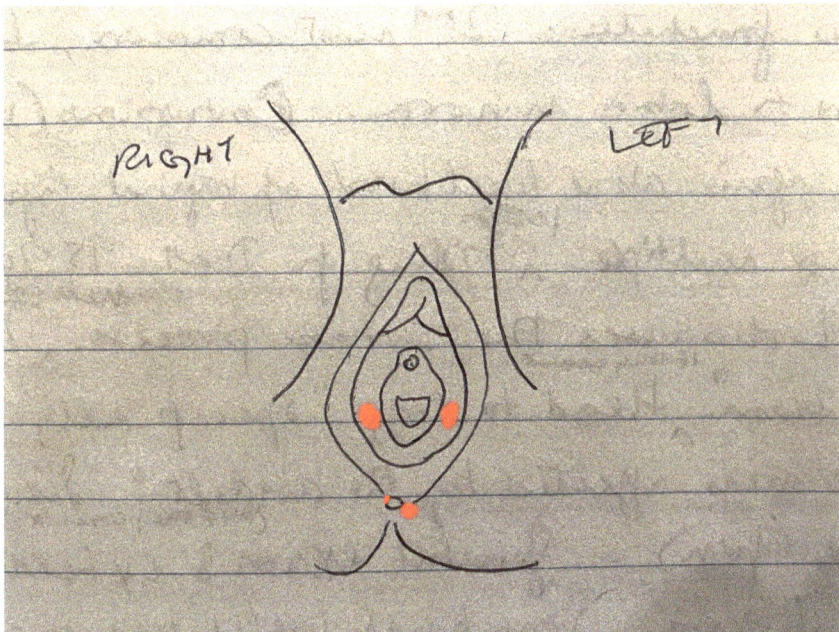

FIG. 9.2 The anthropologist's rendering of a marked body map, in which injuries are indicated in red

the jury to see when there are no visible wounds to mark the assaulted body. In the course of the sexual assault trial, the truth of sexual assault must be established through the painstaking and deliberate introduction of testimony. Between the nurses, social workers, police detectives and crime lab analysts who are the most frequent expert witnesses participating in the trial, a variety of absences were explained away: the lack of injuries, lack of fingerprints, imperfect DNA matches or the absence of DNA altogether, and delays in disclosure by victims of sexual assault. Whether compelling and insistent, or repetitive and tedious, the parade of witnesses who testify to the absence of evidence establishes that the lack of physical evidence is securely normal. The systematic materialisation of the lack of evidence makes way for the testimony of the victim herself (or on occasion, himself). In *A Theory of the Trial*, Robert Burns writes,

> evidence is logically relevant if [the link between evidence and the propo-sition being offered] is supported by 'experience or science', or, somewhat more technically, if that link, which constitutes the 'probative value' of the evidence presented, is secured by a 'major premise' that exists in our common sense (the 'web of belief') and which a reasonable jury could conclude was applicable to the evidence submitted (1999: 22).

In the case of the sexual assault trial, the notion of what we can call vaginal durability is evidenced by supplementing jurors' common sense with suggestive analogues: their mouths or a stretchy scrunchy or a reflection on the notion that women who bear children most often recover from labour and birthing.

Here, courtroom ethnography illuminates the day-to-day practices of the trial court, ordinary events which are rarely captured in other forms of legal scholarship that focus on case law, or law at the level of precedent. This is how law is lived. Seated in a trial court for many months, I took note of the ceremony of repetition, the formulas that are proffered when adjudicants are on the record, and the care and thought that attorneys invested in selecting their witnesses, sequencing their witnesses, eliciting testimony on direct and cross-examination and emphasising unmarked body maps. My fieldwork frequently circled back to the ways in which forms of knowledge-making during the sexual assault trial normalised the absence of injury by deploying a scaffolding for interpreting the findings of a pelvic examination, reinscribing a gendered understanding of the 'vagina'. The conventions of the examination, such as draping, were conveyed through the court's practice of witness sequestration, and its use of expert testimony that follows the complainant's testimony, speaking to the victim-witness' experience. It was the prosecution's goal that the jury, compelled by the argument that a lack of physical evidence is normal, would then rely on the victim-witness's testimony to make their findings. In the circumscribed space of a criminal trial, the justice system became one more space in which the singular experiences of particular victim-witnesses are shaped into familiar and normative narratives of gendered violence, while, regardless of the outcome of a legal case, nursing expertise serves to impart and normalise the 'vagina' itself through a universalised rendering that can only be understood through the nurse's expert intervention.

REFERENCES

Baxi, P., *Public Secrets of Law: Rape Trials in India* (Delhi and London: Oxford University Press, 2014).

Burns, R. P., *A Theory of the Trial* (Princeton and Oxford: Princeton University Press, 1999).

Canguilhem, G., *The Normal and the Pathological* (New York: Zone Books, 1989).

Gavey, N., *Just Sex? The Cultural Scaffolding of Rape* (New York: Routledge, 2005).

Kapsalis, T., *Public Privates: Performing Gynecology from Both Ends of the Speculum* (Raleigh and Durham: Duke University Press, 1997).

Martin, E., 'The Egg and the Sperm: How Science Has Constructed a Romance Based on Stereotypical Male-Female Roles', *Signs*, 16.3 (1991), 485–501.

Mulla, S., *The Violence of Care: Rape Victims, Forensic Nurses, and Sexual Assault Victims* (New York: New York University Press, 2014).

10

CASE BY CASE

Jason Danely

'THE QUESTION FOR ME OF WHETHER TO GET A STOMACH TUBE FOR MY mother was whether or not she has lived her natural life completely.[1] Maybe her time has come and maybe not. The tube just makes a natural life last longer… But it is really difficult! It just has to be case by case'.

Yasuda-san pursed his lips silently, as if to make sure his words would not change their minds and return to his mouth. Then he turned to the older man dressed in a baggy beige cardigan at the table next to him and gestured to his mid-section.

'Stomach tubes! It is really case by case, right?'

'Case by case!', the man replied, nodding, 'But it is at least something that you can do. If they need a lot of hydration or something, they can put the tube in so that they don't get oesophageal pneumonia'.

'If you get pneumonia it is really bad', Yasuda-san agreed, 'but the thing is, once you do [the surgery], you might have regrets. That's just the human condition I guess… most people, once they put it in, they leave it there until the end. At my mother's care home most, well, really *everyone* has a stomach tube. *Every single one*! In my mother's case, [when I think about the tube] what I think about is whether this person is needed on this earth. I'm not sure'.

The two friends appraised their respective narratives, taking turns like playing a game of catch. Although I had been conducting participant observation in this men's caregiver support group for several months, and was aware that Yasuda-san's mother and Takeda-san's wife were both living with advanced

FIG. 10.1 'It's meal time!' announces the nurse holding a bag of artificial nutrition, while family and friends look on

FIG. 10.2 The patient's daughter is shocked when her father's eyes open when he is given food

dementia, this was the first time I realised that the men had also made the decision to give artificial hydration and nutrition to the ones they cared for. The ethical uncertainty of the decision lingered. Yasuda-san was worried that perhaps he was not merely preserving her life but extending it too long. These decisions about life-extending care could only be appreciated, as the two men agreed, case by case.

Yasuda-san turned back to Takeda-san, who had been listening quietly.

Yasuda: Your wife, can she still speak?

Takeda: No, she hasn't been able to speak for over a year. But I still visit. She still knows.

Yasuda: Her eyes?

Takeda: Yes, right.

I quickly learned that conversations like these would spring up constantly once people learned that I was interested in the subject of elder care. Some caregivers, like Yasuda-san, leapt at the chance to talk about their experiences, but often ended up circling around an unresolved sense of bewilderment, uncertain futures, ambivalent feelings, thoughtful, and elliptical eddies. At times it seemed

FIG. 10.3 About three-quarters of older people in Japan with care needs are cared for primarily by family members, one-third of whom are men

like the experience of care was as simple and as heart-breaking as the flash of a mother's glance, silently looking up at her son from a hospital bed. At other times it was so complex that each caregiver's circumstances, their family relationships, the nature of the illnesses involved, their religious background or insurance status—all of it could potentially shift the fragile stability of the care situation.

Along the way, decisions had to be made. For Yasuda-san, the choice of having a feeding tube inserted into his mother's stomach was not taken lightly; in making his decision he was making a choice to become a kind of 'case', to himself, as much as to me or to his friends. Becoming a case means becoming a possibility, different from but linked to a coterie of other possibilities. As an anthropologist, it is this sense of possibility that draws me toward each new case, but I had not considered that my interlocutors were also aware of themselves as cases. Indeed, becoming a case meant deflecting bioethical judgement, since each case was its own constellation of contingencies.

Becoming a case motivates a further self-crafting of one's first-person narrative (see Mattingly 2014). For Yasuda-san, this meant engaging with some heavy emotional and existential issues, such as weighing his mother's destiny in this world and his responsibility for what he called her 'soul' (*tamashi*), whose gaze he could not escape. Although a small percentage of those receiving a stomach tube are able to regain the ability to take in adequate nutrition by mouth (about 6.5.%), Yasuda-san was nearly certain that once the tube was in, it was never coming out. He could only wait until the stomach failed completely (maybe a matter of years) before his mother could die a natural death. Within this window of time, between the decision and the death, his case provided a point of conversation with other caregivers, like Takeda-san, whose story was similar, but also somewhat different, neither better, nor worse.

Another case among many, neither tragedy nor comedy, Yasuda-san's case gives flesh to the often polarised debate around end-of-life care and the boundaries of the 'natural' or 'good' death in the oldest and longest-lived country in the world. As of 21 September 2015 (national 'Respect for the Aged Day' in Japan), 26.7% of Japan's population were 65 or older.

I had been following debates about the stomach tube already for a few months before Yasuda-san opened up to me at the support group. Nurses and care aides had at various times told me that the widespread use of stomach tubes among persons with dementia was an indication of staff shortage rather than an actual need or a sign of respect for the life and well-being of patients. 'We are keeping [patients] alive to fit our own circumstances', one nurse explained, 'we would be in trouble if we let them just die, but it is just miserable'. Another care aide told me, 'The family doesn't visit but as long as the patient is alive and we are taking care of them, the family keeps on getting the pension, so of course they are going to get a tube'. He then asked if Americans were still using the tubes, since those used in Japan appeared to be American-made.

The case, in my research, cannot help but be a case for the ordinary as a site of moral work (Das 2007; Mattingly 2014: 26). Michael Lambek has argued that 'Ethnography supplies case material that speaks to the urgency and imme-diacy yet ordinariness of the ethical' (2010, 4). But this ordinariness is not to be seen in contrast with some abstract notion of the unusual or exceptional. As more and more stories surfaced, not only about tubes, but other forms of care and abuse as well, I began to hear fewer and fewer 'exceptional' cases. I began to wonder what might constitute the exceptional. Each case was different, to be sure, but at the same time, ordinary in the sense that it was grounded in the texture of everyday life.

Yasuda-san and Takeda-san practised care in ways that afforded them chances to reflect on themselves, their care, their roles as men, as sons, as husbands. They experimented with possible selves as their circumstances changed, as potentials of life emerged as one thing and then became another. Becoming a case meant that they could share in this process of mutual reflection and recognition without being identical. Instead, they embodied two possibilities of the ordinary, each following a logic of care when taken case by case.

ENDNOTES

1 I use the term 'stomach tubes' as a translation of the Japanese *irō* 胃ろう, which in all cases mentioned refer to Percutaneous Endoscopic Gastrostomy (PEG) feeding. See Aita et al. 2007; Nakanishi and Hattori 2014 for more on their prevalence in Japan.

ACKNOWLEDGEMENT

This publication was made possible through the support of the John Templeton Foundation, via The Enhancing Life Project. The opinions expressed in this publication are those of the author(s) and do not necessarily reflect the views of the John Templeton Foundation.

REFERENCES

Aita, K., M. Takahashi, H. Miyata, I. Kai, and T. E. Finucane, 'Physicians' Attitudes about Artificial Feeding in Older Patients with Severe Cognitive Impairment in Japan: A Qualitative Study', *BMC Geriatrics*, 7.1 (2007), 22. doi:10.1186/1471-2318-7-22.

Das, V., *Life and Words: Violence and the Descent into the Ordinary* (Berkeley: University of California Press, 2007).

Lambek, M., Introduction, in M. Lambek, ed., *Ordinary Ethics: Anthropology, Language, and Action* (New York: Fordham University Press, 2010), pp. 1–36.

Mattingly, C., *Moral Laboratories: Family Peril and the Struggle for a Good Life* (Berkeley: University of California Press, 2014).

Nakanishi, M., and K. Hattori, 'Percutaneous Endoscopic Gastrostomy (PEG) Tubes Are Placed in Elderly Adults in Japan with Advanced Dementia Regardless of Expectation of Improvement of Quality of Life', *Journal of Nutrition, Health & Aging*, 18 (2014), 503–09.

I I

THE CASE OF THE UGLY SPERM

Janelle Lamoreaux

THE CHINESE FILM, *UNDER THE DOME*, TELLS THE STORY OF A FORMER CCTV (China Central Television) news anchor's struggle to understand and deal with smog in the wake of her pregnancy and motherhood. The filmmaker and narrator, Chai Jing, makes a case for reducing pollution in China by highlighting the potential correlation between Beijing's smog and the tumour found in her developing foetus, diagnosed in utero. The film was released on video streaming websites in 2015, and quickly went viral. According to *China Dialogue*, the video was viewed hundreds of millions of times before being removed from major streaming portals one week later. This viral appeal could be attributed to the film's concentration on reproductive health, along with the ways environmental and personal narratives intersect at this critical juncture. Case in point: At a screening of *Under the Dome* that I attended in London, our host introduced the film by relating Chai's story to her own difficult experience of finding out she was pregnant while living in smog-filled Beijing. In her case, as in Chai's, tackling pollution in China became more pressing when its potential consequences threatened future generations.

There are other, less personalised, less narrativised approaches to making a case for reducing pollution in China via reproductive health. One of these is developmental and reproductive toxicology. Since the mid-twentieth century, this branch of toxicology has focused on studying correlations between toxic exposures and reproductive ability, as well as congenital disorders in developing offspring. Among the group of toxicologists I researched while conducting field-work in Nanjing, China, who I refer to as the DeTox Lab, the case for reducing China's pollution was initially made through male infertility. More specifically, the case was made through sperm.

By the early 2000s, many toxicologists in the US and Europe had shown through animal experiments that indirect exposure to synthetic pesticides leads to reduced sperm quality and quantity. The DeTox Lab was one of the first research groups able to conduct similar research on humans because of the amount of pesticide factory labour taking place in China's Yangtze River delta and its surroundings. Comparing the sperm of pesticide factory workers to those outside the occupational environment, the DeTox Lab found that human males who were indirectly exposed to synthetic pesticides in the factory were more likely to have sperm with chromosomal abnormalities, a condition linked to infertility, stillbirths and spontaneous abortion. Through this study, the lab made its first case for the harmful impacts of China's environment on sperm, focusing on the 'occupational environment'. Results were published in an international toxicology journal and, the laboratory director told me, shared at public health forums where they could potentially impact industrial regulations.

Was sperm an effective vehicle through which a case could be made for the regulation of pesticides and pollutants in China? It seems the DeTox Lab chose to first focus on male infertility partially because a broader discussion of post-industrial sperm decline was already occurring in many nations around the world. In China, the nuances of this conversation connected rising rates of male and female infertility to rapid social and economic transformations that had occurred since Reform and Opening began in the late 1970s. Under what the Chinese government called Socialism with Chinese Characteristics, the organisation of economies, labour and other aspects of daily life shifted. Male reproductive health specialists and media outlets listed lifestyle changes and increased stress as potential reasons for the accompanying post-Reform and Opening shifts in sperm counts: in one study, from approximately 100 million per ml in the 1970s to 40 million per ml in 2007.[1] Since then, the degradation of Chinese sperm has been explicitly linked to a degradation of the 'Chinese environment'. A 2013 green paper on climate change released by the China

Meteorological Administration made passing reference to reproductive health problems brought about by exposure to smog, resulting in renewed media coverage of the declining quality and quantity of Chinese sperm. One news article quotes Li Zheng, an andrologist and sperm bank coordinator from Shanghai, who states '[if] the environment is bad, sperm become ugly'.[2] Here, 'the environment' – more broadly defined – is again seen as a causal factor in sperm's decline.

Since their initial studies of the occupational environment, the DeTox Lab's research has raised the stakes of this toxic connection between human substances and their environments. In epigenetic studies of sperm quality and quantity, which I observed while doing research in 2011, toxicologists tried to understand how the contexts surrounding Chinese sperm become incorporated into and inherited by future generations.[3] Toxicologists would breed mice and rats that had been exposed to chemicals known to bring about sperm decline, and then analyse the sperm of their offspring. Though no statistically significant results were found during the time of my research, an experimental formula was being established which they hoped could be used to make a case for reducing pollution by emphasising the threat to future generations. Today, making a case for changing the environmental present seems to increasingly be done by making a case for the future.

Whether utilising film, toxicology or ethnography, when making a case one usually considers what will capture the imagination of an audience. How will one seize upon existing values, expectations and structures of feeling in order to move readers, colleagues or viewers? As Annemarie Mol writes, 'A case carries knowledge, not in the form of firm rules or statistically salient regularities, but in the form of a story about an occurrence that, even though it may have happened just once, is still telling, indicative, suggestive. It condenses expertise that is not general, but inspirational' (this volume: 44). Unlike Chai Jing's story, which suggests a relationship between her child's tumour and Beijing's smog, the DeTox Lab attempts to make its case through statistically significant correlations between increasing toxic exposures and decreasing sperm quality. Perhaps one is more inspirational than the other, and perhaps this has to do with their relationships to specificity and generality – with the degree to which a case is made through a personal account (a mother's first-person documentary) or by depersonalised accounting (the male-oriented scientific 'view from nowhere').

But what these two cases of case-making have in common is that they draw upon concerns about China's 'environment' – how it is defined is part of the problem – inhibiting the ability to bring forth healthy future generations. Like the threat of a congenital disorder, the threat of male infertility is, in a sense, inspirational. Sperm is a figure that inspires toxicologists in the DeTox Lab to seek the generalities that might allow others to make specific policy recommendations. Through sperm they also hope to better understand and inspire others to understand the intimate connections that exist between biological, economic and political domains, as well as the future stakes of ignoring these connections.

ENDNOTES

1 Xinhua, 'Experts Warn of Lower Fertility because of Stress, Lifestyle', *China Daily*, 4 October 2007.

2 Liyu Chen, 'Last 10 Years of Sperm Donor's Sperm Does Not Reach Set Standards', *Shanghai Morning Post*, 11 June 2013.

3 Epigenetics is often defined as (the study of) modifications to the genes that impact gene expression, but do not alter DNA sequence. Epigenetic research often studies the way DNA expression is influenced by extra-genetic factors such as diet, lifestyle or toxic exposures.

12

WAITING IN THE FACE OF BARE LIFE

Aaron Ansell

ADVOCATES OF A MORE ROBUST DEMOCRATIC CITIZENSHIP IN BRAZIL OFTEN point bitterly to the frequent practice of cutting ahead of others in line. Such line-cutting, they lament, indicates a popular attachment to patronage-styled hierarchy and a disregard of one's fellow citizens. Democratic citizenship, so this line of thought goes, inheres in one's respect for the stranger's time, body and life-world, a far cry from the daily humiliations (e.g., physical access restrictions) that poor people suffer within Brazil's anonymous metropolitan spaces (Caldeira 2000: 367–377). Waiting for services is thus 'a privileged site for studying performances of citizenship' because it reveals popular dispositions toward the generic citizen's rights and vulnerabilities (Holston 2008: 15).

I want to consider the possibility that waiting one's turn in line, what we might call waiting democratically, brings with it the threat of disarticulation from those social relations that give value to particular lives. Reflecting on Brazilians' invocations and subversions of egalitarian waiting opens a window into a mode of suffering that liberal institutions sometimes elicit, especially in a context of austerity. In what Javier Auyero calls the 'patient model' of governance, the neoliberal state imposes long waits and thus 'manipulates poor people's time' to produce their docility (Auyero 2012: 157). Here I suggest that poor people who inhabit democracy face another form of suffering, one associated with the threat of being reduced to a variant of 'bare life' (a lá Giorgio Agamben) as they anticipate the materialisation of their rights.

The incident I take for my ethnographic case occurred in March 2015 in the northeastern state of Piauí. There I witnessed an argument between two people waiting in line for curative consultation with a local spirit medium.

One party to the argument was 'Dora', a retired caretaker in her late fifties, who had been suffering from knee pain for months. Dora frequently complained that she lacked the money for private doctors. She had debated accessing free services through Brazil's 'Unified Health System' (*Sistema Única da Saúde*, or SUS), but was wary. SUS healthcare is hampered by insufficient state investment throughout Brazil, especially in the rural northeast. The one public hospital in Dora's town was chronically understaffed by medical personnel, many of whom routinely ditched their posts to attend to wealthier patients in their private clinics. I had overheard Dora and her friends complaining about waiting in line for days in the hot sun outside the public hospital. When she did go to that hospital, she returned complaining that the wait was insufferably long, that the visit 'Didn't do anything [for me]', and that 'the doctor just looked at me quick and said to take [a non-prescription pain killer]'.

I was glad to drive Dora to the remote home of a spiritual medium, 'Medium João', that March day. When we got there, we had to wait for two hours on the front porch behind a young man in his twenties, but the waiting area itself was quite congenial. It was a sort of garden with comfortable benches, palm trees for shade, and a pitcher of ice-water. Alongside these comforts was an ornate shrine to St Sebastian, who is often syncretised with the African deity, Oxôssi, guardian of herbalists and physicians against evil spirits. The waiting area was also bedecked with peppers, cow horns and other protections against the malignant power of envy (the evil eye). As she approached the house, Dora briefly greeted the young man who had been waiting there, and he smiled back. Then he grew agitated when she walked right by him, knocked on the door, and presented the lady of the house with four litres of fresh milk to give to medium João. After João's wife disappeared into the house, the young man protested to Dora that he had been waiting for some time. She responded,

> I just went to give some stuff. Don't worry, kid. You could be here ten years
> in front of me, if he wants, he'll see me (first); if he wants, he'll see you

(first). I just gave him some stuff. Medium João is [like] my brother. There's none of that stuff.

Still upset, the young man stopped talking and João's wife soon called him in for his consultation. Though he attended to the young man first, the medium gave him only a fraction of the time that he would later spend with Dora.

But let me dwell on Dora's words. Her concluding phrase, 'There's none of that stuff', begs the question, What stuff? The phrase refers to the norm of egalitarianism that the young man invokes when he implicitly accuses Dora of trying to cut ahead of him in line. Consider that the earlier statements of Dora's response sketch several, partially overlapping arguments that defend her choice to bypass the young man on her approach to the door. The first phrase suggests that she was there to carry out a personal exchange relationship with the healer, rather than wait for his services. The second is a normative claim that charismatic healers (most of whom are men) enjoy the prerogative to see people in whatever order suits them. The third is a descriptive claim that she has a personal relationship to the healer (troped as siblinghood) that both legitimates her gift of milk and preemptively justifies to the man why he might find himself passed over.

Sociable exchange, the healer's prerogative, and personal affinity – Dora was mobilising the forms of agency and value proper to patron-client relationships in order to frame the social space. And to me it seemed that Medium João's waiting area itself corroborated Dora's framing – with its material comforts, warm hostess and invitations to spiritual humility (supplication before the saint and caution with one's own evil).

The logic of Dora's 'active waiting' (see Han 2012: 31) contrasts sharply with that of the public hospital waiting room, and this contrast illuminates the mode of suffering that Dora and others experience when accessing public healthcare. It's not just the long hours and uncomfortable conditions of hospital waiting rooms that bother Brazilians like Dora who seek public healthcare; it's also the feeling (uttered by another consultant) that waiting for SUS 'is like being dead'. I read this feeling in light of the centrality of the reciprocal networks of care and favour that produce each person's social particularity and value (not unlike Marilyn Strathern's 'dividual'). Patients waiting for SUS services sometimes try to mobilise these networks to gain faster service: they ask local politicians to place phone calls to the hospital on their behalf, and they approach the staff with personal, sympathy-inducing stories that support their appeals for a *jeitinho* (the colloquial term for a suspension of the rules, literally 'a little way'). But through the optics of liberal bureaucracy, these practices appear selfish and atavistic. Several front desk workers at the local public hospital told me that they routinely rejected such efforts. Perhaps it is they, more than the doctors or administrators, who enforce an ethic of formal equality in the waiting room.

Left to wait just like the stranger next to them, Dora and others become liberal individuals, both in the sense that they become 'rights-bearing' citizens and in the sense that they are cut off from the articulations that organise their lives as patronage dividuals. Giorgio Agamben (2017) offers a provocative analytic for this situation: patronage hierarchy (rather than rights-enriched equality) constitutes Dora's particular form-of-life (bios) with its attendant protocols of negotiating faster health services such as Medium João's. To the extent that the public hospital's waiting room prohibits Dora from mobilising those relations, it reduces her to a version of bare life, not the killable subject of the literal camp, but rather one whose ignorable suffering indicates her 'dislocating localization [in] the hidden matrix of… the camp… in all its metamorphoses' (144). In the hospital waiting room, Dora feels herself to be a mere vessel for generic rights. Her familiar mode of agency has been foreclosed for a painfully indefinite period by an institutional authority that promises to eventually provide her worthwhile care on the basis of her generic personhood. It usually doesn't deliver.

None of this exonerates the very real failures of patronage-based service access. Moreover, if Brazil's public healthcare system were better stocked with doctors, my guess is nobody would fret about a few hours of quiet waiting. Still, this case forces our consideration of what liberal citizenship feels like when introduced into contexts marked both by patronage and limited state resources.

Granted, 'bare life' suggests a deep inertness that is rarely ethnographically adequate: those waiting in this fashion may continually reassert new social articulations in the face of social service frustrations (see Biehl 2005: 318; Han 2012: 88–89). But they do so swimming upstream against the socially disarticulated subjectivity construed by liberal institutional authority.

While many of us are tempted to demand that Dora and others gain more rights to healthcare, it's worth knowing that Dora knows what 'having rights' in the public hospital waiting room feels like and it's an experience she wants to avoid.

1 3

CROSSING BOUNDARIES: THE CASE FOR MAKING SENSE WITH THE SENSE-ABLE

Christy Spackman

A BLACK PLASTIC RUBBISH BAG, HELD IN PLACE BY MASKING TAPE, COVERED the drinking fountain jutting out from the brick wall. It was an incongruous sight in the otherwise clean, carpeted church hallway on the outskirts of Charleston, West Virginia. The thick covering separated observer from object, calling attention to what it ostensibly sought to obfuscate. '[Facilities and Maintenance] still haven't replaced the filters', I was told, as I sopped up the syrup under my pancake and drank bottled water with the congregation members; 'The bag is to keep anyone from accidentally drinking contaminated water'.

Five months earlier (on 9 January 2014), the county's municipal water supply was abruptly declared off limits for *all* use due to contamination with crude MCHM (4-methylchycloheanemethanol), a chemical used in the cleaning of coal. No brushing teeth with the water. No showers. No clothes washing. One could still flush the toilet, but even then it was advised to avoid standing over the toilet. Underlying these restrictions was an uncomfortable reality: no one knew whether the chemical threatened human health, and if so, at what levels.

Remembering to follow the blanket restriction on use did not come easily. 'I would forget and brush my teeth with it', one coal-worker who lived at the end of the water distribution line told me, noting that he'd got the chemical all over himself at work before. A retired nurse living at the top of a hill reported that her neighbours had complained of the smell, but she never noticed it. Yet for many, the smell helped them remember. In fact, the chemical leak that caused the contamination was first identified due to crude MCHM's intense odour, characterised by journalists as, sharp, sweet, and liquorice-like. The odour permeated downtown Charleston, lingering for days as the chemical plume passed. 'I could smell it', a local baker told me. 'Outside. All the time. I joked after everything had happened about having to go home to Sissenville (a suburb of Charleston) to get water, "home sweet smell"'. A middle school teacher noted that she could still smell the MCHM in bathrooms and her classroom despite the coverings.

In the days and weeks that followed, citizens faced a paradox: although experts quickly declared the water free of crude MCHM, and thus safe to use, the bodies of many throughout the Charleston area said otherwise. The authorities and scientists tasked with monitoring the presence of crude MCHM based their safety determination on levels of the chemical dropping below methodological and instrumental detection limits. As the concentration dropped, crude MCHM proved ghostlike: detected by many human bodies, but invisible to the officially recognised scientific, instrumental methods of detection. The water is safe, official discourse said. Yet bodies throughout Kanawha County disagreed, appearing in the emergency rooms with rashes and headaches in the early days of flushing. Noses continued to identify the 'liquorice' smell for weeks after the crisis was declared over. 'It was maybe two months before [we] stopped detecting it coming out of the spigot', one interlocutor told me.

Before 9 January, the exact smell of crude MCHM did not matter. However, as the odour continued to persist despite its apparent absence as measured by instrumentation, it became apparent that the methodologies put in place for detecting and responding to sense-able chemical contamination were inadequate. Instrumental insensibility undermined and negated experiences of bodily sensibility, and in the process pitted individuals against the authoritative agencies ostensibly there to protect them.

These moments where instrumental insensibility collide with bodily sensing call for methodological approaches that can capture the rich detail of individual experiences, while also acknowledging the unevenness of the sensory world. Although the sciences dedicated to mapping the sensory world seek subjects that fit within a sensory norm by screening for ability to taste or smell, by its very nature sensing is difficult to quantify: even the ideal sensing body changes, gets sick, is injured or carries genes that make coriander leaves taste like soap or inhibit the detection of bitterness. As such, the uneven nature of sensing complicates large-scale efforts to make sensory knowledge universally available, even as sensory scientists and researchers attempt to quantify and standardise sensory knowledge. Translation devices for bridging individual and group sensory experience abound – from printed tasting guides to professional tasting classes – all united by the goal of allowing the specifics of an individual's sensory experience to be broadened through creation of a shared sensory vocabulary. Authorities in West Virginia turned to sensory science to try to grasp the exact sensory nature of crude MCHM and determine whether continuing reports of liquorice-like odours had merit.

Yet contemporary practices of sensory analysis remove individuals from the very environments that stimulate the senses in the first place (c.f. Howes 2015; Lahne 2016). Sensory science seeks test subjects who fit an objective, laboratory-based model of ideal tasters. Participants are screened for ability to smell or taste, and those who cannot are excluded. It is notable that the standardised sensory science approach eventually justified citizen claims that crude MCHM was still present despite instrumental measurements that said otherwise (McGuire, Suffet, and Rosen 2014). In accordance with the scientific demands of contemporary sensory science, the consumers selected to characterise the sensory experience of smelling crude MCHM diluted in water had no knowledge of the contexts in which sensing crude MCHM had – or might – occur. While these practices are useful for the deconstruction and reconstruction of flavours at the heart of industrial taste-making, and also provide critical information about how the human body can or cannot detect odours or tastes, they fail to account for the ways that sensory information is embedded in lived contexts. In the case of the West Virginia crisis, inhabitants did not encounter the smell of crude MCHM in the anonymous confines of a lab. They encountered it in their homes, churches, workplaces, and further developed and solidified how they sensorially understood the chemical through conversations with each other and media attention.

To restate this in more familiar terms, if we were together in the same room instead of separated by time and distance, I could hand you my favourite black liquorice or hold out a sample of Viktor & Rolfe's Flowerbomb perfume for you to sniff.[1] We could taste and smell these things and imagine ourselves in the valley surrounding Charleston on a cold, early January day waiting in line to receive water from the National Guard. We could even suspend our smelly substitutes for crude MCHM in hot water and spray the mixture into the air in the bathroom, envisioning ourselves sensing an unwanted chemical intruder in our home as we follow the steps for flushing provided by the water supplier. Despite these efforts, neither of us would be able to comprehend the experience of those in Charleston during the days and weeks and even months following the spill. Our outsider bodies do not carry the greenhouse manager's memory of watching massive fish die-offs in the Elk River as a child, or of the woman learning to watch the flames at the chemical plants to determine whether one should feel safe or worried. Our bodies do not know the fear or discomfort of a mother smelling crude MCHM in the water as she weighs the government's claims to safety against her nose's warning of danger and debates giving the water to her daughter. Our bodies have not become attuned to the chemical's presence. As West Virginia Public Broadcasting's Scott Finn noted in late February 2014, 'After state officials finally stopped the MCHM from entering the water supply, after they told us to flush our pipes, you could still smell it in the water for weeks. I would engage in a nervous ritual: run the tap, lean in a little and sniff three times – and there it would be'. As such, the resulting knowledge of crude MCHM's sensory characteristics generated by the scientific studies failed to capture the cultural or environmental aspects so critical to the experience of West Virginians.

Sensory science's inability to capture the cultural and environmental aspects of sensing also threatens the ethnographer of sensory experience. As Nicholas Shapiro noted of his own sensorial experience interviewing people exposed to formaldehyde in their homes, the ethnographer's sensory exposure may 'intimate the costs of apprehending chemical others' while nonetheless remaining ephemeral due to the researcher's ability to enter and exit the field (2015: 371). Examining the sensory offers a continual conundrum: how can the ethnographer effectively participate, observe and make meaning of their interlocutors' sensory experiences given the limits imposed by each individual's accumulated sensory knowledge and the ethnographers own sensory naiveté?

It is precisely thinking in cases that opens a path through the thick forest of accumulated sensory knowledge: Thinking in cases prioritises the unevenness of sensory experience, allowing the voices of those who sense and those who do not the possibility of participation. Thinking in cases resists the flattening of sensory knowledge for commercial purposes by bringing excluded voices back into the conversation. And perhaps most importantly, thinking in cases pushes the ethnographer to acknowledge the limits of participation and observation when it comes to embodied experience, opening the doors for new types and forms of interlocution.

ENDNOTES

1   One of the crude MCHM-naive panellists recruited to participate in the consumer panel assembled to estimate the odour threshold of the chemical described the odour as that of her favourite perfume, 'Flowerbomb'.

REFERENCES

Howes, D., 'The Science of Sensory Evaluation: An Ethnographic Critique', in A. Drazin and S. Küchler, eds., *Social Life of Materials: Studies in Materials and Society* (London: Bloomsbury, 2015), pp. 81–97.

Lahne, J., 'Sensory Science, the Food Industry and the Objectification of Taste', *Anthropology of Food* 10 (2016).

McGuire, M. I. H. Suffet, and J. Rosen, 'Consumer Panel Estimates of Odor Threshold for Crude 4-Methylcyclohexanemethanol', *Journal AWWA*, 106 (October 2014), 10: E445–E458.

Shapiro, N., 'Attuning to the Chemosphere: Domestic Formaldehyde, Bodily Reasoning, and the Chemical Sublime', *Cultural Anthropology*, 30.3 (2015), 368–93.

HOME *Sweet* SMELL

14

SWAMP DIALOGUES: FILMING ETHNOGRAPHY

Ildikó Zonga Plájás

IN RECENT ANTHROPOLOGICAL FILM PRACTICE WE SEE A SHIFT FROM ESTAB-
lished visual ethnographic paradigms focused on discursive representation
(Crawford 1992), towards the realm of interdisciplinary cooperation and
experimentation. Working with filmmakers and artists has a long history in visual
anthropology; however, recent theoretical debates open up new terrains for
cooperation with various fields like science and technology studies, bio-medical
sciences, forensic science and architecture. As attention is directed towards the
corporeal experience that informs intellectual understanding (Suhr-Willerslev
2013; Postma 2006; MacDougall 2006) the role of visual perception and representation is revaluated once again. In this discussion I interweave clips from my
film and text to make a case for post-representational anthropology, that is, an
anthropology that does not reveal the truth, but which advocates for different
and intersecting ways of engaging with the worlds we inhabit.

I spent several months in the Romanian Danube delta conducting fieldwork
about the manifold ways people engage with 'wilderness'.[1] Upon returning from
the field, before setting pen to paper, I started to work with the audio-visual data
and to compile a narrative in image and sound. The anthropological film *Swamp
Dialogues* (2015, 53 min.) thus became part of the analysis and the outcome of
the research. Though the text and images of this 'filmic thesis' are aimed at an
academic audience, it might still be useful, or perhaps necessary, to emphasise
that the film is not an imprint or a document of reality, and neither are the 36

hours of footage which I recorded in the Danube delta. Also, the film is not an illustration of the written analysis, and therefore it is not subordinated to the text. As MacDougall puts it, 'visual anthropology may offer different ways of understanding, but also different things to understand' (MacDougall 2006: 220). Throughout the fieldwork I used audio-visual methods, not only because of the ethnographic knowledge they generated, but also because they enriched the possibility of the ethnographic field itself.

Whether approached as text or as object, the visual medium of film functions through implication, visual resonance, identification and shifting perspectives that differ from the principles of most conventional anthropological writing. Film necessarily involves the audience in a heuristic process of meaning creation. A filmed field encounter can be communicated to viewers in many places, adding to the validation and reliability of findings as well as providing a more visceral kind of knowledge than academic writing tends to deliver. *Swamp Dialogues* brings the sensorial aspect of being in the Danube delta to the audience, making almost palpable the cold, the foggy mornings and the hardship of the fishermen's work, but also the beauty, humour and vitality of daily life in the marshlands. A camera, if used in a reflexive way, can make apparent that the fields we work within are not out there, but assembled through the documentary process.

FIG. 14.1 Excerpt from the film *Swamp Dialogues* where Nelson catches the big fish

She sleeps in my house,
and then she goes to other villages.

FIG. 14.2 Excerpt from the film *Swamp Dialogues* reflecting on the position of the ethnographer in the field

The themes of my analysis, which later became the building blocks of the storyline for the film, emerged from the same anthropological curiosity which shaped other fieldwork decisions. This happened sometimes accidentally even while filming. In the village C. A. Rosetti, for example, I was accompanying Tanti Dumitra for the umpteenth time to walk the cattle at dawn. On this specific morning, the foggy weather and beautifully filtered light made me take the camera with me. Having already worked with the cows alongside my hosts for two weeks, I was confident with the animals, which did not run away, but obeyed my voice and long stick. This morning, however, I was carrying an unknown object with a big furry microphone and paid more attention to filming than to herding. For this reason the cows took a slightly different path, leading us into a highly polluted region of the fabled nature reserve.

I did not know about the rubbish dumped in the fields and I happened upon it while I was filming Tanti Dumitra. When I noticed the backdrop of my carefully framed image, the focus of the frame shifted to the waste. 'Do they dump the garbage here?' I asked a few minutes later, after we had walked on. In the editing, I placed this question immediately after the visual encounter, while the viewer is still looking at the garbage. This is a unique moment of the film when I invite the audience to participate in my wonderment. Here, the camera becomes not only a tool to provoke or catalyse field-interaction, but also an exploratory tool to literally co-create the situations that then demand comprehension.

What could be a better medium to highlight the communicative aspect of ethnographic understanding than the audio-visual 'records' of field-situations? 'Dialogues' in the title reflects the dialogical setting of fieldwork, but also 'being

FIG. 14.3 Excerpt from the film *Swamp Dialogues* where we walk the cattle

FIG. 14.4 Excerpt from the film *Swamp Dialogues* in which we accompany fishermen in winter time

in dialogue' with different scientific discourses and the multiple layers of intentions and interpretations emerging from the field site.

Pels notes that the 'romance of harmonious collaboration is [...] an ethical injunction that intervenes in, rather than represents, the methodology of an ethnographic research project' (Pels 2014: 230). Perhaps while doing away with the imperative to represent (a singular truth), we can still keep alive the problem of representation – that is, the problem of how we advocate for different ways of knowing.

It would be hypocritical to claim that *Swamp Dialogues* was produced in a harmonious collaboration. Many of the people I met refused or were just not so keen to be filmed. This happened often when talking to fishermen who were using illegal plastic nets or fishing without permits. Although I sometimes inadvertently filmed people who were obviously not happy with what I was doing, I always turned off the camera and never used any footage without consent. But more importantly, throughout the entire process of the research I did my best to lay my cards on the table. Everyone knew there were risks for all involved, since we could not always anticipate the directions we would go.

The ethnographic film produced by this research gives room for reflection upon the ways field interactions shape ethnographic knowledge, emphasising the deeply relational character of the understanding that ensues. At the same time, it offers a medium where no verdict has to be given, where the contradictions and incongruities can be present within the same filmic landscape. In this sense, it evokes the complexity of the Danube Delta Biosphere Reserve, which is characterised by the 'polytheism of the scattered practices' (Mosse 2005) elaborated in the written part of the thesis.

The evocative character of the film is also performative, bringing into being a film-object which functions as a contribution to the mainstream environmentalist discourse, while also offering a platform for ethnographic debate that makes room for confusion and misunderstandings. Due to its sensorial richness, *Swamp Dialogues* adds to the quality and complexity of perception and understanding and represents an intervention through which new insights are materialised. But above all, it is a testimony to how nature and the environment are constantly produced by different practices, including the dialogue provoked by the anthropologist-filmmaker.

ENDNOTES

1 *Swamp Dialogues* film synopsis:

The Danube delta in Romania – the last European sanctuary' – is a UNESCO World Heritage Site. While major efforts are made to protect biodiversity, the plight of local communities is largely overlooked. Social scientists claim that the traumatic nature of the swamp bears heavily on the villagers' lives. But is nature really to blame? *Swamp Dialogues* is based on extensive field-research in the Danube Delta Biosphere Reserve. Through 'an argument montage' built entirely on cinematic language the film entails an anthropological reflection on knowledge production in social sciences. All content was filmed by the author, with permission of the Danube Delta Reserve Authority and the protagonists.

To watch the full film, scan the QR code below or visit: https://vimeo.com/127259241:

REFERENCES

Crawford, P. I., 'Film as Discourse: The Invention of Anthropological Realities', in P. Crawford and D. Turton, eds., *Film as Ethnography* (Manchester: Manchester University Press, 1992), pp. 66–84.

MacDougall, D., *The Corporeal Image. Film, Ethnography, and the Senses* (Princeton, NJ: Princeton University Press, 2006).

Mosse, D., *Cultivating Development: An Ethnography of Aid Policy and Practice* (London: Pluto Press, 2005).

Pels, P., 'After Objectivity: An Historical Approach to the Intersubjectivity in Ethnography', *HAU: Journal of Ethnographic Theory*, 4.1 (2014), 211–36.

Postma, M., 'From Description to Narrative: What's Left of Ethnography?', in M. Postma and P. Crawford, eds., *Reflecting Visual Anthropology: Using the Camera in Anthropological Research* (Leiden/Højbjerg: CNWS Publications/Intervention Press, 2006), pp. 319–57.

Suhr, C., and R. Willerslev, eds., *Transcultural Montage* (New York/Oxford: Berghahn Books, 2013).

WHAT IS A FAMILY? REFUGEE DNA AND THE POSSIBLE TRUTHS OF KINSHIP

Carole McGranahan

TASHI THOUGHT THEY WERE HIS KIDS.[1] THEY WERE HIS KIDS. HE WAS THE only father they had ever known. He had been their father since the day each of his four children was born. After being recognised as a Convention Refugee in Canada, he applied for permanent residence and listed his wife and children as his 'overseas dependents' on his application. Finally he would be reunited with his family who had waited in a Tibetan refugee camp in South Asia while he made the uncertain journey to Canada via a well-worn route through the USA. He had dutifully written down their names, sexes, ages and dates of birth on his application. He had told the truth. But then the Canadian government asked for a DNA test as proof that the children were his. His claiming them was not enough because, as the government asserts, refugees lie. And then a different truth was revealed. He was not the genetic father of two of his children, although his wife was their genetic mother. Canadian government officials decided that Tashi had been untruthful in claiming these children – his children – on his permanent resident application. His request to bring his family to Canada was denied.

What sort of truths do DNA tests provide? What are the social and family truths that precede and exceed DNA? What is the responsibility of the anthropologist to confirm or challenge these truths?

Tashi's struggle to reunite his family came to me as a legal case in need of anthropological expertise. It was a legal case that needed to also be an ethnographic one. Questions put to me by his attorney included: Do Tibetans have a tradition of infidelity? Would a husband know if his wife was having an affair? What makes someone a parent in Tibetan society? In some ways these are classic anthropological questions about marriage, kinship and social relations (Carsten 2000), and in other ways, they are anthropological questions repurposed for the legal system, designed to speak back to DNA findings by showing family is not solely determined by shared genetic markers. The presumption of the Canadian government official was that Tashi knew about his wife's infidelity and lied about it. However, while DNA may suggest infidelity, it does not decide family.

WHAT IS A FAMILY?

Family is kin, but kin is not only genetic. Tibetan kinship is patrilineal; belonging is formally reckoned through the father, but genetic fatherhood may go unclaimed and non-genetic fatherhood may be claimed. Outside marriage, men may choose or not to claim their genetic offspring as their children. Identifying offspring as children enters them into one's patriline, and thus into certain familial obligations and relationships. In the case of polyandrous marriages, which in Tibet mostly consist of a woman married to brothers, all of her husbands are the fathers of her children regardless of which husband is the genetic parent; each would be referred to as 'father'. In terms of non-genetic fatherhood, Tibetan practices of adoption, of step-parenting and of grandparents raising grandchildren as their children (rather than as their grandchildren) are all examples of relationships for which the terms father, mother, son and daughter are used. How does infidelity factor into any of this? It depends.

Extramarital affairs are not condoned in Tibetan society. Some affairs remain secret, while others become known to members of the community, including spouses. A wife may learn about her husband's infidelity and feel there is nothing she can do. Or she might confront him or leave him, or confront his mistress, or worse. A husband may learn of his wife's infidelity and do nothing about it or may confront her or her lover. Or he may also do something worse. Graphic physical abuse in cases of discovered extramarital affairs is not gendered. Both men and women participate in this. There is no single disciplinary rule for infidelity. Historically, Tibetans do have socially acceptable forms of sexuality outside marriage that are not secret, such as being a religious consort to a tantric practitioner; such sexual practices are not categorised as infidelity. In contrast, infidelity is hidden from one's spouse. In the case of a married woman who becomes pregnant by her secret lover, as long as she is also having sexual intercourse with her husband, then it is entirely possible her husband might never know her genetic children are not also his genetic children. Until, of course, a DNA test is done.

A growing number of governments use DNA tests to assess refugee claims for family reunification (Heinemann and Lemke 2012, 2013; Holland 2011). Such testing resembles efforts in the US to determine tribal belonging through DNA tests. In *Native American DNA: Tribal Belonging and the False Promise of Genetic Science*, Kim TallBear (2013: 4, 201) argues that DNA testing is reconfiguring the concept of the tribe in ways that do not cohere with the nongenetic ways Indigenous peoples 'assert their inherent self-determination as peoples'. Her incisive critique of genetic testing rests in part on its supposed scientific neutrality that frees it from cultural or other bias. Instead, she finds that such tests are deeply cultural: 'the populations and population-specified markers that are identified and studied mirror the cultural, racial, ethnic, national, and tribal understandings of the humans who study them' (TallBear 2013: 5). That is, DNA testing rests on categories of belonging that do not necessarily belong to the group being tested. The genetic presumptuousness demanded of tribal belonging is similarly demanded of parents and children in Canadian family reunification programmes.

Why does genetic knowing have such power for Canadian immigration officials? Part of this has to do with the modern truth claims of science, and another part rests on the twenty-first-century fascination with new technologies. One such invention, according to Louise Amoore (2013: 82), is the biometric border in which 'digital technologies, molecular techniques, and data analytics ... simultaneously dissect bodies into granular degrees of risk'. The association of risk with refugees, and the mistrust of them, is not something new (Daniel and Knudsen 1995). What is new here are forms of authorisation such as biometrics and genetic testing that promise expert truths. Amoore contends these new forms of knowing 'act as though they were sovereign, as proxy forms of sovereignty' (2013: 6). These new forms of knowing enable Canadian officials to say no. No, you have not told the truth. No, you are not a family.

In the case of Tibetan refugees looking to reunite their families, DNA testing provides proxy expertise to the immigration official. This is an expertise not congruent with either cultural or legal truths of the family. It is an immigration practice which denies family beyond genetics. If DNA testing shows that parent and child do not share enough of the same chromosomal patterns, there is no automatic immigration process to continue the investigation of the claim. Instead, the burden of proof is placed on the applicant through the process of appeal, but documents that might be expected by the Canadian government are often not available. For Tibetans, birth and marriage have long been life events that take place at home without the involvement or certification of the state, the monastery or any other institution. Even today, in the refugee community in South Asia, most Tibetans do not possess birth or marriage certificates, and many do not even have identity documents. Building an appeal case thus involves telling one's story through the help of an immigration attorney, through the testimonial letters of neighbours, friends and Tibetan government officials, and through the services of an expert witness like me. The use of DNA testing to determine family is an effort to foreclose these lived, narrative truths of family.

Narrative is at the heart of the ethnographic case. In their Introduction to this book, Emily Yates-Doerr and Christine Labuski explain that a case becomes ethnographic in the way that it situates the narrative of any given event within other narratives. The ethnographic case is necessarily one that is multi-layered, in which expertise as singular truth rests on a series of multiple truths. In the case of determining family, of assessing who is parent to a child, a singular 'yes' or 'no' truth cannot rest solely on a DNA test. Such a formulation works in neither the Tibetan cultural system nor the Canadian legal one; in both systems, logics of family are multiple, involving systems of legitimation and recognition beyond the genetic. In the Tibetan case, unknown infidelity on behalf of a wife does not cancel out a husband's paternity claims to her children. Given that the infidelity was unknown, given that the genetic father did not at the time of birth or any time since claim the children as his own, and given that Tashi was the only father any of the four children had ever known, in Tibetan terms he was their father. Tashi was their father.

As with so many other families, with those formed through adoption or second marriages or reproductive technologies or some other means, genetic belonging is not what holds Tashi's family together. Care, commitment, shared stories and social recognition of claimed family status do. Tashi came to Canada to seek a better life for his family. Tibetans have been refugees since 1959, constituting a now multi-generational diaspora spread around the world. Theirs is a continuing story of loss and separation, of families fragmented and of dreams of reunion. Rather than facilitating a reunion, DNA testing now threatens to pull this family apart.

Can anthropological knowledge make a difference? It should be able to. Ethnographic truths about kinship and family, about sexuality and secrets provide the substance and the nuance needed to understand why DNA tests might not find familial relationships even in situations where they thrive. And yet the ethnographic case is one that disrupts. It is one that challenges the easy no, and that thus is read and put aside by immigration officials untrained in the kinship, marriage or other practices of the individuals whose files cross their desks. Or, in anticipation of inconvenient disruption or delay of bureaucratic work, the ethnographic case might be the one that remains unread. As Marnie Thomson (2012) writes, the international refugee system is predisposed to say no, to have authored and authorised its own series of loopholes and rules that enable a denial of status, or perhaps a denial of family. In consular offices and refugee camps around the world, this is a familiar story. Disruption is not welcome. Disruption is risky.

For Tashi and his family, who remain in South Asia, disruption in the form of ethnographic truths is necessary. But even together with legal truths, taken out of the consular office and brought into the courtroom, will these be enough? And what happens if they are not?

ENDNOTES

1 Names and details of this story have been changed.

REFERENCES

Amoore, L., *The Politics of Possibility: Risk and Security Beyond Probability* (Durham, NC: Duke University Press, 2013).

Carsten, J., 'Introduction: Cultures of Relatedness', in J. Carsten, ed., *Cultures of Relatedness: New Approaches to the Study of Kinship* (Cambridge: Cambridge University Press, 2000), pp. 1–36.

Heinemann, T., and T. Lemke, 'Biological Citizenship Reconsidered: The Use of DNA Analysis by Immigration Authorities in Germany', *Science, Technology, and Human Values*, 39.4 (2013), 488–510.

——, 'Suspect Families: DNA Kinship Testing in German Immigration Policy', *Sociology*, 47.4 (2012): 810–26.

TallBear, K., *Native American DNA: Tribal Belonging and the False Promise of Genetic Science* (Minneapolis, MN: University of Minnesota Press, 2013).

Thomson, M., 'Black Boxes of Bureaucracy: Transparency and Opacity in the Resettlement Process of Congolese Refugees', *PoLAR: Political and Legal Anthropology Review*, 35.2 (2012), 185–204.

Valentine, D. E., and J. Knudsen, eds., *Mistrusting Refugees* (Berkeley, CA: University of California Press, 1995).

I 6

A POLYGRAPHIC CASEBOOK

Susan Reynolds Whyte

THERE WAS A GLITCH when our book *Second Chances* was almost ready to go to press. It was a layout problem. The Table of Contents was congested with too many chapters, too many stand-alone case stories, and too many authors. We had to drop the authors' names and, in the end, for technical reasons, the good people at Duke set the case stories instead of the chapter titles in bold.

The Table of Contents that went to press gives the impression that we have made a casebook – a set of descriptive

FIG. 16.1 Table of Contents for *Second Chances*

instances of individual people who survived AIDS when antiretroviral medicines became widely accessible. The layout problem was transformed into an authorial problem: the cases were highlighted, and *we* who had authored them were in shadow.

'We' is a definitely plural pronoun. We were eight people, four from Denmark (Lotte Meinert, Hanne O. Mogensen, Michael Whyte, Susan Whyte) and four from Uganda (Phoebe Kajubi, David Kyaddondo, Godfrey Etyang Siu, Jenipher Twebaze), who did a study and together wrote a book about it. All eight of us were authors, but our book is neither a monograph nor an edited volume in the conventional sense. We call it a polygraph. It resembles a lie detector – but not because it reports *a* singular truth or discerns untruths. A lie detector works by simultaneously measuring different physiological indicators (pulse, respiration, blood pressure, skin conductivity) and translating bodies to marks on a page. Similarly, our polygraphic methodology examines vital processes at different points in a social body over one time period. The locations are varied social positions and different treatment programmes; the processes are social activities such as connecting, partnering, eating, working, travelling, medicating and so on. Moreover, our book is based on polygraphy in the old sense of copious writing – piles of handwritten fieldnotes transcribed to electronic text. The classic polygraph was a person who commanded broad knowledge and wrote on many topics. The scholars of today are far more specialised. Still, compared to other researchers, many anthropologists take a broad perspective on social and cultural life. We wanted to put HIV treatment in the context of political and personal histories, rather than focus narrowly on some aspect of its medical effectiveness.

We had worked together for years before we decided to systematically document a dramatic turn in Ugandan history: the 'rollout' of free antiretroviral medicines. In one way or another, we had all been touched by the AIDS epidemic – by the feelings of helplessness and injustice as people we cared about suffered and died while medicine was saving lives in richer parts of the world. When the antiretrovirals (the ARVs) were finally provided for free around 2005, a whole generation of people who expected to die of AIDS got a second chance to live. We wanted to write about those people.

We never doubted that the way to do it was to start with life stories. It seemed obvious because HIV had already become a narrativised condition. Positive people were encouraged to open up, to testify about their experiences to their peers and their treatment providers. News media were eager for the existential dramas of sex, life and death. Organisations supplying the medicines needed the personal accounts to justify the enormous expenses being poured into the effort. Public health researchers, as well as social scientists, found that experience-near descriptions made their analyses compelling and credible.

Case stories also seemed evident as an anthropological method. We were Africanists for whom the extended case and the situational analysis of the Manchester School were exemplary. We had seen the power of carefully unfolding a situation, progressively contextualising it so as to portray a political economy or a broader pattern. It was a way to do ethnography.

The narrative possibilities pulled us as well. We saw the chronological potential in retrospective life histories combined with prospective following along through visits over a period of time. Stories of individuals would allow us to make connections over time, to see how one thing led to another, and more importantly, to listen to how our interlocutors knitted yarns together or dropped stitches. So it was with the woman we call Jackie, whom our colleague David Kyaddondo visited over a year and a half. In a strikingly frank manner, she confided her experiences and the surprising turns that her life took.

Early in their acquaintance Jackie told David how unhappy she was that Joseph, the father of her younger children, kept their relationship a secret. He refused to introduce Jackie to his parents, thus disallowing her recognition as a daughter-in-law and denying their children acknowledgment as grandchildren. Although he clandestinely paid for the treatment of their HIV positive child, he would not publicly admit that he was the father. She was torn, wanting to leave him, but reluctant to forego the support he was giving her. On one occasion, Jackie even asked David for advice about what to do.

Finally she decided to make a break; she got 'saved' in a Pentecostal church and began saying that Joseph had demons, and that they were committing the sin of adultery. Indeed, Joseph was formally married; his first wife had made a point of asking Jackie if she knew why all of the children of this first marriage had died, implying that Joseph was HIV positive. At one visit, David found that Jackie had moved out of the rooms she shared with Joseph. But the split did not last long; she remarked that perhaps it was God's plan that she should stay with Joseph. Still they quarrelled regularly; she insinuated to him that he was the one who had infected her, even though she had earlier told David about the HIV diagnosis of her first partner, father of her eldest child.

At the last visit, she gave David the startling news that Joseph had died. Hoping at last to gain recognition from his family, she gathered the children and took them to the funeral where they could be presented as his only living heirs. Surprisingly, however, three other women showed up with children who all claimed Joseph as their father. His family knew nothing of these women either, but said they were prepared to provide support for all of his children. Thus it was only upon his death, that Joseph's children gained paternal grandparents.

There were many stories as fascinating as Jackie's. We could have concentrated our efforts on fewer. But we wanted diversity, which we felt was often lacking in the studies we had read of AIDS patients. We wanted to talk to men and women, poor and better off, rural and urban, clients of different treatment programmes, including some who had tried to pay for their treatment in the days before it was available for free.

We contacted forty-eight people on antiretroviral therapy, through seven different treatment facilities, and asked them to tell us their life stories, not just their sickness stories. How did you grow up, what about your family, your work? From the beginning we tried to talk to people in their everyday settings, not at their places of treatment, a strategy that decentred AIDS and brought out what people were making of their second chances. Among these forty-eight, we identified twenty-three whom we visited seven more times. And here I should write 'they' instead of 'we', because the Ugandan members of our team did most of the talking and visiting. From Denmark we followed along, reading the notes as they ticked in on our computers. And whenever we were in Uganda, we went along on the visits. But by and large, it was David and Jenipher and Phoebe and Godfrey who got to know the individuals, homes, families and workplaces of the people who became our cases.

FIG. 16.2 Jenipher Twebaze listening to an interlocutor's story

The visits and revisits developed differently. Some interlocutors became friends and the researchers got involved with their lives and problems as friends do. There were phone conversations and text messages between visits; the researchers got to know other members of the family and followed the tensions and détentes that are a normal part of family life. Other interlocutors remained acquaintances, who were welcoming on some occasions and more reserved on others. There were dramatic moments, as when Jenipher arrived to find the man she was visiting in jail on allegations of stealing a sheep. And there were routine calls 'just checking in' when there was not much new to report.

When a year and a half had passed, the visits ended, and we faced hundreds of pages of notes. Brainstorms and difficult choices and attempted divisions of responsibility followed, resolving into the plan that became *Second Chances*. The lives we had documented became cases as we began to treat them as source material – all twenty-three arranged neatly in ring binders. They were ready for polygraphic examination: a varied set of positions in the social body and coverage of the different topics and processes that would become the book chapters. At this point they formed the stuff of classical extended cases, based on retrospective histories and prospective follow-ups over eighteen months.

However, our plan was not to work from case to case, but to abstract from this material in order to illuminate – and also to illustrate – our analytical points about generational consciousness, sociality and chanciness. Our extended cases provided both analytical insight and, when chopped into pieces, useful and hopefully 'apt' examples.

We also wanted to preserve some cases as longer texts that could convey to readers the individuality and diversity of the people whose lives were prolonged by ARVs. We hit on the idea of letting one case introduce each chapter – easy enough since the chapters themselves provided analytical discussions of everyday concerns like families, partners, food, work and so on. We selected cases for their evocation of the chapter topics, but they were always about all kinds of other themes as well. That is why we set them up as stand-alone sections that could be read on their own. The longer texts provided singularities we sought to reason about, rather than mere material that could be assimilated to theories. Almost every case had a theme about children – children being the most important second chance for nearly everyone – but Jackie's case showed with particular clarity how HIV played into the social recognition of children in this patrilineal society.

In many ways those cases are what capture readers, especially students, and allow them to see how we made the analyses that followed. One of the manuscript reviewers had cautioned us against presenting the material as 'an array of cases laid out for the reader to inspect'. He thought it was a disservice to the material to exhibit people like butterflies. In the end though, we did lay out an array and made a virtue of it. We found that the casebook format allowed us to discuss a corresponding assortment of analytical issues, while still 'making a case' in the sense of an overall argument about second chances. The polygraphic casebook also permitted us to capture what was essential about our enterprise: assembling evidence through multi-sighted investigation at several locations in the social body.

Looking back six years after *Second Chances* was published, I still regret the glitch. At the book launch in Kampala, a senior Ugandan academic was disappointed that there were no Ugandan names immediately evident on the cover or Contents page. Although authors were clearly shown on the case studies and chapters within the book, the Table of Contents is remarkably anonymous. This is also unfortunate in that an opportunity is missed to remind readers that the cases were assembled, chosen and edited by subjective researchers interacting with protagonists and concerned to analyse selected vital processes. Next time we will integrate the cases in the chapters so that there are fewer separate entries in the Table of Contents. But we will retain and emphasise the part authors play in making cases.

There has been enough interest in our attempt to make a polygraph that we are already working on a 'next time'. Perhaps the polygraph will even become a new ethnographic genre. As ethnographers increasingly work in teams on common projects, we need a form that is less mono- than the monograph and more collaborative than the edited volume. Polygraphs are one solution. They need not be casebooks, of course, but for the purpose of making a case in a vital and compelling way, the polygraphic casebook has shown its uses. As a form, it is inclusive of our interlocutors and our co-researchers. It is carried by individual stories but still, we hope, provides an over-arching narrative about generations, sociality and chanciness.

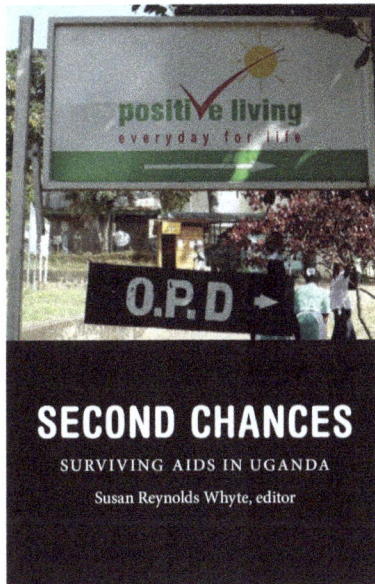

FIG. 16.3 Susan Reynolds Whyte (ed.) 2014. *Second chances: Surviving AIDS in Uganda.* Durham, NC: Duke University Press

TRAVELLING WITHIN THE CASE

Atsuro Morita

ON A BOAT SAILING THROUGH THE STILL WATERS OF THE NOI RIVER, A tributary of the Chao Phraya River in Thailand, Miura-san, a senior male engineer from a Japanese engineering consulting company, grows increasingly excited about the legendary Dutch irrigation engineer Homan van der Heide, who designed the basic plan for the entire water infrastructure of the delta in the early twentieth century (Ishii 1978). At the moment, we are traveling in the dense and complicated network of watercourses in the western part of the upper Chao Phraya delta. Here a maze-like network of small channels connects the Noi with the Chao Phraya. Although this entire delta area has long been the object of human intervention, the dense vegetation on the banks and meandering watercourses seem far from an artificial landscape.

Miura-san is comparing these seemingly chaotic channels with the map in front of us (Figure 17.1). More precisely, he is comparing the canal network of the eastern bank of the Chao Phraya River, whose tributaries appear orderly and grid-like on the map, with the labyrinthine watercourses of the western bank, where we are traveling. The delta, which has been cultivated to become these two contrasting areas – the carefully ordered network of canals of the Chao Phraya's eastern bank, and the more chaotic waterways of the western bank – is especially effective as flood management systems go. The maze-like network in the west functions as a huge retention zone to store excess water, protecting the canal grid on the opposite bank. Thus, Miura-san was doubly impressed, both by the skill of the Dutch engineer to design the modern canal network of the eastern bank, and by the ingenuity of this heterogeneous system that hinges on the distinct features of the eastern and western landscapes.

One way to think about a case is as an epistemic object that a practitioner manipulates, in the way that a medical provider records, classifies and compares clinical cases. However, as I learned on this boat trip, environmental scientists, civil engineers and infrastructure designers engaged with the case in a different

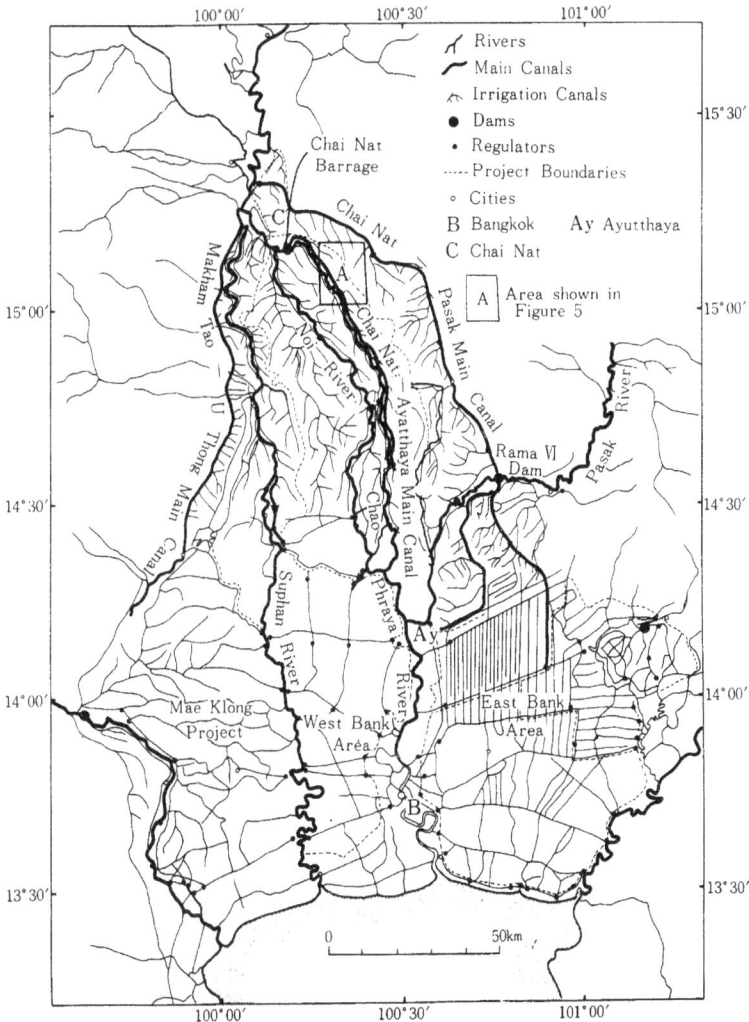

FIG. 17.1 Map of the Chao Phraya delta

149

way. Because they deal with objects with extensive spatial and geographic ranges, the act of a fieldtrip lets them travel *into* the case. This case unpacks the question: how does traveling within a case differ from the treatment of cases as objects to be compared? And how does this traveling shape our understanding of what constitutes a whole object?

The fieldtrip to the Chao Phraya River was organised by a Japanese engineering consulting company, mainly for Japanese participants of a conference on flood mitigation held in Bangkok. The seminar was held by the Japanese International Cooperation Agency, with the goal of developing a new mitigation plan in the Chao Phraya delta after the devastating 2011 floods. With the exception of myself, the participants of the boat trip were engineers, hydrologists and computer scientists. More than half were based in Japan, visiting Thailand only occasionally for meetings and conferences such as this. The fieldtrip was planned by the consulting company, which acted both as a subcontractor of the infrastructure design and as a coordinator of the project, to facilitate a shared understanding of the 'case' of flood management with which these various people were engaging.

But what does 'case' actually mean in this context? The project aimed to develop a new delta flood management plan by focusing on three major aspects: an assessment of the river hydrology, the design of basin-wide infrastructures and the development of a flood forecast system. These diverse components were brought together to improve responses to future flooding in the Chao Phraya delta. In the report that came out as the final product of the project, an imagined future flood is called the 'design flood'. The report takes the actual 2011 flood as a template for the design flood because it is the largest flood in the recorded past. So the case of flood management here is a composite of a geographical entity, the Chao Phraya delta, and an imagined flood, which is at once a probabilistic entity in the future and an actual event in the past.

This is what the case looks like *on paper*. In practice the case is both an instance of intervention and the object upon which to intervene. Donald Schön indicated more than thirty years ago that 'case' and similar words 'denote units which make up a practice' (Schön 1983: 60). For him, a central feature of professional practice is the use of cases to frame a problem. Professionals draw analogies and make comparisons between the problem at hand and other cases they know from experience, in order to figure out how to deal with the current situation. Annemarie Mol also touches on this point in her contribution to this book: '[a] case carries knowledge [...] about an occurrence that, even though it may have happened just once, is still telling, indicative, suggestive' (this volume: 44). In short, the case is an opportunity to consider the very practice of intervention.

In one sense, past cases gain their meaning in relation to a problem. But through comparison with past cases, the problem situation *becomes* one of the cases. Thus, the case of the Chao Phraya floods takes different forms, depending on what other cases practitioners conjure up. For the hydrologists, the 'case' is a drainage basin of the Chao Phraya River whose hydrological characteristics need to be explored; for the engineers, it is a set of infrastructural interventions to control the river flow.

The flood's multiplicity (Mol 2002) is what made the fieldtrip less straight-forward than I had initially imagined. It quickly became clear to me that hydrologists and engineers were not naive enough to believe that going out to the field would allow them to reach a single, shared solution. In fact, rather than reaching a consensus among the diverse expert viewpoints, Miura-san encouraged the participants to explore their own questions on the boat trip. As the engineer's lack of interest in the coherent whole suggests, what I found during the trip was rather complex relations between the situated and traveling viewpoints and the overviews of the delta water system, which itself is multiple. These complex relations resemble what Donna Haraway (1988) argues in her well-known essay on situated (and partial) visions.

It was actually hard to see commonality between what we would see around us while sailing and what the hydrologists and engineers discussed and treated as 'the delta' in other sites of practice, such as in labs, project workshops and formal conferences. Their discussions typically focused on combinations of maps and diagrams on paper and PowerPoint slides that represented various aspects of the delta's hydrological patterns. These artefacts were connected with water flows, topography and precipitation observed in the 'field' by automatic measuring devices. These discussions were occasions where I could observe them behaving like Shön's practitioners: they conjured up cases they knew from personal experience or from the literature, and they relied on comparisons to highlight characteristics of the Chao Phraya case, or to examine the possibility of applying existing infrastructure designs to problems in the delta.

However, in the boat trip the participants approached the case quite differently. In contrast to manipulating the case in the labs and conference rooms, on the river delta we found ourselves *traveling within the case*. During the fieldtrip, the delta became our entire environment. It was very difficult to imagine the delta and its water flows as the objects of practice, when we were literally encompassed by them. The conversation among hydrologists and engineers also reflected this fact and had a very different sensibility from those discussions held in other sites, where they were able to characterise the delta as an object of intervention by connecting it with other cases. In order to connect the present case with past ones, we needed to draw external relations between the two – a difficult task when you are located inside the case being examined. Instead, what we were doing on the boat was seeing the case *from within*.

This inside view has some distinct characteristics. In the trip the vision of the entire delta such as maps and diagrams, which was so visible and salient in the labs and conference rooms, receded into the margin. Instead our attention was constantly drawn to the smaller parts of the delta that we ran into and passed through, including the meandering canal network between the Noi and the Chao Phraya. But this does not mean that we were working on 'smaller' cases or objects during the trip. The encompassing existence of the delta, taking the form of the watery landscape around us, as well as the project's formal aim to formulate a plan for the entire delta, constantly drew our attention back to the overview of the delta gained in the labs and conference rooms. Thus, most of the participants never parted with maps, since they acted as essential artefacts to get back to the 'delta as a whole'. Just like Miura-san did in his comparison between the meandering watercourses we traversed in the west and the canal grid in the east, we constantly moved between the scenes around us and what we imagined as the entire delta.

This constant shift between the immediate scenes and the maps led to another distinguishing characteristic of the view from within the case. On the trip, we encountered many scenes that we had never imagined in the conference room: trains of huge barges dragged by tugboats; numerous quarries on the banks, which seemed to be providing building materials to the barges; an old, mysterious riparian town where most of the houses were built almost on the water (Figure 17.2); a huge number of water hyacinths covering the surface of the Noi River; and the jungle-like canal network between the Noi and the Chao Phraya.

These unexpected scenes provoked a lot of questions, some of which seemed only vaguely related to the issue of flood protection in the delta. But because we were surrounded by the undeniable material existence of the delta and its water, many of us were somehow forced to think more carefully about these seemingly marginal scenes. For example, my friend Omori-san, a hydrologist who had kindly invited me to the conference, was fascinated by the riparian commerce in the delta, which had a longer history than land transport. Using old hydrographs he found in a library, he started thinking about these networks of trade in relation to the broader changes of the river course over time and

FIG. 17.2 Houses along the Noi River

ended up formulating a hypothesis about historical changes of water flow in which canal digging acted as a central factor that induced the change of the course of the river.

The constant shifts between those unexpected scenes and the topographic overviews urged the hydrologists and engineers to see the delta as a dynamic and ever-changing entity. How did those diverse human and non-human activities, ranging from pre-modern canal digging, to modern infrastructure building, to the proliferation of water hyacinths, constitute what we were calling the delta? This is a dual question, because the 'delta as a whole' denotes both an object we could see on the map and the environment we were traveling through. Eventually this movement led both Miura-san and Omori-san to rethink the specific dynamic forces that formed the present delta. For Miura-san, the civil engineer, this took the form of Homan van der Hiede's engagement with the delta through infrastructure building, while for Omori-san it was the historical change of the river course brought about by both human and natural forces. Apparently, their inclination toward historical explanations was at least partly the product of their conversations with me, the anthropologist who acted as a guide to the social and cultural background of the local area.

These engagements with the delta seem to explain why fieldtrips are often given a place of importance in civil engineering and water management projects. It is not because such trips allow practitioners to encounter the 'true' or 'real' delta, but because these encounters push the practitioners toward more experimental thinking, as they face the constant back and forth of unexpected scenes and the imagined whole of the case. Of course, at the same time, this whole is not a singular entity. Just as the professionals are always engaging with a multiple case when they meet in the conference room or laboratory, during a fieldtrip they conjure up different versions of the whole. For the hydrologists, it is primarily a river network and drainage basin; for the engineers, it is the total of infrastructures, and for me, when acting as their guide, it is a historical landscape.

What, then, can anthropologists and ethnographers learn from this version of a fieldtrip? There are certainly commonalities with our own fieldwork practices. An anthropologist also treats his/her case both as an object of analysis and a place to travel and live. As Marilyn Strathern notes, this distinction corresponds to 'the desk' and 'the field': two central sites of ethnographic practice (Strathern 1999). Many anthropologists treat the field as more 'real' than the desk. Engineers and hydrologists, however, usually do not take such a view. For them, the archetype of the real is based on data gathered in the field by measuring devices. Because the cases presented in labs, workshops and conferences are tightly connected to these data sets, they are more real than the practitioners' own travel experiences, which do not in themselves yield what they think of as data. However, partly because of this marginality in their practice, fieldtrips have significance for engineers and hydrologists as sites for experimental thinking.

At the end of the trip, we landed on the bank at a closed sluice gate in the upper delta. We found the final surprise there. Attached to the sluice gate, there was a huge machine to collect water hyacinths gathering on the water surface (Figure 17.3). A Thai colleague explained how water hyacinths, which were introduced long ago as decorative plants, had now become an environmental threat and a hindrance to infrastructural operations. Such plants never appeared

FIG. 17.3 Sluice gate and water hyacinths, Chao Phraya delta

in the reports or in conference room discussions. But momentarily, at least, as we paused near the sluice gate at dusk, the hydrologists and engineers quietly reflected on how this multispecies presence might affect the delta and its floods. This scene and conversation with them also led to my own experimental thinking, as I envisioned a cyborgian infrastructure consisting of plants and sluice gates (Morita 2015). This wild image sheds light on the anthropological meaning of traveling within the case. While often overshadowed by the issue of the 'real' nature of the field versus our representations of it, the field has also been an experimental space for anthropology. Journeying through these fields, anthropologists and their interlocutors have become fellow travellers, encountering surprises and engaging in partially connected experimentations.

REFERENCES

Haraway, D., 'Situated Knowledges – the Science Question in Feminism and the Privilege of Partial Perspective', *Feminist Studies*, 14.3 (1988), 575–99.

Ishii, Y., *Thailand: A Rice-growing Society* (Honolulu, HI: University Press of Hawaii, 1978).

Japan International Cooperation Agency, CTI Engineering International, Oriental Consultants, Nippon Koei, and CTI Engineering. 'Project for Comprehensive Flood Management Plan for the Chao Phraya River Basin: Final Report', Japanese International Cooperation Agency, 2013.

Mol, A., *The Body Multiple: Ontology in Medical Practice, Science and Cultural Theory* (Durham, NC: Duke University Press, 2002).

——, 'Exemplary: The Case of the Farmer and the Turpentine', *The Ethnographic Case: Second Edition*, Manchester: Mattering Press, 2023.

Morita, A., 'Multispecies Infrastructure: Infrastructural Inversion and Involutionary Entanglements in the Chao Phraya Delta, Thailand', *Ethnos*, 82.4 (2015), 738–57.

Schön, D. A., *The Reflective Practitioner: How Professionals Think in Action* (New York: Basic Books, 1983).

Strathern, M., *Property, Substance, and Effect: Anthropological Essays on Persons and Things* (New Brunswick, NJ: Athlone Press, 1999).

THE CASE OF THE CAKE: DILEMMAS OF GIVING AND TAKING

Rima Praspaliauskiene

IN MY FIELDWORK AT THE CARDIOLOGY UNIT AT VILNIUS PUBLIC HOSPITAL I encountered what I call 'the cake case'. In 2009–2010 I was in Lithuania to study how medical care was transforming as the state embarked on health care reform that aimed to rationalise and privatise public services. In particular, the neoliberal reform projects targeted the informal payments, or 'bribes', that were prevalent in public health care. The state sought to transform these transactions into a system of transparent co-payments, one of many efficiency-producing transitions underway, including the introduction of private health care insurance and increasing the number of private clinics. Meanwhile, I observed how doctors, patients and their relatives engaged in ambiguous practices of giving that policy makers and some scholars would define as non-transparent, informal and corrupt. The cake case helped me understand how multiple forms of care coexist in any exchange, such that what counts as efficient and acceptable care is not stable or solid.

'Did you see that?' nurse Violeta asked another nurse and a resident at the nursing station when a tall and sizable woman in high heels, carrying an oversized black bag, marched into the four-bed male patient room. They nodded. 'What do we do now?' asked Violeta. Her colleagues rolled their eyes. The medical staff was clearly uncomfortable, unsure of how to react to the situation.

Shortly afterwards, the woman emerged from the room proudly carrying a large chocolate cake with a red rose on the top and entered the nurse assistants' office. I recognised the woman, Galina, as the wife of a man in his late fifties who had been hospitalised twice in the previous two months. He was a former alcoholic with a liver condition that further complicated his heart problems. After both of his previous discharges, Galina brought three cakes as a gesture of gratitude. After the first time, nurse Violeta thanked Galina and told her that it was 'really unnecessary'. Later she explained to me that the patient's family was barely making ends meet: the warehouse where Galina worked was cutting hours, her husband's disability payment was very modest, and their heating bills were increasingly high.

When Galina rolled out her husband in a wheelchair and the sound of her high heels faded away, a doctor named Regina commented, 'I don't know what to do with her; they will be back soon. I told her not to bring the cakes or anything else even though they are so tasty but you know their situation. I feel so sorry for the wife'.

Violeta nodded in affirmation. 'I told her: your life is hard, don't do that, but she just doesn't listen'.

'She is a good baker, I gave her extra diapers', the nursing assistant Irena added.

'I packed an extra supply of medications for the poor woman, she has to suffer because of that alcoholic', concluded Regina.

In the cardiology unit, patients from across the economic spectrum waited for pacemakers, medications and tests, or were recovering from heart surgery. All day long, family members, friends and acquaintances came and left. Many of these visitors brought their favourite foods – not only for the patients, but for the medical staff as well. Boxes and bars of chocolate, coffee, cakes, home-made cottage cheese, jars of honey, apples and smoked meats and fish were objects that patients and caregivers offered to the doctors and nurses. I saw bottles of wine and brandy visibly sticking out of paper and plastic bags. A few times I smelled smoked eel, ham and sausages. Their smell sharply contrasted with the sterility of the corridors and the blandness of the hospital food.

I also saw quite a few boxes of chocolates that were gifted to the doctors and nurses. The less expensive chocolates were often shared immediately, while the ones from gourmet chocolate stores in Vilnius would be quietly taken home. Sometimes, these boxes were paired with envelopes that contained money destined for doctors' pockets. At the end of the week, when many patients were discharged, boxes would pile up on desks and shelves. Residents and interns, constantly on the run between the ER and the hospital's multiple units, consumed most of these chocolates. They saved leftovers for night shifts and gave chocolates to their fellow residents. At other times, boxes were left unopened: the medical staff had been saturated with too many, were too busy, or were (possibly, I thought) inhibited by my presence.

Stories about giving, anxiety, humiliation and gratitude in medical encounters are a shared memory and a present practice in Lithuania. I am not innocent of these practices. My mother worked at a hospital during Soviet times in Lithuania and occasionally brought home sweets that she had received from discharged patients. When my father was sick, she took gift bags and envelopes with money to the medical staff. At the cardiology unit, giving and taking – however ambiguous – constitutes a form of life and caring in the Lithuanian public health system.[1]

Things, money and people are enmeshed within these circuits and constitute a specific form of 'enveloped care'.[2] The 'little envelope' (*vokelis*) is the most common form of handing money to doctors in public health care. The envelope with money, along with boxes of chocolates, cakes and other food items, carries more than just money or sweets. It encapsulates the linkages between notions of health, relations to medical power, belief, hope, vernacular history and political economy. It is not only an economic transaction, but also an aesthetics of communication and a form of care embedded in social relations and driven by webs of obligation that both exceed and are included in notions of the gift, the commodity or the bribe. We might understand Galina's cake to be a sign of gratitude, a gift given *after* hospital care was received. Yet chronic patients, like Galina's husband, will be returning to the hospital. The temporal markers – before and after – that are often applied (by doctors, patients and anthropologists) to distinguish gifts from bribes cannot be applied in illness encounters. 'After' is also 'before' for the sick and their caretakers.

While observing the work of doctors and nurses and their interactions with patients and their social networks, I realised that accepting these 'thank yous' was as complex as giving them. The cake case is an example of such tensions. Cakes or envelopes with money can be both signs of attention and expressions of sincere gratitude for the nurses and doctors. They might also be neither, but rather an expression or display of care towards the patient. Both and neither.

The encounter I described might be read as an economic transaction where the cake is exchanged for a bag of diapers and compassion. Indeed, medical practitioners' act of giving diapers and medication to Galina resembles a way 'to settle accounts', to acknowledge and make visible exchange and reciprocity, to prevent Galina from bringing another cake in the future, and thus continuing the pattern of her relationships with the doctor, nurse and the aid. However, Galina's encounters do not fit within these rational logics of exchange. Galina, like other carers, was concerned about being a caring wife, daughter or friend. Giving the cake was a way of caring for her kin as well as for the doctors. Both and neither: breaking the logic of equivalence and staying within it could each, at once, be true.

Galina's cake was indeed very tasty: not too sweet and not too rich. It was a special cake, different from other cakes shared by medical staff at the unit. The story of Galina and her husband was embedded in it. On that day, the cake was shared with other medical practitioners who came into the unit. At the end of the day the nurses and doctors took the leftovers of Galina's cake home to their own children, along with bits of an ongoing story.

ENDNOTES

1 Things and money have been an important part of clinical relationships in other post-socialist contexts as well. See, for example, Andaya, E., 'The Gift of Health. Socialist Medical Practice and Shifting Material and Moral Economies in Post-Soviet Cuba', *Medical Anthropology Quarterly*, 23.4 (2009), 357–74; Bazylevych, M., 'Prestige Concept Reconsidered. Hybridity of Prestige in Post-Socialist Biomedical Profession', *International Journal of Social Inquiry*, 3.2 (2010), 75–99; Patico, J., 'Chocolate and Cognac: Gifts and the Recognition of Social Worlds in Post-Soviet Russia', *Ethnos*, 67.3 (2002), 345–68; Rivkin-Fish, M., *Women's Health in Post-Soviet Russia. The Politics of Intervention* (Bloomington and Indianapolis: Indiana University Press, 2005); Salmi, A. M., 'Health in Exchange. Teachers, Doctors, and the Strength of

Informal Practices in Russia', *Culture, Medicine, and Psychiatry*, 27 (2013), 109–30; Sabina, S., 'Neither Commodities nor Gifts: Post-Socialist Informal Exchanges in the Romanian Healthcare system', *Journal of the Royal Anthropological Institute (N.S.)*, 18 (2012), 65–82.

2 Praspaliauskiene, R., 'Enveloped Lives: Giving, Caring and Relating in Lithuanian Health Care' (Cornell University Press, 2022).

19

FROM FISH LIVES TO FISH LAW: LEARNING TO SEE INDIGENOUS LEGAL ORDERS IN CANADA

Zoe Todd

'THE NECESSITY OF RESPECTING GAME IS STILL WIDELY ACKNOWLEDGED BY Inuit. The awareness, that the continuity of society depends on the maintenance of correct relationships with animals and the land, is still very strong' (Aupilaarjuk et al. 1999: 2).

In 2012, I spent eight months living and working in the Inuvialuit hamlet of Paulatuuq, which is situated on the coast of the Beaufort Sea in the Inuvialuit Settlement Region, in Canada's Northwest Territories. I was interested in people's relationships to fish, and how fishing relationships were being asserted within the community in the face of cumulative colonial and environmental impacts, including looming mining interests, affecting the region. My first two degrees are in Biology and Rural Sociology and when I started ethnographic work in Paulatuuq, I still saw the relationships between humans and their environments with colonial eyes: fish were food, fish were specimens, fish were inputs in surveys and dry policy documents.

I knew better than to see fish this way. I grew up fishing with my parents and sisters on Baptiste Lake in north-central Alberta through the 1980s and 1990s. I swam with the fish in that green prairie kettle lake every summer throughout my entire childhood. I dreamt about fish and their fish-lives beneath the inscrutable, rippled lake-surface. I squealed with joy at the silver flash of minnows in the shallows on lazy July days and, for many dinners through my adolescence, we ate fish my stepdad caught in the Red Deer River, Pepper's Lake, and on his own re-watered wetland in central Alberta. But even with fish woven so intimately into every part of my life, it had never occurred to me that fish were also citizens, interlocutors, storytellers and beings to whom I owed reciprocal legal-governance and social duties. These lessons had been deeply erased from dominant (non-Indigenous) public discourse in Alberta and I had not recognised the implicit ways fish were woven into my own life as more than food. This is the thing about colonisation: it tries to erase the relationships and reciprocal duties we share across boundaries, across stories, across species, across space, and it inserts new logics, new principles and new ideologies in their place.

Anishinaabe legal scholar John Borrows (Pohlmann 2014) argues that Canada is enlivened by legal pluralities. By this, he means that Canada is not governed only by laws derived from French and English legal systems, but that the country is deeply shaped by the legal orders of First Peoples in North America whose territories were dispossessed by the colonisers. But through colonial sleight of hand, the Canadian State has tried to get us to forget that fish, too, are citizens within the territories we inhabit, that we share treaties and governance relationships with fish, plants and other more-than-human agents.[1] Colonialism has worked tirelessly to erase the Indigenous laws that govern Indigenous territories across Canada. This erasure obscures Indigenous legal orders and thinking in which humans, animals, water and land are integrated into nuanced and duty-full relationships with one another,[2] replacing these legal-governance realities with ones that draw solely on anthropo-centric French and English legal paradigms.

FIG. 19.1 Humpback whitefish

Part of the struggle in identifying Indigenous law owes to their *implicit* nature, as Indigenous legal scholar Val Napoleon (2007: 8) points out:

> [M]any Indigenous peoples are not aware of the law they know—they just take it for granted and act on their legal obligations without talking about it. This is in contrast to explicit law, in which everything is explained and talked about and written down. Sometimes Indigenous peoples think that their laws have to look like western laws and so they try to describe them in western terms.

It took me nearly my entire lifetime as a Red River Métis (otipemisiw, Michif) woman to learn to see the implicit Indigenous laws operating all around me throughout Indigenous territories in Canada. It was the experience of doing ethnography in Paulatuuq that taught me, finally, of the urgency and necessity of honouring Indigenous laws and the beautiful ways that they incorporate the more-than-human into legal-governance paradigms and discourses. In my work, I went looking for *human* responses to colonial relations, but quickly learned that resistance to colonial dispossession is articulated and mobilised not only through human means, but also through the bones, bodies and movement of fish.

In addition to focusing on the relation between fish, people, law and colonialism, my work also dwells on the complexities and paradoxes of doing ethnographic work as a Métis woman within the homeland of another Indigenous people.[3] The greatest challenge I face in 'doing ethnography' is in becoming familiar and contending with tensions between, first, my obligations to Euro-Western academic research structures, paradigms and ideals and, second, those

LAKE TROUT (anaaKłiq)

FIG. 19.2 Lake trout

duties I am bound to across, within and between Indigenous legal orders and philosophies in Canada. In this tension lies the underlying reality that before I am a researcher or philosopher or academic, I am a citizen living within a complex, if at times unspoken, plurality of legal-governance systems – and interrelated histories, philosophies, stories, and ideas – operating in Canada. I draw my understanding of simultaneous interrelatedness and difference across settler-colonial and Indigenous thinking, stories and laws from the work of Papaschase Cree Scholar Dwayne Donald (2009: 6), who outlines a principle of 'ethical relationality' as:

> An ecological understanding of human relationality that does not deny difference, but rather seeks to more deeply understand how our different histories and experiences position us in relation to each other. This form of relationality is ethical because it does not overlook or invisibilize the particular historical, cultural, and social contexts from which a particular person understands and experiences living in the world. It puts these considerations at the forefront of engagements across frontiers of difference.

Ethical relationality encourages me to contend with my research relationships differently than the Canadian and British academies where I was trained. The university, as a structure and a system, is built upon and informed by the laws and ethics of Euro-Western thinking and governance; it also operates to reify laws that are used to dispossess Indigenous peoples. However, to work in Indigenous territories and with Indigenous peoples' cosmologies in North America necessarily brings me into legal-governance and ethical relations across the plurality of laws that enliven these dynamic territories.

Donald's work invites us to attend to the space between and across: a) the Euro-Western legal-ethical paradigms that build and maintain the academy-as-fort (or colonial outpost),[4] fixing it within imaginaries[5] of land as property and data as financial/intellectual transaction, and b) Indigenous legal orders and philosophies which enmesh us in *living* and *ongoing* relationships to one another, to land, to the more-than-human, and which fundamentally challenge the authority of Euro-Western academies which operate within unceded, unsurrendered and *sentient* lands and Indigenous territories in North America. It also brings our anthropological attention to the simultaneous and often contradictory negotiations that Indigenous peoples make across *both* sameness and difference in contending with the colonial nation state in Canada.

In Paulatuuq, interlocutors Andy Thrasher, Millie Thrasher, Annie Illasiak and Edward and Mabel Ruben taught me that fish are more than food. Fish are simultaneously many things: food, sentient beings with whom humans share territory, specimens of study and regulation in wildlife co-management regimes, citizens and agents in legal-governance relationships and examples of what Ann Fienup-Riordan (2000: 57) calls 'active sites of engagement'. Across these sites, human-fish relations inform and capture memory, stories, teaching and philosophies. I also learned that human-fish relations can act as 'micro-sites' across which fish and people, together, actively resist and shape colonial logics and processes within Inuvialuit territories. Just as humans can shape and experience the colonial encounter, so too can animals. Human-fish relations in Paulatuuq therefore present a plurality of meanings, strategies and principles for those enmeshed within them. As a result, fish pluralities in Paulatuuq deeply inform a vibrant and creative set of local strategies through which some community members have refracted colonial state formations of human-animal and human-environmental relations (Todd 2014).

Annie Illasiak, an elder I worked with in Paulautuq, repeated the same lesson to me several times while I was working and living in the community. That teaching was 'you never go hungry in the land if you have fish'.[6] At first, I thought she meant this teaching as a purely utilitarian subsistence or survival lesson: even if every other source of food is unavailable, if you have fish, you won't starve. It wasn't until *after* I had moved back to Scotland to write that I began to untangle my utilitarian understanding of the statement and began to see the fish pluralities she was referencing. This was not a lesson solely about food, but about the many manifestations and articulations of human-fish relations in Paulatuuq: as long as you have fish, you have stories, memories and teachings about how to relate thoughtfully with the world and its constituents. As long as you have fish (and other animals), you are nourished not only physically, but in a plurality of emotional, spiritual and intellectual ways as well. A world without fish is not only a hungry one, but one intellectually and socially bereft.

People I worked with in Paulatuuq demonstrated to me how they employ what Inuvialuit political leader and thinker Rosemarie Kuptana (2014) calls the Inuit practice of 'principled pragmatism'. Working across both sameness and difference, Paulatuuq people employ strategies that incorporate elements of the Canadian state's wildlife scientific co-management system *and* Inuvialuit legal orders and thinking to assert the wellbeing of humans and fish alike. Employing this dynamic strategy, Paulatuuqmiut successfully shut down a government-mandated commercial fishery in a vital local watershed in the 1980s (Todd 2014). The lives and stories of fish and people are tightly woven together in complex ways, and these relationships not only inform what might be glossed as cultural, religious, ontological or ecological concerns, but also shape concrete, gritty, practical, fleshy lived legal-political (decolonial) realities as well.

By working outwards from particular and specific fish stories and memories that interlocutors shared with me in Paulatuuq, I was brought into a rich world of Indigenous legal-governance operating in dynamic ways across Canada. I was taught to see fish as non-human persons who consciously and actively respond to the human and non-human worlds around them. I was taught to understand land, climate/atmospheres, water and animals as sentient and knowing, and to position my engagement with these agents ethically, reciprocally and accountably. My presence as someone entangled in settler-colonial research systems was also made explicit and forced me to question and engage with the uncomfortable question of what my role is (if any) as a southerner working in Arctic Canada. At the end of the day, I realised that I cannot work in the northern research

ARCTIC CHAR (iqalukpik)

Zoe Todd

FIG. 19.3 Arctic Char

industry while research in unceded Indigenous lands remains controlled, in large part, by southern non-Indigenous research institutions which operate under settler-colonial legal constructs (Moffitt et al. 2015). For now, I work in the territories where I grew up. I make this choice so that I can renew and tend to the relationships to fish, people, lands and Indigenous laws that I was raised with but unable to 'see'.

Through my ethnographic experience, I was taught by Inuvialuit interlocutors to train my eyes, ears, heart and mind to honour implicit Indigenous laws long obscured by the dominance of British and French laws employed by the Canadian State. I was also sensitised to the differences between laws, stories and relationships in Paulatuuq and those Métis teachings I grew up with on the green waters of Baptiste Lake in Alberta. Working within the frameworks of Indigenous legal orders re-situates my duties from those that prioritise the academic-research industrial complex to a nuanced and careful negotiation of duties within, across and between Indigenous laws that centre and tend to land, water, fish, humans and climate. For me, ethnography and anthropology remain fraught structures, processes and spaces. However, by tending to my duties to Inuit thinkers, and the philosophies they articulate (and intellectual labour they perform), and in tending to my legal-ethical duties as an Indigenous feminist working within the ongoing settler-colonial realities that shape Canada, I can slowly but insistently untangle some of the forms of violence the academy reproduces in its iterations and interpretations of Indigenous philosophy.[7]

ENDNOTES

1 Vanessa Watts (2013: 23) argues that: 'habitats and ecosystems are better understood as societies from an Indigenous point of view; meaning that they have ethical structures, inter-species treaties and agreements, and further their ability to interpret, understand and implement. Non-human beings are active members of society. Not only are they active, they also directly influence how humans organise themselves into that society'.

2 There is a rich literature on Indigenous legal orders and Indigenous cosmologies to refer to here. I suggest reading the work of Mario Aupilarkuuk et al. (1999); John Borrows, Sarah Hunt, Kahente Horn-Miller, Sylvia McAdam, Val Napoleon, Tracey Lindberg, Jim Tully, Sharon Venne, Vanessa Watts and others.

3 This is a tension that Indigenous scholars Olga Ulturgasheva and Stacy Rasmus (2014) interrogate in their ethnographic work across and between territories in Alaska and Siberia.

4 Donald (2009: 4) interrogates the 'frontier logics' that still operate within Canada to separate Indigenous and non-Indigenous pedagogies and stories, and he employs the Fort as metaphor to illustrate the active way the education system works to keep Indigenous stories and philosophies *outside* the classroom.

5 In a talk in Ottawa, Canada in October 2015, Tracey Lindberg called these the 'colonial legal fictions' that the Canadian state relies upon to dispossess Indigenous peoples from living, thinking and sentient lands.

6 I explore this in depth in my doctoral work and in a recent publication (Todd 2014).

7 For further reading on the negotiations of Indigenous philosophies within and outside Euro-Western academic structures in North America, see the works of John Borrows, Dwayne Donald, Sarah Hunt, Tracey Lindberg, Cutcha Risling Baldy, Erica Violet Lee, Val Napoleon, Audra Simpson, Kim TallBear, Eve Tuck, Vanessa Watts, Kyle Powys Whyte and other contemporary Indigenous thinkers working on these issues.

REFERENCES

Aupilaarjuk, M. and others, *Interviewing Inuit Elders Volume 2: Perspectives on Traditional Law*. 1999. http://tradition-orale.ca/english/pdf/Perspectives-On-Traditional-Law-E.pdf.

Donald, D., 'Forts, Curriculum, and Indigenous Metissage: Imagining Decolonization of Aboriginal-Canadian Relations in Educational Contexts', *First Nations Perspectives*, 2.1 (2009), 1–24.

Fienup-Riordan, A., 'An Anthropologist Reassess Her Methods', in A. Fienup-Riordan and others, eds. *Hunting Tradition in a Changing World: Yup'ik Lives in Alaska Today* (New Brunswick, NJ: Rutgers University Press), pp. 29–57.

Kuptana, R., 'Indigenous Peoples in Canada: Politics, Policy and Human Rights-based Approaches to Development and Relationship-Building', Text from a lecture given at Trent University's 50th Anniversary, Friday 8 August 2014. Full transcript online: https://www.facebook.com/notes/10152653528630909/.

Moffitt, M., C. Chetwynd and Z. Todd, 'Interrupting the Northern Research Industry: Why Northern Research should be in Northern Hands', *Northern Public Affairs*, 4.1 (2015), 12035. http://www.northernpublicaffairs.ca/index/interrupting-the-northern-research-industry-why-northern-research-should-be-in-northern-hands/.

Napoleon, V., 'Thinking About Indigenous Legal Orders', Research Paper for the National Centre for First Nations Governance. http://fngovernance.org/ncfng_research/val_napoleon.pdf.

Pohlmann, M., 'John Borrows on Indigenous Legal Traditions: "We Need to Explore How We Can Take That Law and Carve It in New and Beautiful Ways"', *The Globe and Mail*, 5 December 2014. http://www.theglobeandmail.com/globe-debate/john-borrows-on-Indigenous-legal-traditions-we-need-to-explore-how-we-can-take-that-law-and-carve-it-in-new-and-beautiful-ways/article21960774/.

Todd, Z., 'Fish Pluralities: Human-Animal Relations and Sites of Engagement in Paulatuuq, Arctic Canada', *Etudes/Inuit/Studies*, 38.1–2: (2014), 217–38.

Ultargasheva, O., and S. Rasmus, 'Developing Indigenous Research Methodologies in the Arctic', *Field Notes: The Polar Field Services Newsletter*, 2014. http://polarfield.com/blog/developing-Indigenous-research-methodologies-in-the-arctic/.

Watts, V., 'Indigenous Place-Thought and Agency amongst Humans and Non-humans (First Woman and Sky Woman Go on a European Tour!)', *DIES: Decolonization, Indigeneity, Education and Society*, 2.1 (2013), 20–34.

20

ETHNOGRAPHIC CASE, LEGAL CASE: FROM THE SPIRIT OF THE LAW TO THE LAW OF THE SPIRIT

André Menard and Constanza Tizzoni

IN 1956, CLAUDE LÉVI-STRAUSS ADDRESSED A LETTER TO THE 1ST
International Congress of Black Writers and Artists held in Paris. In the letter,
he stated that 'after the aristocratic humanism of the Renaissance and the bour-
geois humanism of the 19th century' the Congress announced the arrival of 'a
democratic humanism' in which 'every human society must be represented,
not just a few'.[1]

A society's access to the rank of civilisation is, however, neither evident nor
immediate, but requires the presence of representatives. Lévi-Strauss explained
this situation in the following manner: 'these civilizations of which you are the
spokespeople have hardly had any written documents and some only devoted
themselves to the monument's transitory forms. For lack of these so-called noble
productions, in order to comprehend them, one must focus oneself, with the
same degree of passion and respect, on the "popular" manifestations of culture:
those shared by all members of society'.[2]

In this statement from Lévi-Strauss, we can see three things: an expression
of the politics of deracialisation policies promoted by organisations such as
the United Nations and UNESCO since the end of World War II; the promotion of the concept of culture over race as the new tool for the management of

human differences; and the creation of a new subject – Indigenous peoples as an internationally recognised political and legal category.

What is perhaps most meaningful in Levi Strauss' statement, however, is that this new global category takes the shape of a special kind of subject: the anthropological informant – that anonymous person or individual whose name always functions at a secondary level after the authorship of the ethnographer, whose role is to instantiate a collective category, which was understood in the past as race and is today known as culture. Every gesture and word of the inform-ant becomes a sign of the beliefs, mythologies or worldviews of the culture to which he or she supposedly belongs.

Hence the informant assumes the obligation of not only belonging to the group but also representing it, that is to say, *not only being but also appearing* as the authentic representative of a different culture. This mandate of authenticity becomes urgent in the present context of multicultural policies, in which the exemplary form of representation of cultural identity is the dominant form of visibility that Indigenous actors must draw on when dealing with the political, legal and administrative apparatus of their respective national states.

In Chile this model of multicultural management has been implemented since 1993 with the enactment of Law No. 19.253, also known as the 'Indigenous Law', which was subsequently confirmed with the entry into force of ILO Convention 169 in 2009.[3] This is a national law for the protection, promotion and development of Indigenous Peoples, which recognises as Indigenous those individuals who maintain cultural traits of any of the nine Indigenous ethnicities recognised by the Chilean state, and who also self-identify as such (Article 2, letter c). Likewise, the Indigenous Law recognises traditional organisations and specific forms of Indigenous organisation (Articles 61 and 68).

We are interested in addressing the problem of representation of the ethno-graphic case: that a particularity comes to stand in for a (cultural) generality. We address this problem, through an older and more traditional genre – the legal case – where we can also identify a tension between the universality of a law and the specificity of situations to which it applies. However, in the case of the 'Indigenous Law', culture appears as an intermediate category between the universal and the particular that points to a type of untranslatability between cultural and legal systems, while also, as we shall see, introducing the necessity of some special category that will allow for translation.

THE CASE OF MOISÉS MALIQUEO

On 17 August 2013, Mapuche farmer Moisés Maliqueo was sentenced to ten years in prison after being found guilty of killing his wife a year earlier.[4] The case would have been treated like other femicides in the country if it had not been for the cultural belonging of the accused.[5] That he was Mapuche allowed him to benefit from the services of an agency specifically focused on the defence of the Mapuche peoples of southern Chile: the Mapuche Public Defender.[6] The defence requested an anthropological investigation in order to assess the existence of any extenuating cultural aspects for his crime.[7] Along with the anthropologist, a psychiatrist also appeared in the trial acting as an expert, as well as a *machi* (Mapuche shaman) who healed Maliqueo, and who acted as a witness.

The primary concern of the judges and prosecutors (much like that of the ethnographer with the informant) was to confirm the authenticity of the Mapuche defendant, that is to say, his level of attachment to his culture. In the statement made by the psychiatrist, certain suspicions were raised regarding the genuine nature of his cultural belonging, supported by the vagueness that, in the professional's opinion, characterised Maliqueo's explanation of the evil (witchcraft) that had turned him into an alcoholic and driven him to kill his wife. The psychiatrist explained,

> With regard to this story of evil, it struck us that he was too vague when describing what this evil consisted of and how he was treated, so we began to question whether he was really describing a belief rooted in his culture, or if it was something he'd simply made up to justify his actions[8]

From this point of view alcoholism is a sufficient and admissible cause for Maliqueo's violent act in the context of the court. On the other hand, the magical cause implied by the evil eye, works as a supplementary cause with respect to this psychiatric cause.[9] It appears as a cultural supplement of causality in a certain way no less magical than the evil eye, and hence also becomes an object of suspicion.

The psychiatrist continued:

> Finally, we conclude as a team that this is a man of a rural origin [...] We also delved a little into how cross-cultural he is: he considers himself both Mapuche and Chilean, takes part in activities characteristic of his culture and of his ethnicity, but in turn participates quite normally let's say in the more Chilean-Western part of society. The team has its doubts as to whether this is genuine behavior from the point of view of his culture, or is simply an argument that he uses to justify his behavior.[10]

An anthropologist was then called upon. Since his role consists in proving cultural extenuating circumstance for Maliqueo's crime, it may be important to note that in March 2013 the Sernam (the state office devoted to the defence and promotion of women's rights) had denounced the exculpation of seventeen Mapuche accused of domestic violence, who had successfully appealed to Convention 169.[11] In those cases the defence argued that the aggressors' simple assertion of Mapuche customs was enough to exculpate them.[12] Thus, within this contextual and legal background, the anthropologist in Maliqueo's case began by stating the nature of his work: organising a field trip, interviewing people, in short, undertaking ethnography. It was in the course of this work that he realised 'that a sociocultural environment operates within the community'. The judge asked what this meant, to which the anthropologist replied:

> In other words, there exists a Mapuche religiosity called nguillan mawün, according to which, and specifically within this community, they celebrate 'nguillatun' [a collective propitiatory ceremony], the cultural practices characteristic of the Mapuche people, like what is called machitún [a shamanic healing rite].[13]

Here something is described that will be a constant not only in this case, but in most trials of this type; that is, when it comes to proving the cultural belonging of the accused, judicial protagonists refer exclusively to two aspects: use of the Mapuche language and participation in Mapuche religious ceremonies. Both the psychiatrist and the prosecutor were emphatic about establishing that Maliqueo speaks Spanish.

However, and in spite of the fact that Maliqueo does speak Spanish, the defence (in order to perform his cultural identity) managed to get the court to assign him an 'intercultural facilitator', a Mapuche court official responsible for translating the process both linguistically and culturally to the accused. As for the argument about religion, both the defence and the anthropologist confirmed Maliqueo's participation in traditional ceremonies, as well as his trust in the *machi* (shaman) from whom he sought assistance. In fact, in the first intervention of the defence of the accused, the following was stated:

> My client [Maliqueo] is a Mapuche man. I think it is very significant in this context and in this particular case to identify who this person is. Witness statements will be given by an anthropologist who will reveal who this person is, along with a social worker and a machi. My client speaks Mapudungun (translator's note: the Mapuche language), he follows the Mapuche religion and ceremonies; he prays in his own language, this is called 'guillatucar' in Mapuche, and is also a 'pifilquero', that is to say he plays the pifilca [a Mapuche flute], and he takes part in various ceremonies, in nguillatunes, as well as machi ceremonies, as he is also the assistant of a machi.[14]

Thus the trial turned to focus on the actual impact that this cultural condition had in the lead- up to his actions. The *machi* Victor Caniullán, who attended to the defendant after he had been arrested, was called as a witness, where, in addition to providing details about the killing, he was asked to give a quasi-class to the jury on Mapuche ethnology. The judge began by asking him about the conditions required to practise as a *machi*, to which he replied:

> Usually there are two types of spirits: a spirit needed for being a person and one needed for being a machi. When there's a machi within the

family, that spirit normally returns a long time after the death of the old machi.[15]

He then recounted how, in Maliqueo's case, it was the spirit of a grandmother that was transmitted to him. The *machi* was then questioned by the defence and asked to explain the Mapuche concept of health:

Machi: Within the Mapuche classification of health we observe four areas: the physical, spiritual, psychological, and the social.

Defense: Can you explain a little more about each one of these?

Machi: Essentially there is a concept called kutxan, which basically means pain. Sickness is not only physical pain, you know? Rather the physical has to do with the whole issue of a person's body, the physical pain, the ailments, in short. For example, a cough may be a physical illness. When we treat social problems, we include the area where the person develops, grows, lives and coexists. And when we deal with the issue of the psychological, this relates to the issue of consciousness. And in spiritual terms, this is basically how our spirit relates to the surrounding environment, and to all the beings that exist.[16]

Next the machi gave a statement regarding the classification of illnesses according to the Mapuche system. He explained that there are five illnesses, of which Maliqueo suffers from two. The first one was *re kutxan*, a physical ailment of one of the body's organs, and which literally means 'pure illness' or better still 'illness and nothing more'.[17] And the second one was described as *mapu kutxan*, meaning 'land illness' or 'earth illness', but which also, and this is important, means 'Mapuche illness', which is to say an illness imbued with a cultural quality. In other words it is untranslatable in terms of biomedical terminology and its anatomical universality.

Three other illnesses exist: *wingka kutxan*, a Chilean or Western disease, which the *machi* shamans have no ability to treat; *kisu kutran*, which only affects persons of authority such as the longkos [chiefs] and *machis*, and is attributed to the relationship with the spirit associated with their position; and, finally, *wesa kutxan*, or the evil disease or 'evil' caused by supernatural attacks, or directly through poisoning, carried out by a specific person. This last can be translated as 'witchcraft', an issue that is indeed highly present in Mapuche ethnography, and that Maliqueo argued was the final cause of his crime, although this wasn't confirmed by the *machi*.

Now, if we examine the second of these, *mapu kutxan*, we can see that the double meaning of Mapuche illness and earth illness contains the ambivalence of the same Mapuche ethnonym. This is because the word Mapuche has acquired at least three forms, corresponding to three possible positions of enunciation of the Mapuche used in Chilean legal and political discourses throughout its history.

First: Mapuche as people of the land (in former days known as *reche*, 'pure people', or 'people and nothing more'), which may have meant 'people of this place' or 'we the locals', where the word *mapu* refers to a limited territorial specificity.

Second: Mapuche as a people of a nation like Chile or the Basque Country, passing from a limited territorial reference to the idea of a political territory at national level.

And third: the Mapuche as a synonym of an Indigenous people, a globally recognised category, defined by their prior relationship before a national state who can, having been transformed in the second half of the twentieth century into subjects of law at the international level, claim to be inhabitants of the Earth, but this time in capital letters, that is to say as a planet, and with all the romantic connotation of the pre-modern subject, imbued with community, ecological and, of course, spiritual values.

This is why when explaining what *mapu kutxan* consists of, the *machi* did not only refer to the cultural nature of the illness, but also, and especially, its 'energetic' and 'environmental' nature. In his words:

> Mapu kutxan ultimately has to do with the whole concept of the strength
> and the energy that exists in nature. (…) The other element of mapu kutxan
> has to do with energy or forces that are within the earth and which can cause
> some form of alteration in a person, and in the specific case of the person
> I went to examine, it was … He had a lot of difficulty getting to sleep, he
> didn't sleep well; he had certain feelings of persecution, nightmares, and
> basically that was a situation that, at that time on the 15 November, led to
> his instability within his dwelling.[18]

One interesting point here is that the forces and energies of nature seem to be more determinant than the Mapuche (cultural) character of the illness. As the *machi* explained:

> Only the Mapuche health system is ultimately able to understand what mapu kutxan means, due to the religious view we have of our surroundings, of the environment; this does not mean that only the Mapuche are affected by such illnesses.[19]

The force of nature, then, is a cause of illness, but are its quirks enough to explain its appearance? Apparently the ultimate cause finally lies in the behaviour of the sick person, as the forces of nature or the earth upon the sick person depend on certain cultural transgressions. Again quoting the *machi*:

> For us, and from the point of view of our religious beliefs, all visible or invisible beings that exist in nature have life, have a spirit, have a master, and provide in some way energy. And their illnesses are caused by … these things happen when we somehow transgress certain cultural norms, and by transgressing certain cultural norms, these are forces, energies or spirits that in the end approach the body of the person who then begins in one way or another to feel discomfort, in this case referring to spiritual and psychological discomfort.[20]

Ultimately what reappears as the great marker of Mapuche identity is 'religious belief' which can be immediately translated as 'cultural norms'. Not only is nature spiritualised, but also the culture itself, which cannot be understood except from a spiritual perspective as synonymous with religion. Hence, over the course of the trial the use of this spiritual supplement was a way of expressing cultural untranslatability. And, as we can see, once the discourse becomes spiritualised, the translation appears transparent. When the judge sought to elicit the testimony of the accused, which justified his actions due to the intervention of a third party that had exposed him to 'the evil eye', and asked the *machi* whether Maliqueo suffered from the fifth kind of illness (*wesa kutxan*), the machi replied:

No, in this case, no evil has been caused by a third party. Rather it mainly depends on the behaviour of people, basically with regard to their surroundings, with the earth, the waters, etc. Often the spirit begins to weaken the spirit of the person himself, and in this case that's what was happening according to the diagnosis made at the time.

Judge: It's like saying the energies were not aligned within him and it was because of that that he became unbalanced.

Machi: Exactly.[21]

Exactly. The judge understood perfectly the meaning of *mapu kutxan*: that in the absence of matter, spiritual energies take over.[22] The same can be said of Indigenous peoples, who once they are deracialised lose the material reference of the body as a mark of their untranslatability. Thus culture rises up as an heir of this function, which not having the material reference of a race, has no other choice but to resort to the spiritual reference as the only way to translate their untranslatability. In fact this was even outlined by the same *machi*, when asked by the defence about the translatability of Mapuche categories:

Defence: Is it easy or difficult, and this is specifically for you to answer, to translate Mapuche concepts into Spanish?

Machi: There are concepts that have no translation, as they would lose their essence, their idea, (but) there are concepts that are easy to translate, such as 'pülli' – to assimilate to the spirit, for example.[23]

Thus we can see how the cultural supplement sought by the defence, the same supplement marked by the *mapu* of *mapu kutxan*, can only be 'materialised', that is to say translated, by the spiritual. Here there is no great difference with what happens in terms of international instruments used for the protection of Indigenous peoples. Many articles in both ILO Convention 169 (1989) and the UN Declaration on the Rights of Indigenous Peoples (2007) refer to this spiritual dimension as part of the heritage of such peoples that must be protected.[24] However, every time they do so, the spiritual appears supplemented by other rights, and not only those that are economic and political, but also cultural, symbolic or religious rights. Or rather, the spiritual always appears as an effort to highlight those untranslatable features that all other categories fail to contain.

Between the universality of Chilean law and the specificity of the judicial case, we come across the ethnographic case, that is, the figure of the accused as an informant of a particular culture, which in turn acts as universal, i.e., as a collective category represented within an Indigenous individual. However, unlike the universality of Chilean law, the universality of Mapuche culture lacks the formal recognition of its own autonomous judicial apparatus which would mediate, through the legal decision, the step that is always contingent between that cultural universal and the particular case.

Devoid of this political body that would allow for the realisation of cultural (but also, and above all, social and historical) content in an effective practice of Mapuche judicial decisions, culture remains floating as a pure spirit, a spiritual supplement that the accused must prove (ethnographically, that is to say in a representative fashion) before the Chilean courts.

Thus the multicultural spiritualisation of differences can immunise decision-making structures established by the laws of Chilean sovereignty, relegating the political dimension of the Indigenous condition, that is, the problem of formal and territorial – or even national –autonomy, to a problem between individuals, i.e., a condition which, although invoking a collective dimension, does not cease to be individual.

In this context, the only way to affirm the Indigenous status of the individual is to fall back on the legal argument of diminished responsibility by invoking forces outside their will; in other words, by removing individual agency. Perhaps that explains why the defence has symptomatically resorted to Article 10 No. 1 of the criminal procedural code,[25] which exempts (a person) from criminal responsibility due to insanity. But what insanity could this be, if the purpose was to prove cultural rather than psychiatric motivations for what took place? Perhaps it was the colonial, multicultural or anthropological insanity of assigning to each gesture and each thought of the subject the obligation to represent a collective, to be authentic – in other words, the insanity of the informant.

ENDNOTES

1 This article is based on the results of the Project Fondecyt 1140921. We would like to thank Fabien Lebonniec for his generosity in sharing with us the documents of Moisés Maliqueo's trial.

2 Lévi-Strauss C., 'Lettre au I Congrès d'artistes et écrivains noirs', *Présence Africaine*, 8–9–10 (1956), 384–85.

3 International legal instrument promulgated by the International Labour Organisation (ILO) in 1989, which outlines the rights of Indigenous Peoples and the ensuing obligations of states.

4 Oral Criminal Court of Temuco. Case of Moisés Maliqueo Quidel. Femicide trial. R.I.T.:107/2013. 17 August 2013.

5 The Chilean state signed in 1994 the 'Inter-American Convention on the Prevention, Punishment and Eradication of Violence against Women Convention of Belem do Para', and since 2008 the SERNAM (the state office devoted to the defence and promotion of Women's rights) has developed a campaign for preventing and denouncing violence against women. In this context, and along with public campaigns for denouncing acts of violence against women, cases of femicides are normally denounced in the media.

6 Forming part of the Criminal Justice Reform, the Mapuche Public Defender's Office was created in 2001. It represents the first specialised mechanism for the criminal defence of Indigenous defendants and has been implemented only in the Araucanía region of Chile. The body is staffed by lawyers who specialise in the defence of native peoples, along with intercultural facilitators who provide translation and cultural services and who share Mapuche ethnicity with those whom they defend.

7 The aforementioned 'Indigenous Law' for criminal matters requires the accreditation during trial of Indigenous customs, carried out to prove that the unlawful conduct of an individual, recognised as Indigenous, would have been influenced by the socio-judicial impact on that person of rules of conduct within the community to which he or she belongs. Said Indigenous custom must be accredited by an anthropological investigation, carried out by an expert in that field, and then submitted to the court as judicial evidence (Article 54 of the aforementioned law). Furthermore, as a result of the Criminal Procedural Reform, the investigation of such anthropological experts 'cannot be presented solely in a written report. Rather its main form of presentation should take place in an oral hearing during the trial' (Le Bonniec 2014).

8 Transcript of the statement made by psychiatric expert Sergio Duran during the second day of the oral hearing. Criminal Court of Temuco: Case of Moisés Maliqueo Quidel, Femicide Trial. R.I.T.: 107/2013.

9 Here we are working with the Derridean notion of the supplement in the sense of a paradoxical (and eventually empty) feature that can both function as the supplement for a lack, and as an extra element added to the whole.

10 Idem.

11 We don't have room here, but it would be important to develop all the legal and anthropological implications of the conflict of rights that such a case involves, as far as the cultural rights, claimed by Maliqueo's defence based on the international conventions signed by the Chilean state, collide with the human rights of his victim. The victim's rights are also based in a specific international convention, the 'Inter-American Convention on the Prevention, Punishment and Eradication of Violence against Women Convention of Belem do Para', as the prosecutor argued in his accusation.

12 Here it is also important to note that citizen organisations, including Mapuche political organisations, denounced this legal strategy as a misuse of Convention 169. As we'll try to show in this text, the possibility of this type of legal 'misuse' is based on a rather esoteric use of the category of culture, instead of providing institutionalised spaces (that is, autonomously produced and officially recognised spaces) for the Mapuche people to elaborate, discuss and perform their legal solutions.

13 Transcript of the statement made by the anthropological investigator, Paulo Castro, in the court hearing on the second day of the trial. Criminal Court of Temuco. Case of Moisés Maliqueo Quidel. Femicide Trial. R.I.T.: 107/2013.

14 Transcript of the opening statement by Maria Salamanca for the defence on the first day of the trial. Criminal Court of Temuco. Case of Moisés Maliqueo Quidel. Femicide Trial. R.I.T.: 107/2013.

15 Transcript of the statement by the witness Victor Caniullán on the second day of the trial. Criminal Court of Temuco. Case of Moisés Maliqueo Quidel. Femicide Trial. R.I.T.: 107/2013.

16 Idem.

17 Which is symptomatic of a system that distinguishes between a pure illness and one that includes a cultural supplement that differentiates it from some universal organic illness.

18 Idem.

19 Idem.

20 Idem.

21 Idem.

22 Augé, M., *Le Dieu Objet* (Paris: Flammarion, 1988).

23 Idem.

24 Within ILO Convention 169: Articles 5, 7, 13 and 32. Within the UN Declaration on the Rights of Indigenous Peoples: Articles 11, 12, 25 and 34.

25 Art. 10: 'Those exempt from criminal responsibility are: 1. the mad or insane, unless they have acted with lucidity during an intervening period, and who, for whatever cause independent of their will, have been completely deprived of all reason.' *Código Penal de la República de Chile* [Criminal Code of the Republic of Chile].

REFERENCES

Augé, M., *Le Dieu Objet* (Paris: Flammarion, 1988).

Código Penal de la República de Chile, http://www.leychile.cl/Navegar?idNorma=1984 (accessed January 2015).

Criminal Court of Temuco 2013, Transcript of the statement by the witness Victor Caniullán on the second day of the trial. Criminal Court of Temuco. Case of Moisés Maliqueo Quidel. Femicide Trial. R.I.T.: 107/2013.

Criminal Court of Temuco 2013, Transcript of the statement made by the anthropological investigator, Paulo Castro, in the court hearing on the second day of the trial. Criminal Court of Temuco. Case of Moisés Maliqueo Quidel. Femicide Trial. R.I.T.: 107/2013.

Criminal Court of Temuco 2013, Transcript of the statement made by psychiatric expert Sergio Duran during the second day of the oral hearing. Criminal Court of Temuco: Case of Moisés Maliqueo Quidel, Femicide Trial. R.I.T.: 107/2013.

Criminal Court of Temuco 2013, Case of Moisés Maliqueo Quidel. Femicide trial. R.I.T.:107/2013. 17 August 2013. http://www.ilo.org/indigenous/Conventions/no169/lang–en/index.htm.

Criminal Court of Temuco 2013, Transcript of the opening statement by Maria Salamanca for the defence on the first day of the trial. Criminal Court of Temuco. Case of Moisés Maliqueo Quidel. Femicide Trial. R.I.T.: 107/2013.

Defensoría Penal Pública, *Modelo de Defensa Penal para Imputados Indígenas* (Santiago: Defensoría Penal Pública, 2012).

International Labour Organisation 1989, *Convention 169*.

Le Bonniec, F., 'Interrogantes en torno a la emergencia del peritaje antropológico en Chile', Paper presented in the frame of the project FONDECYT Iniciación N°11121578: *Justicia e interculturalidad: etnografía del campo jurídico en situaciones de relaciones interétnicas en la Araucanía, en el contexto de reforma procesal penal* (Temuco: Universidad Católica de Temuco, 2014).

Lévi-Strauss C., 'Lettre au I Congrès d'artistes et écrivains noirs', *Présence Africaine*, 8–9–10 (1956), 384–85.

Pouillon, J., 'Fétiches sans fétichisme', *Nouvelle revue de psychanalyse*, 2 (autumn 1970), 135–47.

United Nations 2007, *United Nations Declaration on the Rights of Indigenous Peoples*, http://www.un.org/esa/socdev/unpfii/documents/DRIPS_en.pdf.

21

THE ENCLOSED CASE

Elizabeth Lewis

THE CASE THAT FOLLOWS ILLUSTRATES AN ETHNOGRAPHIC FLASHPOINT IN my work on disability. Here, I offer an account of a single morning during my first research trip to Central America. The day marked my only visit to a particularly well-known institution (or shelter) for children and adults with disabilities. The following summer, I would learn that the scenes depicted below were not necessarily representative of other shelters in the country.

Still, several years later, this particular case – this single morning – continues to shape my thinking on the making and unmaking of disability personhood in everyday life. I use it not to highlight the plight of an individual or probe the lived experience of disability in certain economic and sociopolitical contexts. Rather, I approach it as the first of several encounters that prompted me to examine my preconceptions of disability outliers – cases that originally struck me as so extreme they couldn't possibly happen closer to home, back in the US. People kept in closets? Surely not. Children abandoned to live in nursing homes? Impossible. A suspicion that disability was contagious? Come on. Having spent my entire life immersed in the disability community, whether personally, as an ally, or through my research, I naively assumed that I knew better.

Yet I heard such stories again and again as I moved forward with my work on family experiences with rare and undiagnosed disabilities, those confusing puzzles of sensory, physical and intellectual difference that do not correspond to a clear label – the bodies that fall outside diagnostic common sense. The themes persisted long after I transitioned to fieldwork in the US. They weren't discussed as openly, yet simmered below the surface in many of my ethnographic encounters.

I have continuously revisited this case as a cautionary reminder of the materiality of bodily difference and enclosure, and of an ethnographic caution about attributing exceptionalism to an encounter. Each case tells a story, and this one is no different. But the story of a single morning has continued to reverberate through multiple years of a single project, despite my efforts to leave it behind.

The Centro was a clumsily crowded institution housing people of all ages with disabilities. Locals spoke of the kindness and generosity of the Church-run facility, noting its constantly changing international cadre of mission groups and gap-year volunteers. After all, where else could the Centro's abandoned disabled residents live, and who would care for them otherwise? The building's facade stood in typical colonial splendour, layers of sharply flowing lines doused in cheerful hues overlooking food vendors in the adjacent plaza. Anyone who has been to this well-frequented city has most likely passed by.

I met my local contact, V., a physical therapist based in the capital, outside the facility. She worked there twice weekly through an innovative programme developed by a well-connected national disability non-profit (with significant international backing). The programme brought experts from the capital city to other areas within a day's travel that lacked specialised disability service providers. Her formal job was to provide basic therapies to a handful of the residents, but there was more to her work – the simple act of attention, sitting with a person and communicating with them however possible, whether using sign language, speech, gesture or touch. In this space, where residents far outnumbered staff and volunteers, such encounters were a luxury.

Leading me through the maze of partially locked gates, V. narrated the space as we walked. Hundreds of people lived between these walls, hidden from the humming city life outside. The Centro's residents appeared to have a dizzying array of disabilities, and according to V., many did not have a concrete diagnosis – an under-examined, yet quite common, occurrence in global disability. I saw wheelchairs, straightjackets, the whole bit. The children's quarters stretched around a standard open-air courtyard, a deceptively beautiful by-product of the architecture. There were flowers, grass and a small jungle gym. A swing designed for kids in wheelchairs sat vacant, and a collection of multi-coloured beach balls rested under a small tree.

V. and I stopped to greet clients as we walked, shaking hands and patting arms along the way. Almost all were in wheelchairs. She said this was a requirement for residents, including those without mobility challenges. We walked toward a structure the size of a walk-in closet, a small wooden shed in yet another court-yard. My companion knocked. *Tok. Tok. Tok.* Without waiting for a response, she opened the door. A woman in her early twenties was curled on a wooden plank bed lined with a foam mattress. I will call her Maria. She had cropped black hair that stood straight up. V. had told me that she was blind, presumably since birth. I believe her eyes were closed when we arrived.

Maria had lived at the Centro since she was fifteen. She had quite a reputation and was widely feared by staff. She was said to be uncontrollable, unhinged and full of rage. She was violent, I was told, and took her wrath out quite physically on anyone who dared to come too close, especially when she was younger. Having heard all of this, I struggled to make sense of her small frame resting silently in this darkened closet. V. told me that Maria spent most of her days in this position.

Maria's room had no windows, but light slipped in through the uneven cracks where the rough wooden walls reached up toward the flat ceiling. The heat wasn't as oppressive as I expected. I noticed a small latch on the outside of the door. With force, Maria could have pushed her way out. The room was almost empty. A single light bulb hung from the ceiling and the bed sat next to a toilet with no lid or seat.

V. had first met Maria the previous year, and had visited her weekly ever since, following her brief therapy sessions in the children's wing. Her other clients were primarily young kids with multiple disabilities – mostly combined sensory, intellectual and physical impairments – but Maria was different. First, she was a young adult. Second, she lacked the diagnostic ambiguity of V's other patients. On paper, Maria sounded misleadingly clear cut: she was blind. As with the other Centro residents, however, Maria's impairment was enmeshed in a personal history of neglect and isolation that could not be separated from her lived experience with disability. Blindness, as a diagnosis, flattened her every day. Maria's disability had become inextricably linked to life in the closet, rumours (or truths) about aggressive behaviours and an inability to communicate verbally.

As V. had learned from the staff at the Centro, Maria had been abandoned by her parents as a small child. She somehow made her way from town to town and ended up in the main market of a small city. From there, she was sent to the Centro, where she had lived since she was around five. I had heard similar stories elsewhere – the disabled child found in a market stall or public bathroom. V. hadn't heard Maria speak and she didn't utter a sound during our visit that day. V. had been told she spoke a Mayan language when she arrived at the Centro as a girl, but never learned to speak Spanish. Again, I do not know. With us, she communicated through gesture, bodily movements and facial expression. And yet, I could see that she listened to every word we said.

After sitting in her room for a while, Maria stood up. She and I walked outside, slowly making our way across the courtyard. V. trailed behind. The nurses stared openly. When V. started to visit Maria, Centro staff uniformly warned her to be careful. 'She'll hurt you', they said. 'She's like an animal, biting and clawing'. Behaviours were individualised as nameless and decontextualised, yet fixed. Maria was just *like that*, the logic held, and we were all to be careful.

I sat with Maria on the concrete patio. The sun snuck out from rainy season clouds for a few moments. I recall Maria breathing slowly, in and out, always silent. I did the same, not wanting to make additional noise. One of her hands rested softly on my arm, physically keeping tabs on my presence in the space.

I met a man several weeks after this visit, a physical therapy student who had interned previously at the Centro. He immediately asked if I'd met Maria. He snickered as he spoke, recalling the stories of the notoriously wild and uncontrollable patient – this grown man with children of his own. He told me that everyone was afraid of Maria, that she was capable of anything. I asked if he'd ever seen one of her rumoured explosions. He said no.

Maria and I moved to the grass as she relished the rare moments of sunlight. When she was ready, she stood to return to her room. V. and I accompanied her, and we sat on her bed. Maria lowered herself down onto one side, curling into the same position in which I sometimes sleep. V. took out her cell phone and began to play music. I recognised the song instantly, a South American band with soft compositions full of emotion and weight, lots of lost loves and what ifs. The singer pondered the smells that linger once someone departs – of perfume, cigarette smoke, coffee breath, skin. Maria rested motionless, just breathing slowly and rhythmically with the music.

The three of us stayed like this for five minutes, maybe more, sitting there in stillness as the songs wrapped themselves around the small, dark space. Maria's open door caught any breeze it could find, and the air shifted slightly. Maria rested her head on my companion's lap and her hand on my arm. After a few songs, she shifted her weight away from us, creeping closer to the edge of her bed to signal that she was ready to be alone. V. asked softly if she wanted us to leave, telling me that Maria's lack of acknowledgment indicated that it was time. We stood and walked slowly from the space.

'This is always the most difficult part', V. said to me, looking down. I watched as she slowly closed and latched the door, and we left Maria inside her closet.

I did not return to the Centro.

While it was only a single morning in a multi-year project, my encounter with Maria continues to loom large in my thinking. In my work in Latin America and later in the US, including extensive digital ethnography, such outlying or seemingly extreme cases edged closer and closer to the centre of my analysis.

The similarities between this case and my subsequent work in the US were uncanny, most visibly in the convergence of spatial isolation in the crafting of difference in personhood. I returned to these themes repeatedly during later iterations of my fieldwork in Texas, which houses more citizens in large state institutions than any other state, despite a 1999 Supreme Court ruling in favour of community-supported living for people with disabilities. Texas, with thirteen state-supported public residential facilities, institutionalised 2969 residents in 2022 – more residents with intellectual and developmental disabilities than any other state in the US. The situation has grown so dire, including widespread reports of abuse and neglect, that the state was required by the Department of Justice in 2009 to monitor compliance violations. If the state was going to resist federal pressure to close institutions, at the very least it had to improve the treatment of people living inside.

And yet local (and typically left-leaning) news outlets staunchly protested against the proposed closure last year of one local institution, even in the wake of years of well-known problems with the facility. The logic was familiar: 'Where else will these people go? Who will care for them?' The media coverage curiously left out any significant discussion of legal precedent, the ongoing federal involvement, the Americans with Disabilities Act, or the simple fact that many other states had already phased out institutions in favour of community-based alternatives. I recalled my morning with Maria as I struggled to make sense of these renewed calls in favour of disability segregation. I began to think about disability through the lens of Elizabeth Povinelli's (2011) writings on the ordinariness of abandonment and isolation, and Kathleen Stewart's (2010) work on worlding and the everyday. Abandonment not as a jolt, but as the nagging hum of that single bulb in a darkened room, the murmurs of others told to keep away, or the lulling song we played from V.'s cell phone on the day of our visit.

I now approach disability segregation as an ongoing process of bodies and moments, an everyday experience of life in the closet. The slow burn of almost but not quite forgetting a woman made to live apart, and a collective public denial that such cases are not necessarily extreme or, if they are, might somehow be justified. Here, isolation becomes a work in progress, always unfinished, available to the ethnographic lens in snapshots. It is both a process and an act, highlighting disability worlds that are both singular and widely shared, frozen in scenes yet necessarily ongoing.

REFERENCES

Povinelli, E., *Economies of Abandonment: Social Belonging and Endurance in Late Liberalism* (Durham, NC: Duke University Press, 2011).

Stewart, K., 'Afterword: Worlding Refrains', in M. Gregg and G. J. Seigworth, eds., *The Affect Theory Reader* (Durham, NC: Duke University Press 2010), pp. 339–54.

——, *Ordinary Affects* (Durham: Duke University Press, 2007).

22

MAKING CASES FOR A TECHNOLOGICAL FIX: GERMANY'S ENERGY TRANSITION AND THE GREEN GOOD LIFE

Jennifer Carlson

THIS IS A STORY OF WOMEN WHO INVOKE ANOTHER WOMAN'S PSYCHOSO-matic distress to make a case for the 'green good life' and its possibilities. Hailing from a northern German village transformed by sustainable development projects, the people in this story weigh the promises of the *Energiewende,* Germany's "energy turn" from nuclear to renewable energy, through the experience of one woman and her everyday life. At a moment when ecological concern has become a site of capitalist speculation, these women posit investment in renewable energy as a means for better living and, by extension, a solution for their friend's emotional upheaval.

Drawing upon research conducted over a decade of visits to northern Germany, I contend that situations such as this offer insight into the class politics of the unfolding energy transition. Here I interweave two different kinds of thinking in cases. The women in this story invoke their friend's life to make a case for renewable energy, whereas I take their very conversation as a case unto itself: a site where everyday sensibilities about ecocapitalist development are given form and freight.

One Friday morning in the spring of 2011, I sat around a table with four women eating breakfast rolls and mulling over the absence of a friend. Our monthly breakfast circle had evolved out of a preschool playgroup. When the children reached kindergarten age, the mothers wanted to stay in touch and continued to meet without them. I was a later addition to the group, invited by friends when I returned to northern Germany for fieldwork during the previous year. All of us were in our 30s and 40s and all of us lived in Dobbe, a community in Lower Saxony terraformed through wind, solar, and biofuel development. Each of us rotated hosting duties, which meant providing rolls, butter, preserves, cold cuts, coffee, and tea.

While the circle was a leisurely break from our workday tasks, it was also a highly charged space of what Kathleen Stewart (1996) calls "just-talk" a laboratory for working through politics and power in the idiom our own personal lives. Telling stories about ourselves and others, we asked openly what kinds of broader knowledge could be gleaned from the pleasures and frustrations of ordinary life. Ours was a kind of thinking in cases (Forrester, 1996), not in a (scholarly) disciplinary sense, but as a form of therapeutics of everyday living. This aimed at determining what was valuable, just, and beneficial based on our own experience and the lives of those around us.

Regina Janssen was conspicuously absent, having skipped our monthly meeting for the third time that year. Her teenage daughter Angelika had been legally blind since birth, but doctors now warned that her condition had worsened to the point that the last of her partial sight could disappear at any moment. A series of surgeries would be necessary to preserve what was left of her vision. In advance of the procedures, Regina and her husband Volker opted to keep Angelika home from school to prevent undue eyestrain. In the past, Regina had spoken openly to the breakfast circle of her struggles with anxiety, her fears for Angelika, and the stresses of caring for both her children, the younger of whom—Laura—was still in elementary school.

Now her stress was compounded by the fact that Angelika required near-daily trips to the eye doctor in a nearby town to ensure that her eye pressure remained stable while they awaited the green light for her operation in Hamburg. Working long hours at a port on the nearby North Sea, Volker was unavailable to watch Laura while Regina was away from the house, meaning that Regina had to schedule Angelika's trips to the doctor—and the 30 minutes of travel time each way—around Laura's school hours. As such, Regina's free time was severely curtailed, her days subject to the evolving situation with Angelika's eyes. When I mentioned the breakfast circle during our conversations that spring, Regina's tone suggested that all the uncertainty made joining us out of the question.

In Regina's absence, the rest of us shared what we knew about Angelika's condition, but the conversation soon turned to Regina herself. Maike, another member of the group, enumerated a host of concerns including Regina's prior complaints about spinal discomfort, weight trouble, and insomnia with her current stress with Angelika and, more broadly, her domestic life. Maike asserted that the underlying causes of Regina's problems lay not only in the everyday demands of caregiving, but in her relationship with her husband, suggesting that Volker had forsaken Regina for his work. "You know it's because he's always working in the glasshouses," Maike observed, her expression incredulous. "What kind of life is that? They never go anywhere, never do anything special."

The "glasshouses" to which Maike referred were part of a ramshackle plant nursery behind the Janssens' house. Volker and Regina had originally bought the compound with the intention of converting its nine growing houses into a staging area for the reed-cutting business that he and his family had on the side. In the decade since the Janssens moved in, however, Volker's brother had abandoned their joint venture, leaving Volker and his aging father, Enno, with the task of refitting the nursery for other uses.

I found Maike's indictment of Volker as the source of Regina's hardships curious. I had never heard Regina herself suggest such a thing, although Volker's work in the old plant nursery was admittedly time-consuming. On weekdays the men often worked into the night. Enno usually arrived early to have coffee and pastries with Regina and the children before getting a head start on the evening's tasks. During my many visits with the Janssens, I observed that having food on hand for family and friends was a point of pride for Regina. When she hosted the breakfast circle, she recounted in detail buying cold cuts and cheeses from the supermarket and heading to the bakery to buy *Berliner* and doughnuts for

Volker, Enno, and the children. Of all the breakfast circle hosts, myself included, Regina's table was always the most generously set. Maike's statements, and our attendant nods, flattened the pleasures of Regina's life into a story of struggle that could be solved through our analysis.

Perhaps because I had once lived in the house next to the old plant nursery, I found that Dobbeners—and particularly my female acquaintances—were keen to discuss the state of the glasshouses with me when I returned to the area for fieldwork in 2010. I was repeatedly told that Volker was flush with cash, presumably because of his civil servant status at the port authority. Since he had money, some people mused aloud, why not use it to clean up the compound once and for all?

One recurrent suggestion was that the Janssens should convert the old nursery to a solar array by installing photovoltaics on top of the glasshouses. "How much money they'd make if they'd just put solar panels on the roof!" one person exclaimed to me. At the breakfast circle that spring morning, Maike also noted that Volker and Regina should install a solar array, suggesting that the technological fix of solar power might alleviate Regina's distress by "solving" the problem of the glasshouses.

Maike's suggestion pushes other Dobbeners' statements a step further, conflating possible financial gains from solar panel installation with the resolution of other issues the Janssens faced, whether "real" (such as Angelika's blindness) or "perceived" (the perceived harms of Volker's work in the glasshouses). Here I'd like to consider what these assertions imply about Germans' understanding of renewable energy and its promises at a moment when policymakers and popular media depict sustainable development as a key avenue of economic growth, both on the community level and at economies of scale.

By positing solar panel installation as a way out of Regina's troubles, Maike implies that ecocapitalist investment is a path to the good life. Her comments tap into a broader narrative—pervasive in news reports on both sides of the Atlantic—about how the energy transition underway since the 1990s is making Germany a world leader in environmental policy. Germany's energy transition consists of community-based wind, solar and biofuel initiatives that incorporate local energy governance, federal subsidies, and technologies manufactured at increasing economies of scale. The country's Renewable Energy Law, passed in 2000, offers incentives for renewable energy. This includes subsidies for power companies that buy wind and solar power, as well as tax breaks for individuals who invest in rooftop solar panels and other renewable technologies.

Renewable energy advocates in Germany, and elsewhere in Europe, have hailed these measures as a means of transforming energy consumers into "energy citizens," incentivizing people through small-scale development projects. In the words of Hermann Scheer (2013), a chemist and Social Democratic Party member who spearheaded pro-renewable legislation in the 1990s, "Renewable resources will bring a new era of wealth-creating economic development, initiated not by bureaucratic decree, but by the free choices of individuals." Statements like this reveal how Germany's energy turn is a social project as much as a policy initiative. It is a process of "fixing and co-substantiating phenomena, aggregating and assembling disparate elements of social life into a common purpose" (Povinelli, 2013: 38).

In rural areas of Lower Saxony, as elsewhere in Germany, renewable energy development is rapidly replacing farming as the most visible (and in many cases most profitable) economic activity. When I first visited Dobbe in the spring of 2000 a field of twenty wind turbines greeted me as I descended from the autobahn. Today that number has nearly doubled, and other wind parks have spread across the horizon. Fifteen years ago, too, waste from local livestock was used primarily for fertilizer; today, there are three plants around the village where such waste is processed into biofuel. Biofuel development has also led to the "cornification" (*Vermaisung*) of the countryside, as former grazing pastures for dairy cattle are converted into a veritable monoculture of corn for biofuel production. Solar energy incentives spurred many villagers to install solar panels on top of their homes between a research trip to northern Germany in 2007 and my field stay from 2010 to 2011.

By the time I returned for fieldwork in 2010, Dobbe was over 100% sustainable. Its wind park and solar panels produced more electricity than the community consumed—selling the surplus to power companies for distribution beyond the village—although the majority of Dobbeners' cars and home heating systems continue to run on fossil fuels. Dobbe's rapid development speaks to countless reports that renewable energy has transformed sleepy farming communities into hotbeds of economic activity. But despite the fact that renewable technologies dominate the village and its surroundings, comparably few Dobbeners are formally involved in the renewable energy industry. In the county where Dobbe is located, for example, shares of ownership in the "civic wind park" and biofuel processing plants are concentrated in the hands of several large landowners.

Landowning farmers—and more specifically, male landowners–had the most mobility with investments and returns. These farmers had more capital to pay into wind energy cooperatives or to use for installing industrial-sized solar arrays on top of their barns, and many held shares in the biofuel processing plants in the area. Home-owning villagers, on the other hand, invested in rooftop solar panels. While many non-landowning tenant farmers profited from the turn to biofuel crops, few had the resources necessary to invest in large-scale projects.

One could say that only some villagers are able to become "energy citizens," and that citizenship is as contingent on property ownership as it is on the will to preserve the environment, or even the desire to reap a profit. Yet even those who "have money" – that is, those able to marshal capital for investment in civic power generation schemes – may not necessarily wish to do so. As Regina noted on more than one occasion, she and Volker had obtained estimates for photovoltaic installation atop the old plant nursery, but the structures would require extensive work. In order to install the solar panels, she noted, they'd probably have to pay someone to haul the junk away. They remained ambivalent about the promise of solar energy, uncertain whether the benefits of installation would outweigh the hassle and the costs.

Large-scale energy development projects – including those that produce "clean" energy through wind and hydropower – unfold in ways that benefit some people more than others, particularly those who live where the projects are constructed. German energy policy was designed to mitigate this concern by scaling energy governance to the municipal level (recall Hermann Scheer's assertion that the energy transition would be made possible by the "free choices of individuals"). Yet citizen participation remains uneven at many sites of renewable energy development, and provisions for local energy governance is no guarantee that all members of a given community will be included in the siting and planning of development projects.

News reports on the transition's uneven impacts tend to focus on urban areas at the receiving end of power generated elsewhere, with less focus on how people at sites of renewable energy development are affected by the power generation projects in their midst. Less known is the fact that many from the rural middle class are unable to take part in energy development projects, or unwilling to stake claims on such projects regardless of whether they can afford them. My long-term research engages with ordinary affective exchanges to understand how this uneven participation takes form in everyday life. The breakfast circle offers a perspective on this, allowing me to track how renewable energy—and environmental politics more broadly—was indexed in offhand but consequential ways (Carlson and Stewart 2014).

Few of Volker and Regina's neighbors have entered the nursery since it was shut down 15 years ago. Most can only speculate as to what lies beyond the plastic children's pool that sits at the entrance to the structures. Walking through the space itself reveals that each of the glasshouses is its own microclimate of various flora and other materials. The glasshouse closest to the Janssens' house, for example, is alternately a carpenter's workshop, a trash depot, a garage and a playground. On one side, Volker's tools are arranged according to an apparent order; on the other side sit bicycles and the children's pool. Behind this structure are eight more glasshouses, each collapsing into its own form of apparent ruin, with chunks of glass and fiberglass missing from the ceiling and walls, the old cement growing tables covered in dirt and weeds, with irrigation hoses dangling from above, snaking down and around the old growing trays on the tables and floor.

If you kept going all the way to the metal barn on the other end of the compound, you'd find a stockpile of tools and trash, piles of broken glass and old plastic growing trays awaiting new uses, coils of rope and industrial chains with hand-sized links. If you were to walk through these structures with Laura, she would warn you to beware of the glass and the rust. The glasshouses are a lived and lively space, useful to the Janssens, if not in ways that their neighbors could immediately recognize. By linking the apparent disorder of the glasshouses— evident in Volker's work at rehabilitating them—with the disorder in Regina's life, Maike and others create a space for considering how the energy transition offers a horizon of personal possibility.

By arguing that Regina and Volker would have an easier time if they invested in photovoltaics, Dobbeners depict the Janssens as an antimodel for the 'green good life', a cautionary tale of what happens to someone who doesn't use their time or money in the way that they should. At the same time, these comments gloss over the complexities of the Janssens' situation, positing an abstract solution to the concrete and consequential problems posed by Angelika's encroaching blindness. Bypassing the question of how to help Regina at a difficult time, Dobbeners' speculations about the Janssens generated the terms for speaking about the transition as a social project.

Significantly, those who commented on Volker and Regina's situation belonged to middle class families that had yet to invest in renewable energy technology. Their comments work to suspend the question of whether they themselves might invest in renewables by laying the charge of renewable energy investment at the door of absent others who "have money." It's important to note that, in a region where men continue to dominate opportunities for formal participation in the renewable energy sector, the breakfast circle illuminates one way in which women impact the transition's unfolding, namely by shaping how renewable energy is understood in everyday life.

In my writing and thinking I return frequently to the case of the Janssens, who have yet to install solar panels on the roof of the old plant nursery. Although Angelika's sight remains vulnerable (if temporarily preserved through medical intervention), I do not wish to imply that the Janssens' life and circumstances are more exigent than others in Dobbe or the breakfast circle. Nor do I wish to dwell on the question of whether the people of the village were accurate in their assessment of Volker's wealth. Rather I find it remarkable that they presumed the Janssens to be wealthy in the first place, and framed Regina's life as a problem to be solved through ecocapitalist investment. Volker and Regina's life diverges from the expected norm in a region where prosperity is increasingly articulated in terms of ecocapitalism.

Susan Lepselter (2005) notes that "spaces of *departure* from the rooted signs of class position are often the most intricately imagined, as well as the most despised." Through the figure of Regina, her purchasing of the finest groceries, her husband's seemingly senseless work in the glasshouses, and her skipping gatherings because of her daughter's condition, Dobbeners sense out a "parallel shape of desire exposed amid the pervasive narrative culture of class mobility" (ibid: 145) one that does not square with emergent—if implicit—understandings of social and economic citizenship.

Narratives of the green good life suggest that "only outlaws would refuse the gift of state fertility" offered by renewable energy (Tsing, 2012: 146). Yet the Janssens themselves do not speak of their hesitation to install solar panels as a refusal of the transition's fertile gifts. Rather, their actions illuminate alternate ways of living out the transition, without recourse to narratives of ecocapitalist plenty. Even as their neighbors invoke the Janssens' struggles as a case for the 'green good life', Volker and Regina challenge us to consider what stories of the good life conceal and reveal, what they make possible, what (and whom) they deny, and the forms of life that flourish beyond their bounds.

REFERENCES

Carlson, J., and Stewart, K., 'The Legibilities of Mood Work,' *New Formations* 82 (2014): 114–133.

Forrester, P., 'If *p* then what? Thinking in Cases,' *History of the Human Sciences* 9, no. 3 (1996): 1–25.

Lepselter, S., 'The License: Poetics, Power, and the Uncanny,' in *E.T. Culture: Anthropology and Other Spaces,* ed. Debbora Battaglia, Durham (Duke University Press, 2005).

Povinelli, E. A., 'The Social Projects of Late Liberalism,' *Dialogues in Human Geography* 3, no. 2 (2013): 238.

Scheer, H., *The Solar Economy: Renewable Energy for a Sustainable Global Future,* New York (Routledge, 2013), 325.

Stewart, K., *A Space on the Side of the Road,* Princeton (Princeton University Press, 1996); [sociologist Beverley Skeggs offers an extended discussion of the term in 'Imagining Personhood Differently: Person Value and Autonomist Working-Class Value Practices,' *The Sociological Review* 59, no. 3 (2011): 496–513].

Tsing, A., "Unruly Edges: Mushrooms as Companion Species," *Environmental Humanities* 1 (2012): 146.

2 3

FILMING SEX/GENDER: THE ETHICS OF (MIS) REPRESENTATION

Anna Wilking

AS A VISUAL ANTHROPOLOGIST, I WENT TO THE FIELD WITH THE INTENTION of making a documentary film about one of my informants, while also conducting ethnographic research with sex workers who worked on the streets of the historic district of Quito, Ecuador. Over the three years I ended up staying in the field, I spent time with forty women. I examined how they negotiated their multifaceted identities as mothers who were also sex workers – subjectivities frequently viewed as mutually exclusive in Latin America, where religiously inflected gender norms often position mothers as saint-like figures in the social imaginary and sex workers as fallen women, sinners in the eyes of the Catholic Church. I planned to make a film that would use one woman's story to represent the lives I saw around me – a narrative based on a single mother who had turned to sex work to support her children. Instead, I made a film about an exception. This case is about this (mis)representation.

In Ecuador and throughout Latin America, where sex work is decriminalised, prostitution is a viable work option for women who lack formal education. Although they typically earn roughly the same amount as the other jobs they qualify for in the domestic service industry or manufacturing sector, these women chose sex work, and in particular, street prostitution, because as freelance workers they could set their schedules around the needs of their children. Indeed, the women who solicited clients on the streets of Quito's historic centre worked regular nine to five hours, coming and going as they pleased in the middle of the day to shuttle their children between school and daycare.

They also confined their work to daylight hours because they worked in a neighbourhood that transformed into an open drug market at night. They were not organised in any formal way, but due to the rapid gentrification occurring throughout the historic district, my informants were starting to unite to fight for their right to remain in the area. In my film, I wanted my viewers to see that these sex workers were typical Ecuadorian women, who had jobs that they treated like any other.

It will resonate with anyone who has ever made or attempted to make a documentary film, that I had series of false starts. I started filming Javier and his children one day while waiting for my intended protagonist to show up. Eventually, Javier and his children became my primary protagonists. He was the partner of one of the sex workers – Kati – and was always on the streets. Their household was unusual for Ecuador: Javier was the main childcare provider for their three children, while Kati supported the family through sex labour. Their youngest child, Josue, was born with severe cognitive and physical delays and needed full-time care, which Javier lovingly provided. In fact, part of why Javier was the principal parent was that it was he, rather than Kati, who had the patience and skill to care for Josue, as my film depicts in several raw, emotional scenes.

Javier, his children and I spent our days on the streets, so it comes as no surprise that he became one of my closest informants. Javier described the complex social relationships, and in particular, the dynamics of drug trafficking in the neighbourhood. Early on, he established himself as my unofficial bodyguard during fieldwork, a role magnified once I told him my plans to start filming. Javier thought I was extra vulnerable in the area as an outsider, which was probably true, though over my three years in the field I became comfortable and as long I left before sunset, I always felt safe. We made a deal that he would look after me, and in exchange, I would take him and his children to Carmen's cafeteria, where lunches costs $1.50 for soup and a main course.

Even though I had been worried about the ethical issues involved in making a film with any of the sex workers, my discomfort was compounded with Javier and Kati because they were more marginalised than my other intended protagonists. They were both addicted to base, a yellow powder that has a similar effect to crack cocaine. Significantly cheaper than cocaine at $1a baggie, base is the drug of choice of South America's most impoverished citizens. Although the possession of all drugs for personal use is now legal in Ecuador, I was worried about exposing their consumption. Though it was farfetched, I wondered if they could get in trouble with the Ecuadorian child protection services. I was also uncertain to what extent their families knew about their drug use and Kati's involvement in the sex industry.

I discussed my plans with Javier and Kati for the final product – that I hoped the documentary would travel widely on the international film festival circuit, obtain theatrical or televised release, become available publicly online and ultimately receive distribution. There was the potential for countless people to become intimately acquainted with the details of their lives, which anyone, regardless of their subject position, might feel uncomfortable with, but for individuals who were already facing discrimination and stigmatisation, the stakes seemed particularly high.

I was particularly cognisant of how the final product might produce surprising results, as neither my protagonists nor I could have anticipated the success of my first film, *Carmen's Place* (2009), which focused on transgender teenage sex workers living at a homeless shelter run by an Episcopal priest in Queens, New York. It played widely on the international festival circuit, obtained distribution and is still in circulation today. I had thought I was making a film in obscurity that would never amass a public audience, so I had not approached my protagonists with the same caution. The success of *Carmen's Place* caught us all off guard, but luckily, the people in my film had been supportive of me throughout the process and were pleased with the end results.

Having learned my lesson from *Carmen's Place* – that my film with Kati and Javier might circulate more widely than I anticipated and that I would not be able to control its path once it was released – I started running through possible outcomes. What if, for example, Kati's mother was to find out about her drug use by watching my documentary on YouTube one day? (This particular worry turned out to be moot because during the filming, Javier, desperate to get Kati into rehab, told her mother every detail of their lives.) What if my narrative about Kati was viewed as representative of all the sex workers in Quito's historic centre? I did not want my audience to associate drug use with sex work, since most of the women did not consume drugs. Nonetheless, I was intrigued by Kati and Javier's story because they were one of the few dual-parent households I had come across in Ecuador where the father was the primary child provider.

Filming went relatively smoothly for a while, until 'it' happened – the major climax of the story. Kati disappeared. I had become extremely close to them by that time and when Javier called me to say that Kati had not come home in two days, I feared the worst. I was absolutely distraught and as Javier and I checked the city's morgues, hospitals and prisons, continuing my film was the last thing on my mind. I have almost no footage from that day, or the days that followed. The footage I do have is terrible quality; as the snippets I include in the film show, much of it is out of focus, has inconsistent audio tracks and is riddled with other technical difficulties. For many in my filmmaking circles, this wrinkle in the plot was viewed as narrative gold: my film had achieved a punctuated climax that many other filmmakers only dream about. But for me, due to the unusual duration and intensity of my filming Javier and Kati, my interpersonal relationships with them took precedence over getting the story. My professionalism as a filmmaker had worn thin, which I accepted as a natural consequence of this project.

Filming came to a halt in the days and weeks that followed Kati's disappearance as we began to realise what had happened. Kati had moved to a nearby city, Ambato, with her lover and was not coming back. Javier and the children went back to his family's house in Guayaquil –his natal city on the coast, while Kati and her new partner established their lives in Ambato. At this point, I decided to put the film to rest. It had taken an emotional toll on me, and I felt depleted. Now that Kati and Javier were living in different cities in Ecuador, I also knew it was not feasible to continue on a practical level. Kati had left her children and I did not want to make a film about a 'bad' mother.

However, for my own sake, I felt compelled to go to Ambato to find Kati to verify that she was alive and well. I brought my camera in case she wanted to record an interview about the struggles she had faced leading up to her decision to leave. When I finally found her in the red-light district, Kati wished to share her story on camera.

The recording recounted Javier's first week back in Guayaquil, where he was staying with his brother in Kati's absence. Prior to this, Kati and Javier had claimed that Josue's developmental problems were related to Kati having fallen on three different occasions during her pregnancy; this is what they told doctors, family and everyone on the street. But, in the interview Javier shares with the audience that Kati smoked base throughout her pregnancy with Josue, who was born with severe cognitive delays.

Everyone sympathised with Kati, but no one was fooled. It was common knowledge that Kati and Javier were addicts, especially since they procured base from dealers in the neighbourhood and lived in a single occupancy hotel known for its drug consumption. When Javier showed up with Josue in his stroller, the sex workers were always cordial but as soon as they were out of sight, they gossiped wildly about Josue's condition, all of them shaking their heads and tsk-tsking. As a result, the interview is powerful because Javier finally acknowledges that Kati had never fallen during pregnancy.

Immediately following Javier's disclosure, we see Kati share her story. This was the interview I filmed in Ambato after her disappearance. It was one of the last times I ever saw her. In the interview, Kati explains why she abandoned the family: she was fed up with Javier's abuse, of being the breadwinner and of working in the sex industry. The interview ends on a heart-breaking note. When asked whether she would see her children again, Kati wistfully states that she would indeed, once she gets her own apartment, where she will bring them – one day. We later learn that Kati does not contact her children over the next several years.

Although everyone understood why Kati would leave Javier due to abuse or because she fell in love with someone else, no one in their social circles, including her family, could comprehend why she would leave her children. Back on the streets in Quito, the sex workers were horrified by Kati's decision, as many of them were single mothers who had turned to the sex industry to give their children a stable future.

I decided to continue with the film. I took a long break to regroup and figure out how to move forward. The film's narrative arc ended up focusing on Javier's redemption story. Over the next couple of years, I travelled to Guayaquil once a month to film Javier as he got back on his feet. Indeed, he made a lot of positive changes. First and foremost, he became sober after thirty-three years of smoking base. He also applied to government aid for families with special needs children and settled into permanent, family-owned housing.

My story did not turn out to be about a sex worker or the plight of a single mother. Instead, it is the sympathetic portrait of a single father, the ex-partner of a sex worker, who may or may not have been abusive.

While conducting my research and in writing, I had not wanted to present sex workers in a bad light. In hindsight, I can see how problematic it was that I had wanted to construct a decidedly positive portrayal of sex workers' lives, a portrayal reminiscent of the old ethnographic 'noble savage' trope. In turning away from the story of a heroic mother and toward a struggling father, I have also seen the value of focusing on what is neither obvious nor representative.

Javier remains the only single father I have met in Ecuador. That I could have initially overlooked the value of his story strikes me as telling of the lack of space that exists – not only in the gendered politics of Ecuadorian life, but in anthropological stories as well – for men to be caregivers.

This is an important lesson for the anthropology of sex and gender. As a woman interested in gender equality, compelled to study female sex workers because I was drawn to their specific struggles as *women*, it finally dawned on me the extent to which I had privileged the female experience in all my work. Although I had been hesitant about using Javier as the protagonist because I had wanted to make a film about a single mother, the film continues to be a story about parenthood – not a simple, glorious parenthood, but a messy parenthood, fraught with contradiction. In this sense, my documentary is not just a (mis) representation, but it is also an interference, shifting the collective gaze of sex work away from the body of the woman, while making room for vulnerable, nurturing masculinities to be part of the story.

The story I set out to tell never materialised, but as is often the case, I ended up with something much more powerful. Lesson learned. As filmmakers and ethnographers, our most compelling contributions are often those that emerge once we let go of our burdens of representation – in the sociological sense – of having a case stand in for the majority.

I am not suggesting that we no longer think about how we represent our informants. Making the film was arduous, but I am grateful for my anxiety along the way. I still remain unresolved and somewhat uncomfortable about Kati's portrayal, which is part of the reason I write to address these issues. Representation of any sort is fraught, its ethics slippery rather than black or white. Perhaps that discomfort is part of the exchange, something that accompanies the gift of my protagonists' stories; perhaps the question 'could it have been done better?' is something that should haunt us, forming part of our ethical responsibility.

24

THREE MILLIMETRES

Christine Labuski

THE FIRST TIME I ENCOUNTERED JUDY I WAS WITH DR ERLICH, GATHERING fact sheets about vulvar pain conditions. Dr Robichaud, the other physician at the Vulvar Health Clinic (VHC),[1] and a new resident entered the pod in a white-coated blur – animatedly conferring, hastily scribbling on forms that they were pulling from filing cabinets, and getting on the phone to arrange an obviously urgent surgery for the woman whose story they had just heard. Amid the chaos, Dr Robichaud told us that their patient – Judy – had one of the severest cases of lichen planus (LP) that she'd ever seen: her labia were so fused together that she was urinating through a three-millimetre vulvar opening. The procedure that Dr Robichaud was scheduling would both surgically correct the problem and evaluate how much of Judy's vaginal patency it was possible to restore.

Judy was not the first woman I'd met whose genitalia were a source of distress. Prior to the fieldwork that I conducted in the VHC, I had been a nurse practitioner, and for almost fifteen years I managed the gynaecological needs of uninsured and low-income women in several US cities. During those years, I observed that the majority of my patients knew little about their genital anatomy and I frequently attended to the repercussions of this: removing tampons or condoms believed by patients to be 'lost' in their vaginas; excising vulvar warts for patients who struggled to understand their mode of transmission; and describing, often after the fact, the important differences between hormonal and barrier contraceptive methods regarding pregnancy and infection. I chose the VHC as an anthropological field site because I wanted to know if and how the awkward relationships between my patients and their genitals were changed by the presence of life-altering symptoms. I wanted to know, in other words, if a pressing need for clinical attention, as opposed to a less immediate one for bodily awareness, made it easier to ask, 'Can we talk about my genitals?'

Genitalia pose multiple dilemmas for critical gender scholars. Aside from the ongoing project of destabilising the sex/gender binary along which genital anatomy is frequently interpreted, feminist and queer sexuality scholars wrestle with definitional, behavioural and classificatory questions in our analyses of genitalia, and we work both with and against efforts to medicalise and sexualise these overdetermined body parts. We also recognise that advancing greater bodily and sexual self-determination (when that is a goal) may incite a 'sexuality' whose construction Foucault cautioned us to interrogate. In investigating vulvar disease conditions like Judy's, then, I think about the stakes involved in saying more about her labia rather than less: that my work will reify essentialist notions of 'female' genitalia, or that Judy's pain will become a vehicle for ideas about her body that don't resonate with her own experience. I also think about how Judy's knowledge of her vulvar anatomy is cultivated by a broader cultural dis-ease with women's non-reproductive genitalia, and how this can lead to material loss by disease and/or excision. And when I assemble all of these thoughts, I settle on the side of saying more. A whole lot more.

Though perhaps more familiar to anthropologists via its role in female genital cutting debates,[2] the vulva has been an erratic site of investigation for feminists, sexologists and other gender scholars, including its relative role in sex assignation,[3] sexual deviance[4] and bodily aesthetics.[5] Composed of two sets of labia (outer and inner), a clitoris and its hood, urinary and vaginal openings and several sets of secretory glands, vulvas have been both ignored and reclaimed by feminists, often in concert with broader political projects. In my own work, I posit that vulvas in the contemporary United States are best understood as disavowed. The concept of disavowal, in which objects are simultaneously brought to and erased from our attention, helps me to explain the ways that hyper-sexualised vulvas, stripped by cosmetic reduction procedures, contain increasingly less anatomical flesh. It can also explain how even physicians who specialise in vulvar disease conditions contour their definitions of 'getting better' around the ability to engage in penetrative sex, i.e., transforming their object of care from vulvar sensation to heteronormative – and vaginal – behaviour. As genitalia that are irreducible to procreative or heteronormative bodily capacities, as flesh that can be involved in but that ultimately exceeds vaginal penetration, vulvas are anatomy that compel us to 'ask more'[6] about whether and how 'our genitals make us who we are'.[7]

Though there are a host of issues specific to vulvar disease conditions, there were also commonalities between the patients I met as a nurse practitioner and the women I met at the VHC. In both sites, women were paralysed by the embodied knowledge that while good patients compliantly reported their symptoms, nice women refrained from speaking about their genitals. That is, and despite the ubiquity of some forms of genital 'talk' (e.g., pornography; waxed and manicured 'va-jay-jays') the disavowing nature of a word like 'cunt' structures the ways that vulvas are lived. This dis-ease can extend to non-expert clinicians who encounter – and often fail – women like Judy. In this case, I argue that Judy's labia suffer from impoverished definitions of genitalia, definitions that exclude body parts that exceed penetrative sexual activities. I outline how Judy's fused labia tell a story about which bodies are sexual and which are not, and show how a three-millimetre opening in Judy's vulva indexed the harmfully limiting perspectives of providers who were charged with her care.

LOSS

Lichen planus is an autoimmune disease marked by an overproduction of inflammatory discharge that, if not interrupted, can contribute to permanent scarring, compromised patency and decreased elasticity of the vagina. Due to anatomical proximity (and gravitational pull), LP can also lead to vulvar problems, including a loss of suppleness and contour erosion of the labia, and decreased flexibility and mobility around the clitoris and its hood. Narrowed vaginal patency thwarts the efforts of women and their partners to engage in penetrative sexual activity and, for many, this behavioural dimension of their condition – rather than ongoing discomfort or evident contour change – is the reason they ultimately seek care.

Judy told Dr Robichaud that it was 'taking [her] ten minutes to pee', not knowing that medical professionals see vaginal discharge as the likely cause of her problem. Tellingly, Judy's understanding of her disease condition was organised around urinary problems rather than an inflamed vagina in need of treatment. Like other patients at the VHC, she had lived with (and normalised) difficult symptoms for quite some time before trouble emptying her bladder convinced her that something was wrong. What she learned at her first visit was that a 'healthy' genital opening enables a variety of bodily functions, including but not limited to penile penetration; a constricted one, on the other hand, can make vaginal entry difficult as well as trap genital discharge.

The irreversible skin changes sustained by Judy's genitals made me incredibly sad and when I came home from the clinic that day, I told my housemate – a computer programmer who always listened to my stories with genuine curiosity – all about it. After I'd recounted the details, he asked me why and, more precisely, *how* this could happen to a woman with health insurance in the contemporary United States.

In my frustration, I replied 'Because nobody gives a shit about a sixty-two-year-old woman's genitals', a sentiment that I believed wholeheartedly at the time.

And though my assertion was woefully hyperbolic – many people care tremendously about and for the genitals of women of all ages, including women themselves – I nevertheless want to argue that in the case of vulvar neglect, Judy's age compounds rather than causes the disavowal through which her genitalia were clinically apprehended. The compromised access that Judy and the VHC clinicians had to her (sexual) body on the day she came to the clinic resonates with the inadequate capacity of non-expert providers to properly attend to her disease condition.

PRESERVATION

Many autoimmune diseases are notoriously enigmatic, but LP is fairly easy to recognise and manage by knowledgeable gynaecologists and dermatologists. To better understand the ways that Judy's vulva was both seen and not seen, however, it is helpful to know more about the drugs involved in her treatment regimen and, even more importantly, how they were deployed by the providers she saw before seeking treatment at the VHC.

Almost a year before Judy came to the vulvar clinic, she had secured a diagnosis for her condition from a dermatologist I will call Doctor A. Doctor A was a friend of Judy's from her years of working in research hospitals. At the time that her symptoms began, she had just moved. Since she had not yet secured a local health care provider, she called Dr A for what she hoped would be an easy consultation about her genital irritation. Based on what Judy told him, Dr A presumptively diagnosed lichen planus and prescribed a topical steroid, which Judy immediately procured and began using. Cautioning her about some of the more serious side effects of steroids, including immune system compromise, Dr A encouraged Judy to use the medication sparingly, backing off when her symptoms were under control.

Judy complied with this regimen, but it was not long before the steroid could not control her symptoms. When she called Dr A to report this, he referred her to a local colleague – Dr B – who biopsied Judy's vulva and gave her a definitive diagnosis of LP. Dr B switched Judy to a higher-potency steroid and an immune system modulator called *tacrolimus*. But despite the decreased risks associated with this second drug, Judy was encouraged to use the medications only when her symptoms were acute or troublesome.

The problem with this regimen, as the physicians from the VHC well knew, is that LP is an unpredictable and idiosyncratic condition, equally likely to flare in stressful and stress-free situations. For this reason, the vulvar experts at the VHC encouraged patients to use their medications liberally and regularly at first, in order to establish good symptom control; subsequent backing off would then be done under physician guidance and in order to establish whether particular stressors could be identified, predicted and avoided. This seemingly small material difference – the amount of medication prescribed by a physician – is in part a reflection of a provider's clinical orientation, with 'conservative' clinicians wanting to use fewer clinical interventions, including pharmaceutical ones. But in Judy's case, the amount of medication prescribed by Dr Robichaud reflected an acknowledgment that her vulva was relevant and worth preserving – materially and vitally. Here, a less conservative approach toward disease management is simultaneously a queerer stance toward non-reproductive genitalia.

Under Dr B's care, Judy's LP became so severe that her labia fused together. Although not as clinically urgent as the day she presented in the clinic – she could urinate normally, and her vaginal opening was technically patent – Judy's labia were markedly flattened in contour, and she could not accommodate any vaginal penetration. Significantly, and according to Judy, she and her husband were having 'difficulties' at the time, and their sexual activity had more or less ceased. Judy shared this with Dr B, who subsequently recommended that Judy just 'leave it closed' (referring to her vulva and vagina) unless and until she 'needed it' again. Unaware of alternatives, and in a relationship with her genitals that was penetratively circumscribed, Judy agreed to the plan. It was just over a year later, at the start of the more dramatic urinary problems described above, that Dr B referred Judy to the VHC, aware that she now probably needed corrective surgery.

The now of Dr B's decision indexes the differences in kind (rather than degree) between the VHC physicians – Drs Robichaud and Erlich – and more generalist providers through which women without access to specialist care might come to understand their condition. At the VHC, new LP patients were not only encouraged to use liberal amounts of steroids and immune system modulators (like *tacrolimus*) in order to achieve good symptom control, they were also taught to understand the nature of their affliction. Importantly, this included the knowledge that neither medication would halt the (over)production of LP's vaginal discharge. In fact, patients were taught to expect regular exacerbations, even with good pharmaceutical control, and that all people diagnosed with genital LP[8] were at risk of labial contour change, erosion and vaginal scarring. VHC patients and clinicians also knew that in cases like Judy's, where the vagina fuses into a 'classic' apple-core shape, surgically cutting through the fused area was the only way to restore so-called normal vaginal patency.

Drs Robichaud and Erlich, in the role of vulvar experts, consistently and actively worked against disease progression. And though I attribute this practice to their distinct orientation toward vulvar well-being, it is also good preventive medicine. Managing a patient's chronic condition as if it could worsen at any time is standard clinical practice in any speciality area, and most providers routinely do this with a wide variety of diseases (e.g., diabetes and hypertension). In this larger context, managing LP without planning for this kind of complication signals indifference towards the preservation of a symptomatic woman's external genitalia.

Since LP typically afflicts women in their fifties and sixties, decades often reported as a woman's 'post-reproductive' years, an inflammatory obstruction of the vagina can become conflated with the allegedly unnecessary maintenance of robust labia, and women like Judy can get to a point where doctors present 'leaving [their vulvas] closed' as a reasonable option. In contrast, the physicians at the VHC encouraged patients to be proactive in maintaining their vaginal patency, or what they called 'capacity'. This could be done either through regular vaginal intercourse with a partner or, preferably, with the regular (daily) use of a therapeutic dilator; Dr Robichaud, for example, typically recommended that her patients keep a dilator inserted in their vaginas for two fifteen-minute sessions per day. While consensual and desired intercourse was also encouraged, dilators were preferred because they could be used more predictably, with greater patient control and with far fewer problems during the sometimes acutely uncomfortable flares of LP.

This treatment plan, in contrast to the one initially presented to Judy, was derived from an investment in the anatomical and physiological wellbeing of the vulva and vagina, without regard to the 'need' for vaginal penetration or sexual activity. Liberal prescriptions and applications of medications, close monitoring for undesirable side effects, careful instruction about the nature of LP and treatment strategies geared toward maintaining as much vulvar and vaginal anatomy as possible were the material contours through which a patient at the vulvar clinic came to experience her disease condition. These material strategies were obliged to a female genital imaginary in which optimal vaginal patency and vulvar contour were more than simply options to be considered: they were anatomical ground to be preserved.

Although their tools, in the form of immune system modulators, were virtually identical to one another, the physicians described here wielded them with distinct agendas regarding the use-value of female genitalia. Non-expert physicians' lack of information about the condition and treatment of lichen planus evinces how the lines between ill-informed and substandard care often blur. In Judy's case, these unstable boundaries – between conservative clinical management, medical misogyny and casual disregard – convey a casual and pernicious disregard for vulvar integrity. The vulva with which Judy struggled to come to terms was a bodily instantiation of overlapping discourses regarding female sexuality, excess, reproduction, heterosexuality, 'health' (Metzl and Kirkland 2010) and genital normativity. Ethnographic attention to these dynamic boundaries can reveal the disavowing and active nature of discourses that rob many women of a genital 'capacity'. Without explicitly proclaiming that they 'don't give a shit' about the genitals of these women, institutionally located actors convey this sentiment in their everyday acts of evasion, erasure and disparagement.

The last time I saw Judy was when she came to the clinic for a post-operative visit. She was bearing a mountainous basket of blueberry muffins and thanking Dr Robichaud for the genitals she'd 'given back' to her. Of her (sexual) relationship with her husband, she told us, 'We're in a great spot; the best in thirty years'. But what I hope to have made clear is that Judy acquired far more than surgical correction from the vulvar clinic physicians. She also acquired a vulva in which she was now invested. Through this novel imaginary, she could manage her symptoms as well as generate an expanding number of genital behaviours in which her vulva might engage. Her previous casual disregard for her genitalia, cultivated by at least two physicians and through an actively disinvested cultural milieu, had been replaced – at least for the time being – by the practice of getting up 'pretty flippin' early' for the dilator sessions that she knew would help to preserve her genital vitality.

Neurologist Wilder Penfield began mapping the somatosensory cortex in 1932, but it took almost twenty years before genitalia were included on his homunculus, the term he used to describe the brain's proportional representation of various body parts. And though female epileptics were among the patients whose brains he studied, vulvas and vaginas were not depicted in the maps that eventually contained genitalia. I wonder about the genealogy of this absence – how it can be tracked from dermatologists who recommend 'leaving [a vulva] closed' to cosmetic surgeons whose business models depend on widespread vulvar dis-ease. Taking care of women like Judy requires rendering vulvas thinkable irrespective of the penetrative terms of medical and heteronormative discourses. It also requires that we include disregard and disavowal in our list of symptoms to be resolved.

ENDNOTES

1 The names of people and places in this essay are pseudonyms.

2 Shell-Duncan, B., 'From Health to Human Rights: Female Genital Cutting and the Politics of Intervention', *American Anthropologist*, 110.2 (2008), 225–36.

3 Terry, J., 'Anxious Slippages between "Us" and "Them": A Brief History of the Scientific Search for Homosexual Bodies', in J. Terry and J. Urla, eds., *Deviant Bodies: Critical Perspectives on Difference in Science and Popular Culture* (Bloomington, IN: Indiana University Press, 1995), pp. 129–69.

4 Frueh, J., 'Vaginal Aesthetics', *Hypatia*, 18.4 (2003), 137–58.

5 Fields, J., *Risky Lessons: Sex Education and Social Inequality* (New Brunswick, NJ: Rutgers University Press, 2008), 168.

6 Karkazis, K., *Fixing Sex: Intersex, Medical Authority, and Lived Experience* (Durham, NC: Duke University Press, 2008), 13.

7 Lichen planus can also affect oral mucosa.

25

THE DISCERNMENT OF KNOWLEDGE: SEXUALISED VIOLENCE IN THE MENNONITE CHURCH

Stephanie Krehbiel

THIS CASE BEGINS WITH AN UNSETTLING EMAIL. IT CAME FROM A POWERFUL man of the church, a Mennonite executive, and it was a response to an email from me, in which I told this leader that he was perpetuating violence against queer people.

I was an ethnographer writing about the Mennonite movement for queer justice, and I also *was* a Mennonite, at least by background. In the interviews I was doing with LGBTQ Mennonites around the country, I kept hearing the word 'violence': rhetorical violence, spiritual violence, institutional violence, systemic violence. The violence they spoke of was often quiet and subtle, invisible to many. It happened in the wording of denominational statements, in all the ways in which LGBTQ identities were cast as worldly distractions from more important church work; inherited patterns of sexual shame that thrived on the spectre of a monstrous sexual outsider were evident within families. They were made more evident still in the process of what Mennonites call 'discernment'.

Mennonites have little in the way of doctrine. What they do have are committees, some of which are called 'discernment groups'. Listening committees are a regular feature of Mennonite discernment, particularly in the realm of

LGBTQ people, who in the course of the forty-year history of their organising within Mennonite contexts have often been invited to 'share their stories' in front of appointed listeners. I will return to discernment, but for the moment, I will say two things about it.

One, I don't believe I know any LGBTQ Mennonites for whom the word 'discernment' fails to produce groans, eyerolls and other expressions of deep cynicism. For them, discernment about whether they are acceptable to the church has rarely yielded anything more than promises of more discernment. Two, the powerful church leader whose email I am about to quote has written a book about discernment and its role in understanding God's will.

I had initially approached this leader with the presumption that he would be an informant, but when you're doing ethnography on the same religious group that you grew up in, boundaries get fuzzy. Many of the people I could call 'informants' I relate to in multiple ways: friends, family, antagonists, co-conspirators, to name a few. I have not attended a Mennonite church for almost fifteen years, but my last name, Krehbiel, is a common one in Mennonite circles, and thus I can never present myself without revealing some piece of my own history. The name 'Krehbiel' generates questions such as, 'Who are your parents and grand-parents?' 'Where are you from?' and finally, 'Where do you go to church?' To this last one, the answer 'nowhere' is unremarkable for most of my informants. They have their own fraught relationships with church.

But for this leader, I knew immediately that my lack of church attendance would be an issue. His theology was based in binaries. In *The Book of Jerry Falwell*, Susan Harding writes of the evangelicals she studied, 'There is no such thing as a neutral position, no place for an ethnographer who seeks "information". Either you are lost, or you are saved.'[1] As with Harding's evangelical informants, this leader wanted to save me. Given how Mennonites had already marked me, it need not even be a dramatic conversion. It would be more a matter of gently urging me back into a semiotic universe in which I would be suitably chastened by his authority.

Prior to receiving my email, the leader had answered my lengthy questions about church polity and authority structures with a mentorly condescension. I learned about him from these exchanges, and it was invaluable to my work. I learned that he had specialised listening skills. He listened not for content but for rhetoric, the verbal cues that would place a person on the cultural/political map he seemed to carry in his head. Though he presented himself as a mostly power-less servant of the battling forces within his denomination, he communicated as someone who likes to control people, and I could tell he was measuring me, looking for my vulnerabilities. I learned that he prized his notion of himself as a detached intellectual, as the one who interprets what's *really* going on. I saw that he wasn't particularly good at recognising his own limitations; he was almost a parody of a mansplainer at times, used to women performing subservience to him. What did it say about the denomination I was studying, that this man had ascended to power within it? That's what I wanted to know.

But eventually, I got sick of the patronising. I wanted to break out of the rhetorical dance I was doing with this man. I could tell that at some level the exchange was hurting me; I was sleeping badly, unable to shake off the gnaw-ing sense of menace that I felt in the subtext of his communications. So I wrote him another email and told him that his repressive leadership reproduced the same patterns of violence and shame that I saw manifested in my own family. In response to that email, he wrote me this:

> Thank you so much for telling me about your family. This explanation helps me understand the context out of which you are writing. I felt the hot breath of your anger as I read and reread your email. I acknowledge your accusa-tions of violence and abuse. I do not take these accusations and judgments lightly; they strike me like sharp arrows in my heart... Since I am pastor at heart, your story stirs up deep empathy in me. I would love to sit with you in person to explore the ways that your church has failed to be there for your family in times of deepest need.

My memories of reading this email, two years ago, are physical. I was on the couch in my living room, and my body was suffused with adrenaline, pulsing shame, the familiar nausea of feeling an older man's predatory intent: *I fucked up. I brought this on myself.* Why on earth had I addressed him like this, as someone with whom I had a relationship built on any sort of trust? How did that serve me, methodologically speaking? I'd given him an invitation to address me as a pastor might address a lost sheep. I'd tried to break out of his rhetorical cage and walked right into his next trap.

To complicate the situation further, a friend with whom I shared the email I had written to the church leader asked my permission to publish it as an open letter on her popular blog about Mennonite sexual violence. I consented to this, and thus it appeared in a public forum even before he had responded to it. I later regretted allowing it to be posted like this. It wasn't that I was ashamed of what I'd written, but the public nature of the communication no doubt fuelled this leader's embrace of a martyr position in relation to my critiques. He was pierced in the heart by sharp arrows, flung indiscriminately by me in my fit of angry emotion. His response to me, of course, was private. He had to reset the stage, back into a context in which he had the authority to mediate my claims.

I'd written to him of a family incident several generations old, when my grandmother's sister was forced to apologise in front of her church for divorcing a husband who had cheated on her. The incident had a profound effect upon my grandmother, for reasons I suspect are tied to some sexualised abuse in her own past, alluded to but never named outright. She came back to the story of the public apology again and again, in vague fragments I tried to piece together, and when she died, I felt that I'd inherited a puzzle, something to do with the violence of a theology in which a heterosexual marriage bond is so sacred that it must be fed with sacrificial victims.

I was trying to get at something systemic, but this church leader insistently focused on the personal, transforming me into a *case* – not someone with an analysis of anything, just a person with an emotional problem. My academic work that critiqued his leadership and my advocacy for queer justice was just a symptom of something broken in my family; *he* was the one with intellectual remove.

My sense of ethnographic failure in this exchange was layered over something deeper and for me, profoundly Mennonite. I felt vulnerability and violation, coupled as always with an internalised admonition that my feelings of violation were histrionic and paranoid, taking up space in a world where far more consequential violations were taking place. Why did an unwelcome offer of pastoral care trouble me beyond the energy it would take to reject or ignore it? Somehow I could not bear the fact that he presumed.

In order to explain the kind of violence that Mennonites do, I have to start with their love of peace. Born out of the Anabaptist religious movement in sixteenth-century Europe, Mennonites hold nonviolence as a central tenet of their faith. For centuries, separatist Mennonite communities migrated through Europe, and eventually, to North and South America as well, settling wherever governments would accommodate their refusal to serve in militaries. Mennonites in the United States have forged their pacifism in response to the wars of the twentieth century, under the threat of conscription of their young men. Mennonite pacifism developed as a masculinist discourse, not only about men's choices in relation to the state, but about their choices in response to those who called them queers, among other things, for refusing to fight.

Mennonite men have trouble admitting, or even understanding, that they have power. It's a problem that comes with generations of defining themselves against dominant, warrior masculinities. This is a generalisation, of course. I've met plenty of thoughtful and reflexive Mennonite men, some of whom are gay, who recognise the problem of unacknowledged power and work to challenge it. But the problem remains.

Like many religious groups, Mennonites commit a lot of sexualised violence. I use the word 'sexualised' here rather than 'sexual', because it suggests a broader spectrum of violation, encompassing not only what bodies can do to other bodies, but also what theology, institutional structures and communal processes can manifest in the lives of those who are caught up within them. For the past seven years, while carrying out activism aimed at documenting the epidemic of sexual abuse in Mennonite churches, I've been writing about the ways in which Mennonite peace-making practices enable and perpetuate certain kinds of violence. Woven through all this work have been competing claims about what constitutes violence.

Carol Wise, director of the forty-year-old Brethren Mennonite Council on LGBT Interests, speaks of the 'violence of process' in Mennonite practice.[2] In Mennonite theology, God speaks not through divinely-appointed individuals but through community. In order to decide how God is speaking in a given situation, Mennonites engage in the process of 'discernment.' Who is worthy of being in the room when the discernment takes place, and whose claims to truth can be heard as the voice of God? For Mennonites, these questions are the stuff of schism.

Given this focus on discernment practices as a means to access truth, perhaps it is not surprising that when Mennonites want to push back against another Mennonite's claim of violence, they attack at the level of knowledge. It's less, 'you're lying,' and more 'What you think you know is based on a false way of knowing.' Or, with a more pastoral veneer, like the e-mail that so upset me, 'You make the claims that you make not because they are true but because you're damaged. Let's sit down together and talk about how you can be repaired.'

This essay, then, is about how knowledge is legitimised and authorised. In my experiences with Mennonites, nowhere does that contestation feel more acute than in the realm of sexualised violence and survivor advocacy. In the summer of 2015, after finishing my PhD, I helped to assemble a new chapter of the thirty-year-old, largely Catholic, Survivors Network of those Abused by Priests (SNAP). We are a small assemblage of Mennonites and ex-Mennonites, academics and activists. In the course of conducting my research on queer Mennonites, I had heard so many disclosures of sexual violence that I was desperate to act.

Most of us in the group, at some level, are struggling with the effects of trauma, be it primary or secondary. Few of us can walk comfortably into a Mennonite church. None of us has any official role within Mennonite church structures. We try to agitate from the outside, as whistleblowers, although sometimes the line between 'inside' and 'outside' feels as fuzzy in this activism as it does in ethnography. We collect the stories that are told to us: of adult women abused by pastors who offer them counselling, only to be told their experiences were 'consensual'; of students abused by professors at Mennonite colleges, and children abused by church members in congregations that rushed to forgive the perpetrators and isolated the parents of the abused child; of church officials who gaslight survivors and demand that they 'forgive' their abusers; of abusive pastors who manipulate congregations into loving them; and of incest, endless stories of incest, a violation that seems to set up so many of its survivors for a lifetime of encounters with predators. It is soul-searing work to collect these stories, to keep lists of perpetrator names that I can only reveal under the correct legal circumstances, and to see in horrific detail where Mennonite theology and communal practice has failed.

There seems to be no room within the practice of discernment for full acknowledgment of this reality. Mennonites, like so much of the rest of society, are perpetually waiting for the perfect survivor, innocent until violated, whose story can be managed into coherent narrative, unbroken by the memory fragmentation of trauma, that culminates in healing and reconciliation with the community, the perpetrator and God. This expectation is a trap, of course; real human beings never meet its standards of blamelessness. The stories I collect are mixed up with the failures of marriage, with alcohol and drugs that numb PTSD, with sexual yearning that is exploited, with buried queerness that manifests as sexual vulnerability, with thwarted attempts to resist sexual shame. To share and narrate these stories is to bear witness to a fundamental failure of the church's heterosexist sexual ethic. The monstrous sexual outsider has always been inside, and the monster has never been queerness.

Sometimes Mennonites who feel attacked by my work accuse me of having power I don't deserve. Usually these accusations come from angry men on the internet. Sometimes they call me 'Dr Krehbiel' as though it's an epithet, as if they're so affronted by the audacity of my title that they have to spit it out. They're right in a sense: I do have power. It's tied to having a PhD, but it's bigger than that. It's the power that comes from knowing the people for whom the existing sexual ethics aren't working; it comes with naming, with claiming, with pronouncing what is violence and what isn't, what is abuse and what isn't, what is love and what isn't. It is the also the power of secrets, of knowing things I'm not supposed to know. The church is supposed to have that power. The carefully selected discerning committee is supposed to have that power. The men who sneer 'Dr Krehbiel' at me aren't just afraid of what I represent, as a woman with a PhD. They are, I think quite literally, afraid of what I know.

*

My friend Jay Yoder, a queer Mennonite activist as well as a survivor of rape and sexual abuse, breaks down one of the ways that discernment takes power from survivors:

> So, you're the one who has experienced trauma and you have come out the other side with incredible and painfully-earned expertise. And you make yourself vulnerable and share that experience and expertise. Then church officials tell you that they're going to form a panel and serve as judge and jury as to whether your experiences ring true and are worthy of real change or if they just don't matter that much in the eyes of the church, and by turn, God. Where do they get off and just what makes them feel qualified to be an expert on realities that as a rule are not theirs?[3]

'Where do they get off?' That's the question we're always asking, in my Mennonite activist circles, with the double entendre fully intended. Mennonites don't like to talk about power and the way it organises their communities. To talk about power, it seems, is to admit that they are not peaceful. It could become an admission that discernment can be violent, that it can go wrong, that God could misspeak, or that the community could misspeak what God was trying to say. To talk about power might also be to acknowledge that power can be erotic. I suspect that denying the erotics of power makes those erotics all the more destructive.

My files are full of stories of queer people and sexual abuse survivors made to feel shame and then offered that consolation, the private, pastoral words, the words that make a person feel like an individual, aberrant *case*. Those encounters often end with something sexual, or something that feels sexual in a way that also makes the vulnerable person in the situation feel as though they've lost track of reality. When shame permeates sex, then talking about sexual violence or queerness becomes an act of intimacy. When the role of power in that intimacy is ignored, then, to again quote my friend Jay, 'power is a sexy secret.'

This essay began with an unsettling email, and to tell the truth, I'm still unsettled by it. I responded to that email with a finality that ended my correspondence with the presumptuous executive. I wrote, 'There isn't anything exceptional about my family stories. Please just add them to your body of knowledge; let them help you to historicise this particular moment in the denomination that you are directing. That's all I'm asking of you. Personally, I am fine.' I reclaimed my own authority. I asked that he respect what I know.

But what I really wanted to say was straight from my case files, from the many queer people and survivors who shared their story alone in a room to a caring church official, only to say later, after the betrayal, 'I want my story back.'

ENDNOTES

1 See Harding, S. F., *The Book of Jerry Falwell: Fundamentalist Language and Politics* (Princeton and Oxford: Princeton University Press, 2000).
2 Carol Wise, interview with the author, 22 October 2013.
3 Jennifer Yoder, interview with the author, 3 February 2016.

26

EARTHLY TOGETHERNESS: MAKING A CASE FOR LIVING WITH WORMS

Filippo Bertoni

IN THIS SHORT ESSAY, I WILL TRY TO CONVINCE YOU OF THE IMPORTANCE of earthworms in thinking about politics.

If this sounds like an argument, that is because it is. I first organised the materials in this essay to 'make a case'. They were part of a public thesis 'defence' that took place in the Netherlands, a place where, at the culmination of a degree, a researcher will stand before a committee of fully-gowned academics who weigh the evidence presented and, in courtly fashion, bestow an official verdict. This forum, metonymic of much of Euro-American politics, presents truth in terms of a binary relation. There are rights and there are wrongs. Which is why it is important to say at the outset that even as I make an argument, spending time with worms and the scientists who work with them unsettles argumentative politics. What you will see is that the purpose of 'making a case' may not be to be right, but to offer resources that we can use to metabolise and live with the world in alternative ways. Though I make an argument, I do not necessarily want you to agree. This is something I have learned by watching scientists who are watching earthworms. They have helped me to see how we might rework politics as usual, away from dreams of agreement and closer to the dirty and messy ongoings of compost.

Living together has been the focus of Euro-American political theory: from its mythical Greek origins so-called modern society was constructed on the idea that politics is a way to organise social life. Accordingly, the state of nature is violence and war, but political structures and institutions bring order to mankind through a social contract, which stipulates an agreement between members of the society. Politics serves to regulate what is legitimate violence and what forms of violence are in breach of the social contract.

Anthropology has complicated this view: going elsewhere, some Euro-American anthropologists pointed out that people in different places do politics differently. What living together is about in places beyond Euro-America messes with Euro-American categories. It turns out that social organisation is not just about (Euro-American ideas of) agreement and rational discussions but is equally informed by other systems of meanings and different ideas about the world and the cosmos.

In a second and related manoeuvre, Euro-American anthropologists looked not outward but inward. In doing so, they helped in the task of 'provincialising Europe': showing that what is often clumped together as 'the West' is not one thing. Even in the most 'familiar' places politics are already done in many – often surprising – ways.

Challenging this most recognised Euro-American way of doing politics is especially important today, as the limits of established Western democracies become more apparent – their violence morphing into novel neoliberal forms, spreading to engulf the planet and its ecological and geological entanglements. If we have managed to ignore the structural injustices and inequalities of the political systems we live within until now, these have spread too far and are coming back at us, albeit unequally but nonetheless with a vengeance, through planetary forces. As the sea rises to flood ever vaster swaths of land, ecological disruption easily overcomes the conceptual boundaries and categorical barricades erected by the West.

The political as manufactured in and traded by Euro-America relied on agreement (and war upon those who disagreed). But this politics of agreement has structurally excluded nature from its equations. That realm was imagined as categorically separate from politics, ruled by its own 'natural' laws. Defining this was not a political task, but a scientific enterprise. Even anthropologists have struggled to overcome this dualism: when encountering ways of doing politics other than their own, mostly they have remained limited by Euro-American understandings of the human, pinned down onto one unitary world, with one true nature and supposedly still disconnected from politics. It is to remedy the effects of such an expunction of the natural from the political that many scholars in the social sciences have begun to reconsider what nature is and what a politics of nature could be.

It is in this context that worms can be of help. They have certainly not been the object of political theory or anthropology before. And yet they have held a crucial role in the natural sciences, and in particular, in ecological thinking. To see this, it is enough to remember that Darwin himself dedicated over forty years of his life to the study of these invertebrates.

Darwin published the results of these studies in 1881, in his last monograph, *The Formation of Vegetable Mould through the Action of Worms*. There, he unravelled, with his usual meticulous attention, the crucial role of earthworms in all sorts of vital processes in soils. Not surprisingly, he was widely ridiculed by the media of the time for his efforts to introduce what detractors called 'the political worm'. Certainly the old man must have been misguided if he thought that worms were social beings.

And yet, since Darwin's time the centrality of earthworms to ecology has only been reinforced: worms' actions create the structure of our soils and the conditions necessary for soil fertility and plant life. Biologist Scott Turner, in his book *The Extended Organism*, went as far as to show how the evolution of a soil layer that successfully drains and irrigates the landmasses on Earth depends on worms' physiology: their original adaptation to life in water worked poorly as they ventured on land, and forced them to modify their environment to support their ill-adapted organs.

The centrality of worms to ecology also rests on their eating of organic matter. Eating, though, has been often marginalised by a philosophy obsessed with freedom, heroism and thought (the marginalisation often proceeds along the same fault line that splits nature from politics). In my work with ecologists, however, eating was not marginalised, but instead featured as a keystone in the theories that my informants used. Over the last two centuries, ecologists developed a theoretical language as well as practical measuring apparatuses to deal with a world in which life everywhere is engaged in eating and being eaten. They started with early simplifications of a predator-prey world, but their models have become complex, today encompassing trophic systems and nets – and depending on growing computational power.

Scientific descriptions and measures like those found in ecology textbooks offer important ways to imagine the world. But they focus on defining what nature is, true to the conceptual division of labour between politics and natural sciences. This is where my work separated from that of ecologists: I, too, was interested in worms. But, unlike the scientists I worked with, I was not interested in measuring and quantifying earthworms and their activities, but in how earthworms can challenge the way we do politics. I wanted to learn from them about how they are already engaged in politics *otherwise*, living *together with* scientists, and a host of incommensurable and radical others.

By attending to earthworms as they chewed up rocks and defecated fertile soils, I became less concerned with securing definitions about nature and more interested in the diversity of practices of living together that I encountered. The practices of living together I focused on were those that brought earthworms together with ecologists, naturalists, taxonomers, soil scientists and ecotoxicologists. And as I followed their work, I learned that as much as their profession compels them to define nature, to do so they are always-already living together with worms: they engage in earthworm togetherness, as it were. But the kind of politics I began to see there proved to not be exclusive to the ecologist's scientific practices. So, I also took on vermicomposting – the recycling of food waste with worms to make compost – myself. Like the worms in labs and collections, the worms in my bin taught me about living together, and they did so through eating and its metabolic relations.

By engaging in the quotidian, practical activities of composting I learned that to turn food waste into soil agreement is not necessary. Composting is not really about rational choices and democratic consensus. Sure, you can see choice if you want: do I build my own bin, or do I buy one? Do I feed the worms eggshells, or newspaper shreds? But as much as these decisions can be framed as rational and are clearly important to its success, composting is not made by them. Instead, it is the eating, decomposing, composting and rotting that goes on in the bin that runs the togetherness of compost.

Crucially, this togetherness is not about forming consensus around a common good, but about the coexistence of many different worlds that are not merely in agreement but hold together and come apart in differently relational ways. What is relevant in the compost bin is not just one kind of eating, but the complex mixture of microbial activities that go on inside the guts of the worms, how these change the molecular structures of compounds that are found in the bin, how these are then taken up by plant roots or other organisms, and so on. This pushes us to attend to the many different ways in which we can come to know and partake in practices of eating and being eaten.

The living together of worms can serve as a reminder to Euro-American social scientists that there are no guidelines out there on how to live together well. Instead, politics, when understood as living together, calls for makeshift arrangements that are both radical and specific, as well as for experimenting with alternatives. If composting might work through certain standard passages, composting guides never give any final word, but rather suggest some possible alternatives to tinker with.

The kind of politics that attending to earthworm lives makes apparent, then, is not one in which a common good is sought or achieved, but rather an asymmetric one that remains, notwithstanding the asymmetries, reciprocal and relational. This is a politics that does not resolve in a commons, but in togetherness. This politics is in tension with what Bruno Latour, the famous French philosopher and anthropologist of science, claims when he argues that we should 'redefine politics as the progressive composition of the good common world' (Latour 2004). The path Latour lays out for us is, today, an increasingly widespread path to approaching nature. Academics and politicians alike are telling us that to combat unwanted, uncontrollable global forces we should include nature into our political system. It is through this integration that we can face climate change and all sorts of environmental transformations.

But the variegated and asymmetrical 'living togethers' that earthworms participate in are not contingent upon this kind of agreement. Central to the togetherness of earthworms are differences, which are not something to be brushed away or to be made to be similar, but rather something to be appreciated and attended to. A brief example from one of my sites will help make this point clearer.

One of the scientists I worked with was interested in studying earthworms' impact on greenhouse gases. In her work she showed how earthworms contribute to emissions by helping organic matter to decay, a phenomenon she called 'global worming' (e.g., Lubbers et al. 2012). But, while her work consisted in quantifying emissions and searching for statistically convincing data that could help bring this effect to the attention of the climate change science-policy community, it did not stop there. Instead, she worked to describe the minute contingencies of the processes involved: certain functional groups of worms are more important than others; some climates and farming practices are more prone to stimulate the negative impact of worms than others; seasonal dynamics will transform the role of earthworms in some soils; specific details of standards in fertiliser use, farming, dealing with crops and land management will also have different impacts, and so on.

These details are the differences that are crucial to the togetherness earthworms can teach us, and that, I argue, we need to learn to appreciate – a challenge in a time so focused on seeking generalities rather than specificities. This appreciation of differences, again, is something for which there are no guidelines. Studying more won't tell us how to do this better – how to better stay with the differences. It will probably help us in understanding different aspects in other novel ways, but it won't tell us how things 'really' should be. For how things should be is something that doesn't happen once and for all but must be continually experimented and tinkered with. Over and over again.

A science-fiction reference does well in concluding this argument: 'The worm is the spice, the spice is the worm' is a quote from Dune, a 1984 adaptation for the silver screen of Frank Herbert's 1965 novel. In the world in which the movie takes place, giant sandworms on the planet Arrakis are involved in the biogeo-ecology of the spice 'mélange', which is exclusively mined there. Control of the spice means control of the universe, since the spice is essential to space travel. The ecological understanding of interconnectedness that dovetails with this quote – and its whole fictional universe – is the kind of togetherness I suggest. This is a togetherness that is not constrained by the limits of closed systems and of the categories that Euro-Americans commonly use to think about the world. It is instead a togetherness enlarged by the imaginative openings that worms, like anthropology, can offer us.

REFERENCES

Latour, B., *Politics of Nature: How to Bring the Sciences into Democracy* (Cambridge, MA: Harvard University Press, 2004).

Lubbers I. M. and others, 'Greenhouse Gas Emissions from Soils Increased by Earthworms', *Nature Climate Change* (2013).

27

REFUSING EXTRACTION: UNEARTHING THE MESSINESS OF ACTIVIST RESEARCH

Teresa A. Velásquez

FIG. 27.1 Two women walk through the Kimsacocha wetland slated for gold mining; in Quechua, Kimsacocha means 'three lakes'

HOW DO ETHICAL RESEARCH AGENDAS ALIGN WITH THE INTERNAL HETERO-geneity of social movements? If activist research methodologies seek to produce forms of knowledge that advance the political goals of our collaborators, what happens when they refuse to participate in what we believe to be an ethical research process? I ask these questions as a way to tease out the tensions experienced between me and my collaborators that occurred during field research.

In July 2013, I returned to the Southern Ecuadorian Andes to conduct research return: the sharing of findings with participants to seek their critical feedback. Having conducted fieldwork between 2008 and 2010 among anti-mining activists, my impressions were messy: scientific studies of water pollution sparked a local movement against a proposed Canadian-backed gold mine, but gender and racial/ethnic differences divided the movement in antagonistic ways.

Having agreed to participate in my earlier fieldwork, Rosita – one of my closest collaborators – refused to participate in the research return workshop. In this essay, I take the case of Rosita's refusal as a multi-layered feminist practice. In focusing on an act of refusal, I show how my failure to conduct research return among a group of women anti-mining activists is a story of the political conditions that entangle ethnographic research with processes of extraction, i.e., extractivism.

In 2013, I visited some of my closest informants – Doña Patricia, her two daughters and their neighbour Rosita – all of whom form a women's anti-mining group, to seek their participation in a research return workshop. Doña Patricia's home is a modest two-room house nestled in a flat valley surrounded by rolling hills. The zigzag fences created a patchwork of green and brown grassy pastures, demarcating those farms that had irrigation and those that did not. This was an area dominated by dairy farmers – some rich, some poor – who supplied milk to regional and national producers. The women in the group had come together against a proposed gold mine project located upland in their watershed.

They shared the same political goal but were a socially heterogeneous group that varied in ethnic ancestry, access to markets, education and age. Although not all the women were mothers, the organisation used the language of 'motherhood', cast in biological and environmental terms, to oppose the proposed gold mine: they defended 'Mother Earth' and sometimes represented themselves as *madres* [mothers] who worried about the mine's impacts on children.

FIG. 27.2 In the Azuay province of Ecuador, Andean peasant farmland relies upon the Irquis river, fed by upland streams where a gold mine has been proposed

FIG. 27.3 Where the Irquis river runs through the parishes of Victoria del Portete and Tarqui, large landowners, including the hacienda pictured here, have predominant access to irrigation water

Doña Patricia and the others quickly and enthusiastically agreed to participate in a research return workshop, which I referred to as *devolución*. The root word of *devolución* is *devolver*, an adjective that means to give back or return something to its original place. It comprises a little-written-about aspect of activist research methods that values collaborative knowledge production (see Hale 2001). Through research return, I sought to be accountable to systems of privilege and power that structure ethnographic field research (Lewis 1973).

Several days after our initial agreement was reached, Doña Patricia's daughter Ceci phoned to tell me that Rosita, relying on her authority as president of the women's organisation, had called off the meeting. According to Ceci, Rosita believed that the women in the group would have to stand up and provide some sort of testimony that I would document and take away with me to the USA. I called Rosita to talk through and clarify what I was hoping to achieve. After all, I had done extensive interviews with Rosita and thought that if I could just explain *devolución* in local terms of accountability (*rendir cuentas*) she would understand and, ultimately, want to know how I had incorporated their interviews into my study. My goal with *devolución* was to seek the women's validation of my research results in the hope that it could be used in ways to support their political agenda. But Rosita refused.

I was struck by the image that Rosita conjured of the *devolución*. She had evoked a public performance in which the information would circulate beyond her control. While most anthropologists would consider presenting one's research to the community in their native language an ethical act, I suspect that for Rosita the opposite was true. I wondered if Rosita feared the circulation of information within her community. Did she worry that certain information considered private would be made public, or perhaps that she would lose control over the political narrative about the women's group?

Rosita knew that I had been a doctoral student whose writing would be read by a largely English-speaking audience. During my initial fieldwork, she invited me to her home and maize patch many times and granted me two formal interviews. Her refusal to participate in return research belied the collaborative relationship I thought we had developed. Rosita never fully explained her refusal to hold a women's *devolución* workshop. Instead, she translated her concerns with the workshop into an idiom of extractivism – a term with negative implications that we both understood.

Rosita's evocation of extractivism reveals the awkward relationship between collaborators and anthropologists. While some scholars suggest that ethnographic research and the political agendas of activism may be mutually constructive, in my experiences such mutuality was complicated by the political conditions under which both set of actors labour. For instance, my initial research plan in 2008 did not exclusively focus on anti-mining activists, but then everyone wanted to know which side I was on. Some people silently eyed me with suspicion; others were more vocal and demanded to know my intentions. In an effort to earn trust, I let my political views guide my research. I aligned my research with the defence of watersheds from mineral extraction, hoping to use my research to support the rights of farmers who could be displaced by an industrial gold mine upstream.

As I learned in practice, the decision to politically support farmers did not take into account that anti-mining groups were internally fragmented and had competing political agendas. The movement's heterogeneity enabled connections with research that, in their partiality, maintained differences among our agendas. At times my enactment of ethnographic knowledge enabled a connection with the women's group, while at other times, their activist embodiment of refusal underscored the differences between the women's political agenda and my practice of anthropological research.

At the start of my fieldwork in 2008, the women's group allowed me to volunteer with them. I co-organised an international women's anti-mining conference and several popular education workshops on a variety of topics related to environment, health and human rights. Through these events, I documented the process through which, as one woman put it, the diverse group of women learned 'how to speak'. Learning how to speak enabled them to craft their own narratives against mining, grounded in their unique position as agrarian women who defended human and non-human life. They spoke on radio shows, marched in streets, staged protests at government offices and travelled throughout rural areas to share their knowledge about the effects of mineral extraction.

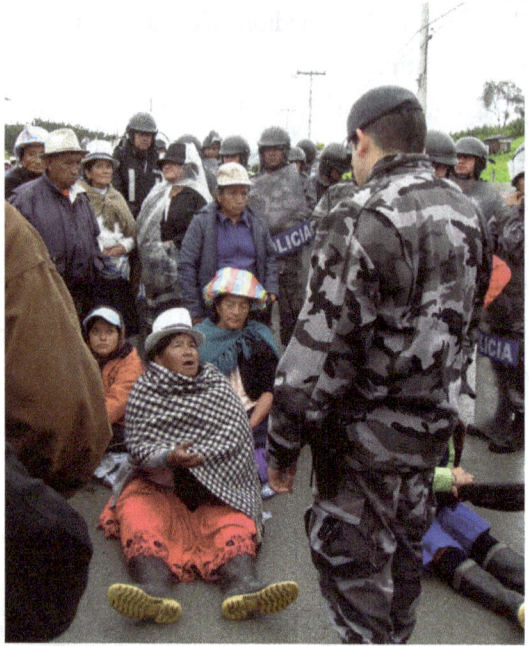

FIG. 27.4 Riot police confront peasant women blocking the Pan-American Highway in a protest against a proposed gold mine

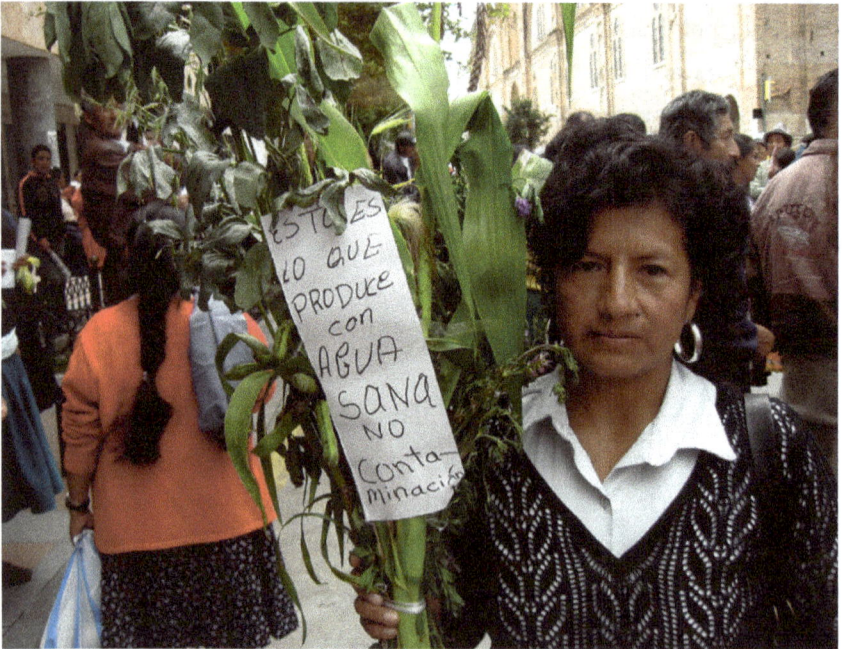

FIG. 27.5 A women's group member holds a picket sign attached to stalks of maize reading 'This is produced with healthy water no contamination'

In learning 'how to speak', their activism challenged the pervasive sexism within an anti-mining movement that was organised by male-dominated communal water boards. While the water-boards were democratically run, Rosita and Doña Patricia told me that they would never be elected to the leadership because of their lack of formal education. In the rural Andes, women are not explicitly barred from participating in water board meetings or holding office, but they become excluded through a common perception that men 'know what to say and how to say it' (Bastidas 2005: 160).

Formal education and the ability to 'speak' becomes a rationale that reinforces gender asymmetries in community politics. The women's group challenged exclusionary political practices by rejecting the masculine standards of speech that can stir up a crowd. A former president of the women's group prided herself on 'speaking' at a rally. She told me that it did not matter if the words came out 'good or bad' as long as she spoke.

When mining conflicts erupted, tensions over the gendered organisation of politics came to the fore. In an interview, Rosita recounted that in 2007 the anti-mining movement blockaded the Pan-American Highway and, in the face of mounting police repression, became split over the decision to continue to protest or to participate in a government dialogue. She criticised Luis, then president of the communal water board, for deciding to participate in a government dialogue. She and other women in the group believed that such dialogues were efforts to manipulate and pacify the movement. In a verbal confrontation with two men from the water-board, Rosita challenged Luis' decision. In response, the men involved defended Luis' actions and called her 'stupid'. Rosita believed that Luis often acted in self-interest, 'to become big, like Herod [from the bible]'.

Rosita and a group of women maintained their membership with the community water board, but politically aligned themselves with the National Coordinating Committee for the Defense of Life and Sovereignty (CNDVS, by its Spanish acronym) – a radical, pro-peasant anti-mining group with Marxist-feminist leanings that favoured street protests over state dialogue. Within CNDVS they established a women's group, *Frente de Mujeres Defensoras de la Pachamama* [Women Defenders of the Pachamama] and routinely identified themselves as *defensoras* [defenders].

FIG. 27.6 Peasants organised by the communal water boards converge upon the city of Cuenca to march against legislation that would permit mining in upland watersheds

I met Rosita through my work with the women's group. In April 2008, she and other members of the CNDVS staged a road-blockade on the Pan-American Highway. She was violently arrested – hit, dragged and stepped on by police before being shoved into a paddy wagon. My writing and research skills became useful to the organisation. I wrote a popular news article about the protest and arrests and documented her story for a human rights legal petition.

Our agendas were not, however, always so closely aligned. Shortly after the protest, the Ministry of Mines and Petroleum organised a consultation meeting with civil society organisations to discuss a draft mining law. While the activist groups rejected the invitation, I opted to attend because at the time I believed it was an important opportunity to understand state discourses around mining and get a better sense of what kind of 'civil society' groups participated in such events.

The event was held in the city of Cuenca on the side of town where rural peasants came to sell their products and in a building that formerly housed an important state agrarian modernisation programme. At the start of the meeting, a group of protestors outside could be heard yelling 'You don't sell the Motherland (la Patria), you defend it'. I stood up to look out of the window and I saw the women's group alongside some of their male allies from the CNDVS. From down below Rosita saw me in the window. At a meeting the following day, she and others were upset with me. They said that I was wearing a tie.

Indeed, I had worn a cowl-necked double-breasted knit jacket to the government consultation forum, which, in their view, stood in for a man's tie. My body was that of a *minero*, a masculine term that can be applied to women. The term is a gendered critique of mining supporters who align themselves with a masculine, imperialist endeavour. The women's group made hard distinctions between themselves as radical anti-mining activists and male/imperialist pro-mining groups. They used this distinction to question my affinity to their cause. I was in drag. I was suspected of betraying the organisation. Yet, without having attended the government dialogue I would have not learned that multinational mining company employees positioned themselves as 'ciudadanos' (national citizens) who called on the government to control 'radical environmental groups' obstructing mineral projects. A couple of months later, rumours broke out that I was a mining company informant and in September 2008, I was asked by CNDVS leadership to cool off my collaboration.

I regained a relationship with Rosita, but she would eventually ask me to exclude her from future research. Her refusal set an ethnographic limit just as other possibilities opened up. My ongoing commitment to collaborative research was enabled by the development of important relationships with urban and foreign anti-mining activists. We established the *Quizha-Quizha* collective, a solidarity group that hosted documentary and panel discussions on mining, carefully tracked concession maps for community leadership and organised a fundraiser for a threatened activist and member of the *Defensoras* group. In the following year, I expanded my collaborators to include the communal water boards that brought together men and women against the mine project.

My relationship with Rosita evinces the ways that the endeavours of ethnographic research and activism diverged and underscores the different ways in which we were positioned. Our relation reveals the potential for 'awkward dissonance between feminist practice and the practice of the discipline' of anthropology (Strathern 1987: 277). Rosita's criticism of my attendance at the mining dialogue exposed the ways in which activists and ethnographers are differently positioned in the field. Jack Halberstam points to a 'shadow' feminism in which 'subjects refuse to cohere; subjects who refuse "being" where being has already been defined in terms of a self-activating, self-knowing liberal subject' (2011: 126). By rejecting the government's proposal in mining policy, Rosita and the activists with whom she was protesting refused to collectively represent themselves as knowable political subjects. As Audra Simpson describes in *Mohawk Interruptus*, refusals enact representational sovereignty in historical contexts where ethnographic knowledge and government legibility entrench the settler colonial state (Simpson 2014). By refusing to participate in the mining dialogue, the *defensoras* enact a politics of refusal that underscores the

FIG. 27.7 The Defensoras enact a refusal to speak and eat in protest against the criminalisation of CNDVS activists; the yellow sign reads 'Down with the fascist and repressor government in service of imperialist miners'

relationships between territorial defence and sovereignty in the representational field. Rosita drew upon the same practice to negate participation in the research return workshop and thereby set limits to the circulation of information that would construct women as ethnographically legible subjects. *Defensoras* practice a form of grassroots feminism that dynamically connects speech and speaking with refusals to speak and be spoken about (Velásquez 2017).

At once collaborating and refusing to collaborate, Rosita's actions can be interpreted in the words of Donna Haraway (cited in De la Cadena 2015): 'we do not need a totality in order to work well. The feminist dream of a common language...is a totalizing and imperial one', (33–34). Rosita and the women's group enact different kinds of feminist practice: speaking at crowds, blocking streets with their bodies and refusing to be 'appropriate' subjects. Feminist practices have implications for politically aligned research, enabling both convergences and divergences between activism and research. Refusals signal a partial connection that emerges under conditions of political division and heterogeneous activist practices. A commitment to work within circuits of partial connections embraces the awkward and messy relationships that energise and confound politically aligned ethnographic research while also enriching methodological possibilities. Embracing the tensions between alignments and refusals as a collaborative research method allowed me to explore anti-mining activism from the perspective of multiple, differently positioned groups. Now, my occasional visits to Rosita entail easy conversations about life, love and delicious gossip that will never make it to a published page.

ACKNOWLEDGEMENTS

I would like to thank the *Defensoras* of Ecuador, especially Rosita. The essay was greatly improved by the colleagues who read generously and commented insightfully: Christine Labuski, Emily Yates-Doerr, Joan Gross, Melissa Biggs, John Bodinger de Uriarte and James Maguire.

REFERENCES

Bastidas, E. P., 'Women and Water in the Northern Ecuadorean Andes', in V. Bennett, S. Dávila-Poblete, and M. Nieves Rico, eds., *Opposing Currents: The Politics of Water and Gender in Latin America* (Pittsburgh: University of Pennsylvania Press, 2005), pp. 154–69.

De la Cadena, M., *Earth Beings: Ecologies of Practice across Andean Worlds* (Durham, NC: Duke University Press, 2015).

Halberstam, J., *The Queer Art of Failure* (Durham: Duke University Press, 2005).

Hale, C. R., 'What Is Activist Research?', *Items and Issues: Social Science Research Council*, 2.1–2 (2001), 13–15.

Lewis, D., 'Anthropology and Colonialism', *Current Anthropology*, 14.5 (1973), 581–602.

Simpson, A., *Mohawk Interruptus: Political Life across the Borders of Settler States* (Durham, NC: Duke University Press, 2014).

Strathern, M., 'An Awkward Relationship: The Case of Feminism and Anthropology', *Signs*, 12.2 (1987), 276–92.

Velásquez, T. A., 'Enacting Refusals: Mestiza Women's Anti-Mining Activism in Andean Ecuador', *Latin American and Caribbean Ethnic Studies*, 12.3 (2017), 250–72.

28

FIXING THINGS, MOVING STORIES

Jenna Grant

DURING HER PREGNANCY, PUTHEA WENT TO A PRIVATE MATERNITY CLINIC for regular ultrasound exams. This clinic was one of the larger and more popular in Phnom Penh at the time (2010) and one that provided *echo poar* – colour ultrasound services.[1] Puthea preferred colour to black and white scans because she could see more detail. Following the doctor's narration, she could recognise feet, legs and face. Of course, she told me, every ultrasound, even colour, has limits to its clarity. 'You have to wait until delivery to see what the baby *looks* like'. Nonetheless, Puthea got one of her later exams at a public hospital, which offered only black and white scans. She did this so that she would be 'in the system' there. Puthea could afford a private clinic – she worked in an upscale hotel and her salary, together with her husband's, placed them in Cambodia's growing middle class. Yet she chose the public hospital because it offered the best delivery services in Phnom Penh and was able to handle emergency or complicated cases.

As many women do, Puthea took a copy of her ultrasound report home with her and showed the report and accompanying image to her auntie, Ming. Ming was the matriarch of the family; she helped to raise Puthea and her brother and owned a popular guesthouse near the riverfront. Puthea was telling me about her most recent experience with ultrasound imaging over dinner at my house, and at this point, she paused. 'Ming looked at the scan, and said, "It [the foetus] looks like a cat!"' The cat comment was distasteful to Puthea, even though she couldn't exactly disagree with her auntie. The foetus had never looked this way in previous colour scans. The black and white image *was* strange.

I was hooked by this story, which came to me in the midst of fieldwork on imaging practices. Puthea's strategies for scanning and delivery were by then familiar – taking into account cost, medical expertise, facility, stage of pregnancy and kind of ultrasound image, among other things. She wanted information that others also wanted from ultrasound exams: information about the sex of the child and when is it due; whether it has its arms and legs, *mean dai mean choeng*, as people commonly put it; whether its head is up or down; the location of the placenta. However, her story of the cat-like appearance in the image was unusual, and it beckoned; it suggested a porousness of life among others – humans, images, animals and machines. I wanted to talk to Ming about it. Puthea laughed at my curiosity but agreed to join me.

When we met in the open lobby of Ming's guesthouse, calm and quiet in the afternoon heat, Ming stood by her original assessment: '*Moel tov?*' she asked me. 'Perhaps you can you see it, too?' She showed the picture to me, and then to a relative who was visiting from Canada. Puthea rolled her eyes impatiently. 'Or, perhaps the doctor was not so good', the relative said. 'Or the machine was old and unable to produce good pictures'. Ming had other ideas: perhaps it was because Puthea loved her small black cat too much; she always had it on her lap, petting it, talking to it. And maybe, too, it was because Puthea did not put up enough pretty pictures on the wall to influence the qualities of the foetus in a different direction. Surrounding oneself with nice images could help bring out vitality, health and beauty.

Puthea was caught between irritation with her auntie's 'superstitious' line of thinking and feeling somewhat under the sway of cultural logics that connect practices of pregnant women with the physicality of the foetus. Here, visual and affective practices – petting the cat and perhaps loving it too much, not looking at pretty pictures – have material effects. In everyday Buddhist philosophy, conception involves the merger of a new physical form with a consciousness or spirit that has lived previous lives; the foetus is both developing and already developed. Pregnancy is a liminal time where a pregnant woman's actions can influence the foetus – its form, its nature.[2] But one need not be committed to Buddhist notions of rebirth and impermanence (or to process ontology) to grasp the plasticity of prenatal life.

This story is not only about the foetus. It is also about the ultrasound image. Ming suggested that Puthea's actions and affect caused the foetus to look like a cat *in the black and white image*. Previous *colour* images had not brought out these qualities. Ming's reading made me wonder: how can an image intervene onto the object, making it come out better or worse, fixing its fate? People look to ultrasound imaging for clues about how the foetus is developing and what its nature might be. Perhaps they also hope that imaging can shift the process of foetal development, just a little?

Exceptional stories have an openness and unruliness to them. They require that we think across, diagonal, in staccato leaps. As I have wondered about transforming Puthea's story into a case, I have looked to quite different conversations for help. Work on 'maternal impressions' could help me think about how the thoughts, feelings and actions of pregnant women affect the physiognomy of foetuses.[3] Work on colour can unravel a bit more about colour as substance, and as part of postcolonial flows of ornament and vibrancy.[4] But then, what about black and white? Some consider black and white to be linked to a period of Cambodia's past, to death, to a notorious set of images, even.[5] Work on portrait photography could help me think about aesthetic practices of relating to images.[6] For example, concerning photo retouching in Ho Chi Minh City, Nina Hien writes: 'Many people considered the photograph as not only as an index of the subject, but also as *a live connection to it*. Following a popular Vietnamese saying, "fixing the image, [could] fix the fate"' (2014: 68). This suggests that images can affect their referents *and* their beholders; is this partly what was at stake for Puthea and Ming?

Khmer has a good expression for stories like these: *kuor aoy chngual* (គួរឱ្យ ឆ្ងល់) a story one should wonder about, a story that is surprising, curious, hinting at a different reality than one is used to. Perhaps wonder is what motivates ethnographic casework, akin to intrigue in medical work.[7] Exceptional cases do require unusual and unruly accomplices. The work of transforming a story into a case is akin to 'fixing' the story, making it come out better or worse. Assembling accomplices shapes what the story is and can be. As I see it, one of the lessons of Puthea's ultrasound scan is about life as process. Ultrasound is a technique for grasping hold of life to get a sense of what it is and what it may be. Another lesson has to do with the work of images. Cases, like the ultrasound image in this story, may intervene in myriad ways. They intervene on the objects they depict – bringing them out better, fixing certain qualities. They also intervene on the readers – how readers sense, think, attune.

There are ways that exceptional stories fix ethnographers, too. I did not hear about another cat-like scan, yet after talking to Puthea and Ming, I listened more closely for image stories. I asked different questions. I worked to make this story into an exemplary ethnographic case. Can it bear this weight? Perhaps. If representations fix – whether with words, images, or as cases – that fixing is a process, impermanent yet consequential. Fixing the image fixes the fate. Fixing the case shifts what is possible.

ENDNOTES

1 'Colour' ultrasound services can refer to Doppler imaging, 3D imaging, or a background tint or platform on 2D images. Puthea was talking about colour 2D images. French and Khmer in the expression *echo poar* indicate the mixtures that make up Cambodian medicine: *echo* is from the French *echographie* for ultrasound and *poar* is the Khmer term for colour. A great history of this medicine is Au, S., *Mixed Medicines: Health and Culture in French Colonial Cambodia* (Chicago, IL: University of Chicago Press, 2011).

2 See Ang, C., 'Grossesse et Accouchement au Cambodge: Aspects Rituels', *ASEMI*, 13.1–4 (1982), 87–109.

3 On maternal impressions see, for example: Morgan, L., 'Embryo Tales', in S. Franklin and M. Lock, eds., *Remaking Life and Death: Toward and Anthropology of the Biosciences* (School of American Research Press, 2013), pp. 261–91.; Stafford, B., *Body Criticism: Imaging the Unseen in Enlightenment Art and Medicine* (Cambridge, MA: MIT Press, 1991); or Taylor, J., *The Public Life of the Fetal Sonogram: Technology, Consumption, and the Politics of Reproduction* (Rutgers University Press, 2008).

4 See Galt, R., *Pretty: Film and the Decorative Image* (New York: Columbia University Press, 2011); or Taussig, M., *What Color Is the Sacred?* (Chicago, IL: University of Chicago Press, 2009).

5 On the Tuol Sleng photographs, see French, L., 'Exhibiting Terror', in M. P. Bradley and P. Petro, eds., *Truth Claims: Representation and Human Rights* (New Brunswick, NJ: Rutgers University Press, 2002), pp. 131–55.

6 I look to Hien, N., 'Photo Retoucher', in J. Barker, E. Harms, and J. Lindquist, eds., *Figures of Southeast Asian Modernity* (Honolulu, HI: University of Hawai'i Press, 2014), pp. 67–69; Pinney, C., 'Notes from the Surface of the Image: Photography, Postcolonialism, and Vernacular Modernism', in C. Pinney, and N. Peterson, eds., *Photography's Other Histories* (Durham, NC: Duke University Press, 2003), pp. 202–20; and Strassler, K., *Refracted Visions: Popular Photography and National Modernity in Java* (Durham, NC: Duke University Press, 2010).

7 On intrigue as a motivation for diagnostic work in medicine, see Saunders, B., *CT Suite: The Work of Diagnosis in the Age of Invasive Cutting* (Durham, NC: Duke University Press, 2008).

29

THE ETHNOGRAPHIC CASE: IN-CONCLUSION

Anna Dowrick, Julien McHardy, Joe Deville

THIS COLLECTION OFFERS LESSONS FROM CASES OF ALL KINDS. WHAT THEY have in common is that they represent experiences considered exceptional by the authors. They defied expectation in some important way, creating a tangible moment of intrigue. Unpacking this intrigue and bringing it to light enables us to share a feeling about it – maybe it unnerves, thrills, saddens, enrages or enlivens us – and from there to examine what holds it in place as the exception rather than the rule.

This book is itself an exception. It is a case of experimental publishing. We wanted to see what might happen if we imagined a book as a dialogue rather than a speech. What if readers engaging in the book wanted to say something? What if authors changed their minds about the text after others read it? What if a book was not finished simply because it had been published? Unlike other publishers, we viewed the publication of the digital first edition of *Ethnographic Case* as a starting rather than end point.

Creating a space of democratic peer review was exciting as a process. Readers considered the essays and offered their thoughts. Authors were free to choose how to revise. The real lesson from this case, however, was about the broader collective work of enacting curiosity.

Mattering Press is able to imagine alternative forms to those presented by for-profit publishers because of the commitment of its editors, authors, typesetters, proof-readers, printers, illustrators and reviewers to forgo profit in the pursuit of different values. The work of producing a book like this is done around the edges of other important practices, such as maintaining a livelihood and fulfilling caring responsibilities. At the best of times these practices push at the edges of experimental work. For instance, our ambition to publish a second edition soon after the first was slowed by the demands of new parenthood. During the pandemic, however, these practices threatened to overwhelm our endeavour. This was both with regard to how to find the time and space for contributors to revise and editors to edit, but also in relation to the larger experimental purpose of the book. What *good* does the experiment do at this moment in time? What is the value of enacting curiosity embodied by this book during a global crisis?

We were not the first to ask these questions. Donna Haraway has explored how to 'stay with the trouble' despite the pressures to turn away. She elaborated on what she meant by this in a talk she gave during the pandemic in 2021[1]:

> I think we need to cultivate in each other a sense of time. This is something that Deborah Bird Rose learned from her Yarralin teachers in Aboriginal Australia. That sense of what it is to be and what Westerners call 'the present' has to look different. It has to be thicker, more engaged with what has been and what is to come. That is the present. And that the work of a serious person is living and dying and working and playing in this thickness. So as to make the world less deadly, more flourishing. Not in some future time, but now. The work really is now. That's what staying with the trouble means. And 'now' is not some vanishing point that now disappears so fast you're never in it. Quite the opposite. We're in now. And things keep resurging.

For us, committing to this ongoing experiment was a way of attending to what remains precious in a time of remarkable uncertainty: making space for alternative ideas and ways of expressing them, and helping these forms and ideas to reach others who might be moved by them. This is our contribution to a flourishing present. Moreover, it remains important for us to actualise these ideas in print. This materially manifests the thickness, the trouble of the work contained within the pages.

That said, the experiment was radically reimagined in light of the pandemic. When we first planned the book, we anticipated a second edition to have moved significantly from the first in light of reader's comments. Instead we encouraged contributors *not to revise* their work during the pandemic. This brought into view a different quality of published work, namely that it represents a specific moment in time that authors might have moved on from, or that is impossible to re-visit at the time of revision. We recognised how the pandemic exacerbated academic precarity, and that while pursuing a second edition offered something potentially valuable to authors, revision might have asked more than they had available to give. What we are left with is a collection that reflects the thickness of the present for our contributors: some pieces revised significantly, some simply brought up to date, some untouched.

We have drawn our greatest learning from the inconclusiveness of this experiment. *The Ethnographic Case* teaches us that each book is unfinished business. Our purpose is not to produce books that are closed cases, but rather to generate literary spaces that fully reflect the troubling, messy, uncertain present, and hopefully begin something good within it.

REFERENCES

Haraway, D., Transcript of event celebrating the fifth anniversary of the journal *Catalyst* (2021). https://catalystjournal.org/index.php/catalyst/announcement/view/829.

MATTERING PRESS TITLES

Democratic Situations
EDITED BY ANDREAS BIRKBAK AND IRINA PAPAZU

Concealing for Freedom: The Making of Encryption, Secure Messaging and Digital Liberties
KSENIA ERMOSHINA AND FRANCESCA MUSIANI

Engineering the Climate: Science, Politics and Visions of Control
JULIA SCHUBERT

With Microbes
EDITED BY CHARLOTTE BRIVES, MATTHÄUS REST AND SALLA SARIOLA

Environmental Alterities
EDITED BY CRISTÓBAL BONELLI AND ANTONIA WALFORD

Sensing In/Security
EDITED BY NINA KLIMBURG-WITJES, NIKOLAUS POECHHACKER & GEOFFREY C. BOWKER

Energy Worlds in Experiment
EDITED BY JAMES MAGUIRE, LAURA WATTS AND BRITT ROSS WINTHEREIK

Boxes: A Field Guide
EDITED BY SUSANNE BAUER, MARTINA SCHLÜNDER AND MARIA RENTETZI

An Anthropology of Common Ground: Awkward Encounters in Heritage Work
NATHALIA SOFIE BRICHET

Ghost-Managed Medicine: Big Pharma's Invisible Hands
SERGIO SISMONDO

Inventing the Social
EDITED BY NOORTJE MARRES, MICHAEL GUGGENHEIM, ALEX WILKIE

Energy Babble
ANDY BOUCHER, BILL GAVER, TOBIE KERRIDGE, MIKE MICHAEL, LILIANA OVALLE, MATTHEW PLUMMER-FERNANDEZ AND ALEX WILKIE

The Ethnographic Case
EDITED BY EMILY YATES-DOERR AND CHRISTINE LABUSKI

On Curiosity: The Art of Market Seduction
FRANCK COCHOY

Practising Comparison: Logics, Relations, Collaborations
EDITED BY JOE DEVILLE, MICHAEL GUGGENHEIM AND ZUZANA HRDLICˇKOVÁ

Modes of Knowing: Resources from the Baroque
EDITED BY JOHN LAW AND EVELYN RUPPERT

Imagining Classrooms: Stories of Children, Teaching and Ethnography
VICKI MACKNIGHT

www.ingramcontent.com/pod-product-compliance
Lightning Source LLC
Chambersburg PA
CBHW050647270326
41927CB00012B/2909